IMAGES
of America

MOUNT SAVAGE

IMAGES
of America

MOUNT SAVAGE

Amanda Paul

ARCADIA
PUBLISHING

ISBN 978-0-7385-1680-6

Published by Arcadia Publishing
Charleston, South Carolina

Printed in the United States of America

Library of Congress Catalog Card Number: 2004106223

For all general information contact Arcadia Publishing at:
Telephone 843-853-2070
Fax 843-853-0044
E-mail sales@arcadiapublishing.com
For customer service and orders:
Toll-Free 1-888-313-2665

Visit us on the Internet at www.arcadiapublishing.com

Contents

ACKNOWLEDGMENTS

The tight-knit community of historians of Mount Savage must be the first to thank for their knowledge and memories of times forgotten. The Mount Savage Historical Society and its efforts in preserving the town's history deserves a huge round of applause. If it were not for their endless hours of volunteer work, much of the town's history and heritage would have been lost for generations to come.

Along with the gratitude towards the society, I must also take a moment to remember a local historian who is only with us in spirit and memory: Mrs. Alice Carney. Her love of the community and its history is what started the preservation of the history of Mount Savage. If it were not for her research and hours of grant writing, there would not be a Mount Savage Museum, which sparked the development of the Old Jail, the Bank, and the Union Mining Company building preservation.

A big "thank you" goes to the community members who allowed the use of their personal photographs and images. Thank you Cora Carter, Joanne Nickel, Earl Pope, Gary Delaney, Joe Carter, Paula Wright, Paula Fuller, Phyllis Reed, Babe Robertson, the James Robison family, Carol Barry, Wilma Delbrook, Theresa Swanson, the Folk's, Buddy Duckworth, and all other friends and community members who helped me find the lost and treasured photographs of our home town.

I am grateful for Shirley Wisenburg, who took the time to complete the first edit of the book. I am also indebted to my husband Sam White for the final edit.

I also have to thank members of my family for having an elephant memory and having the foresight to write events, dates, and names down. A big "thanks" goes to my mother and father, Bonnie and Jim Paul, for making calls and contacts that I could have never made. I am also grateful to my granddad, Wilbert Paul, for writing down his memories of growing up in Mount Savage.

References

Stegmaier, Dean, Kershaw, Wiseman. *Allegany County: A History*. Parston WV: McClain Printing Company, 1976.

Harvey. The Best Dressed Miners: Life and Labor in the Maryland Coal Region, 1835–1910. Ithaca, NY: Cornell University Press, 1969.

INTRODUCTION

Small towns in Allegany County, Maryland, and across the United States are overlooked by the 21st-century eye because the glory years have long passed them. But what most people do not realize is that small towns live and breathe on the citizens who have planted roots and raised their families in them. As in many towns or cities, families move in and out of the area, but there is always a common root of the community that holds the town together.

These rooted families are what make small towns special. If it were not for the community's hard work and love for their town, it would not exist today. There is a pride in the industry that once thrived in the town. There is also a pride in the heritage of the people who built the homes, schools, farms, and churches that still stand along the streets, rows, lanes, and hills of such towns.

Mount Savage, founded in 1759, is known as the oldest existing community in Allegany County. Nestled between Cumberland and Frostburg, the community has changed over the two and half centuries since it was settled. Like many areas in the county, the town started to grow after the Revolutionary War when the soldiers were given military plots as payment for fighting for America's independence. From that point in history the town has almost gone full circle—from its beginning as a farming community to a strong railroad town with the Cumberland and Pennsylvania Railroad, the Iron Works that pressed the first iron rail in the nation in 1844, and the three brick producers in the area. Now the only industry is farming once more.

Through these growing pains the town has seen its share of economic growth and decline, in addition to over-population problems. Yet the town's overall appearance has not changed much from the 19th century. Main Street is still a two-way road, but it is only wide enough for one lane of traffic—just as it was in the 1800s—so remember to yield to oncoming traffic in the center of town. Houses have been destroyed by fire and torn down, and many of the industrial buildings are all but a memory, but the framework of the town is still sturdy as ever.

Although industry was an important component to the town, the school became the center of the town's well being. Education has always been an important factor in the people's lives. They have always supported the school's sports and other activities like drama and chorus. The town has fought to keep the school a center of the town.

Like many industrial-based towns across the country, Mount Savage has had its share of heartache. This has not stopped the town from serving in this fast-paced world. The people have learned to adapt to the socioeconomic changes. Small businesses are still operating, and a bed and breakfast successfully operates in The Castle. The Mount Savage Historical Society and community members have taken it upon themselves to beautify the town. Every year we celebrate our heritage at Old Iron Rail Days during the third weekend of October.

Today's world must view small towns, like Mount Savage, as what makes the town—the people—and not what the town once had been as an economic base. The people are still here and are happy living in the peace and quiet of the beautiful surroundings of the Allegheny Mountains.

The following chapters will unveil Mount Savage as it once was and present how the community has grown and thrived. The photographs will tell various stories of the many eras of growth and downfalls in the town's history. This volume will enlighten readers about Mount Savage's meager beginnings on Old Hinkle Road, the growth of Main Street, the deep spiritual belief in God and the three churches, and the green and gold spirit of Mount Savage School.

One

ARNOLD'S SETTLEMENT A New Community

The town of Mount Savage was first called Lulworth, according to original maps and documents. Lulworth came from the name of the company that owned the land and mineral rights in the 1730s. The town actually had many names over the years—Savage Mount, Jennings Post Office, McDonald's Forge, and Arnold's Settlement—before it was officially named Mount Savage. The official name is believed to have derived from a surveyor, Thomas Savage, who was traveling through the area in 1736.

The winter of that year, Thomas Savage and his group were trapped in a snowstorm on Big Savage Mountain and thought that they might have to resort to cannibalism when their supplies ran low. The group took a vote and felt that Thomas should be the first victim since he was older and had bad eyesight. Fortunately for Thomas, the storm broke and the group made it out of the area safely. The group decided then to name both Big Savage Mountain and Little Savage Mountain after Thomas Savage. The town at the base of Big Savage and the mouth of Jennings Run Valley would also be named for him.

In 1759 the Archibald Arnold family, along with a few other families (Mattinglys, Logsdons, Deans, Gearys, Kimmels, Trimbles, Shaffers, Pratts, Monahans, Rooneys, Brailers, Comses, Porters, Martins, and Blubaughs), settled on an old Native American trail that would soon become a stagecoach route known as Turkey Foot Trail. Arnold's Settlement served as an overnight location, known as Arnold's Hotel, for travelers who were moving westward. The Turkey Foot Trail was used before the development of the National Road in 1811.

All of these pioneer farmers were Catholic and started the first congregation of Catholics west of Cumberland. The unofficial first services were held at Arnold's Hotel. The first mass was not celebrated until 1792, and Father Stephen T. Badin, the first ordained priest in the United States, led it. Father Badin had been traveling by foot through Kentucky and had heard about the Catholic settlement.

The settlement of farmers grew very slowly, and with the development of the National Road from Cumberland to Wheeling, the Turkey Foot Trail was almost abandoned by travelers. The only record of the farmer families were church documents of marriages and a few commerce records that were made when transporting agricultural goods on the National Road. It seems, at first, that Arnold's Settlement was going to stay a small agricultural colony of self-sufficient means.

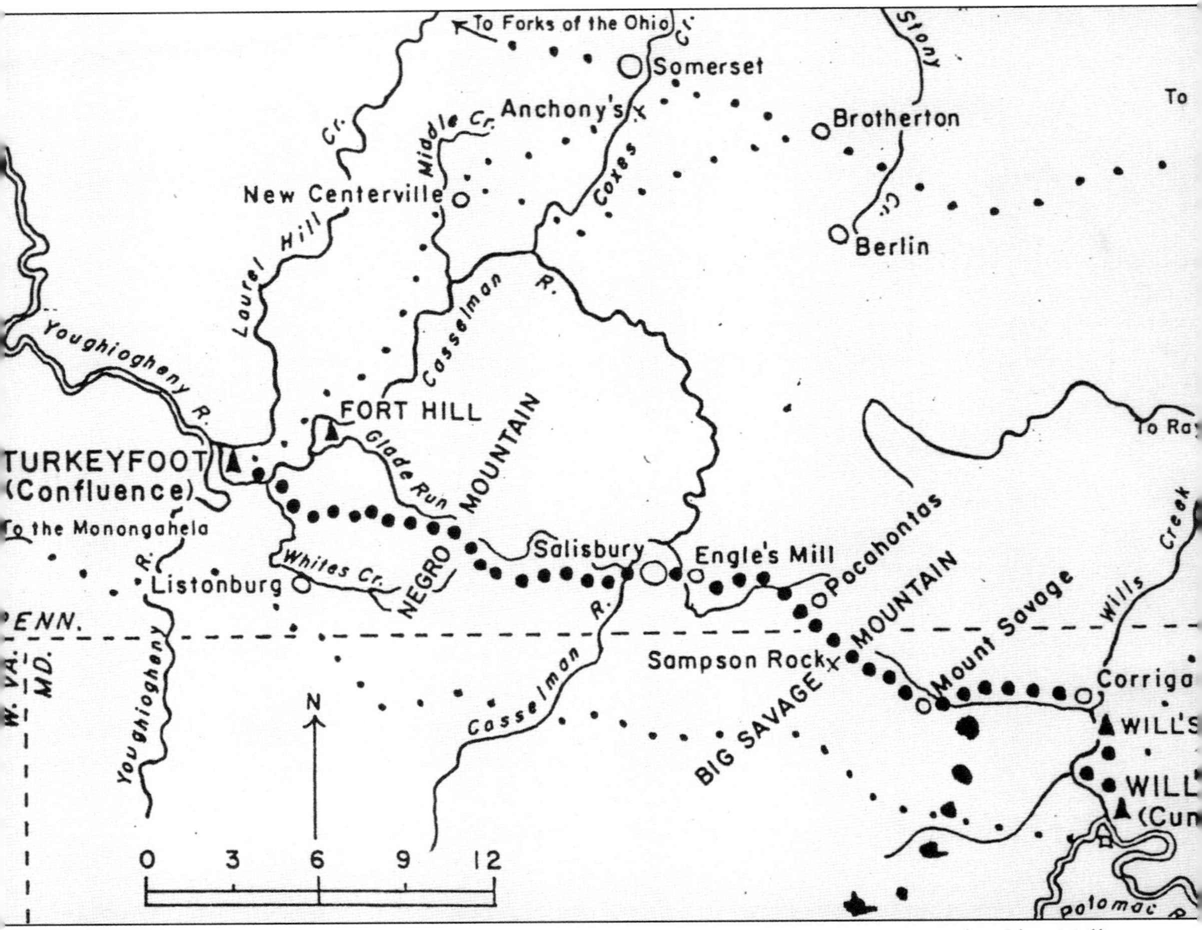

Turkey Foot Trail. This was one of the more popular routes traveling west to the Ohio Valley before Braddock Trail (1755) was cut into the wilderness of the Allegheny Mountains. Turkey Foot Trail was an old Native American trail. (Courtesy of Mount Savage Historical Society.)

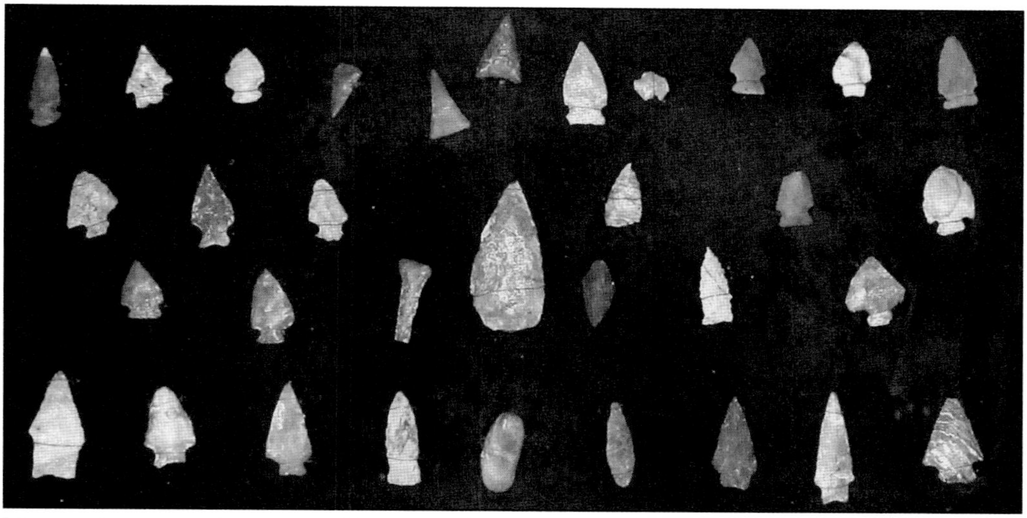

Native American Artifacts. There have been many artifacts found in and around the original Arnold's Settlement. The Shawnee Tribe dwelled in this area around the same time that the Arnolds came into the region. The Shawnees called this place *co-lik-hanna*, the land of sweet waters. (Courtesy of the James Robison family.)

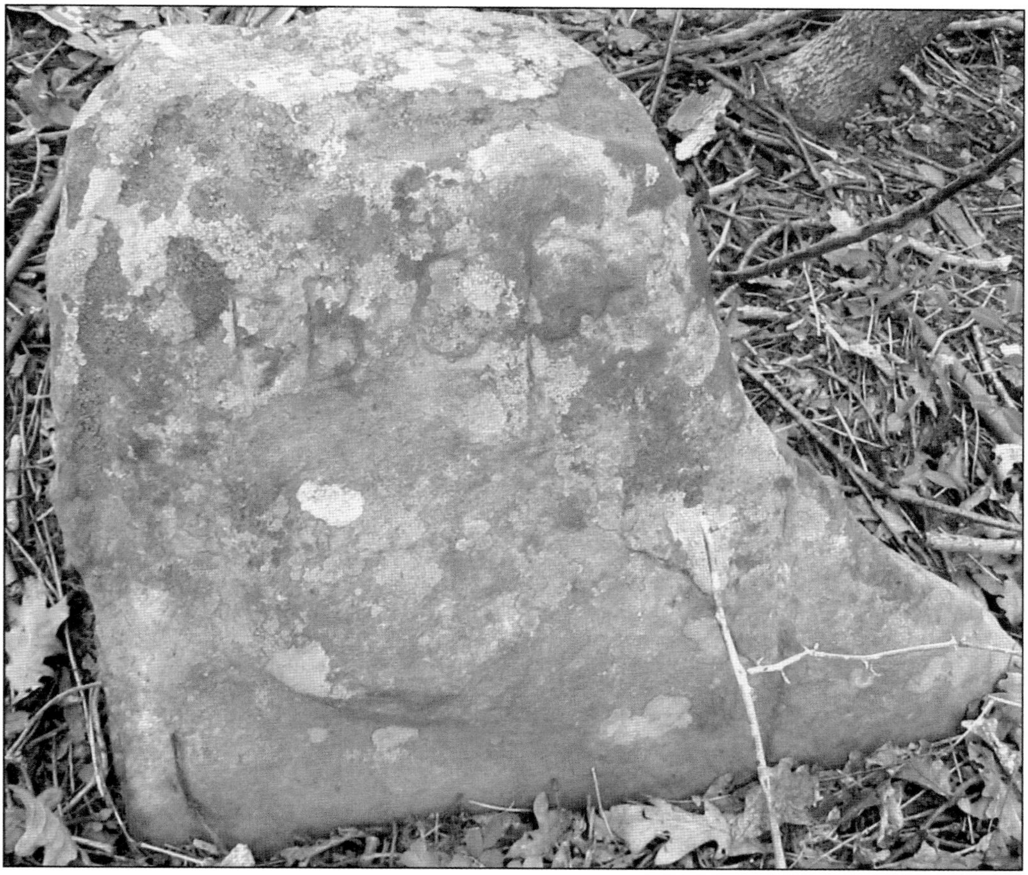

Bear Camp Road Stone. Look closely and the letters *BBCD* can be seen on this marker. The stone was a road marker for the stagecoaches that traveled Bear Camp Road in the 19th century.

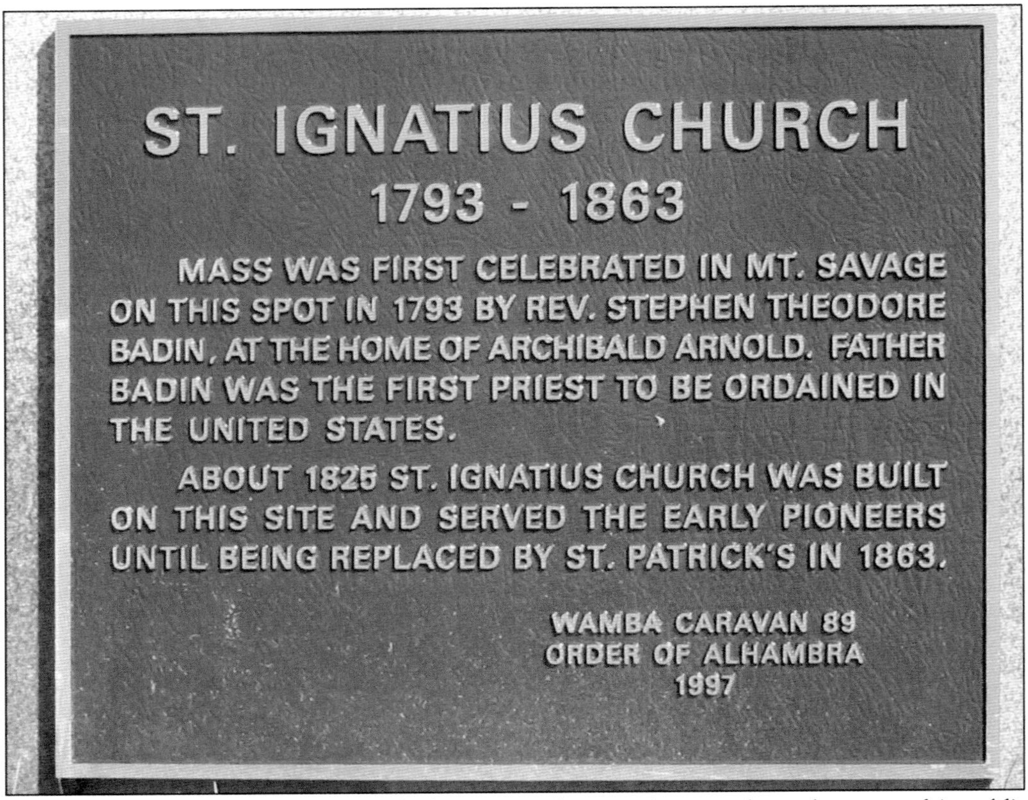

St. Ignatius Church. Unfortunately there are no known photographs or drawings of Arnold's Hotel or the first church. The location of the church, built in Mount Savage around 1825, is designated by this plaque. The families of Arnold's Settlement started this church.

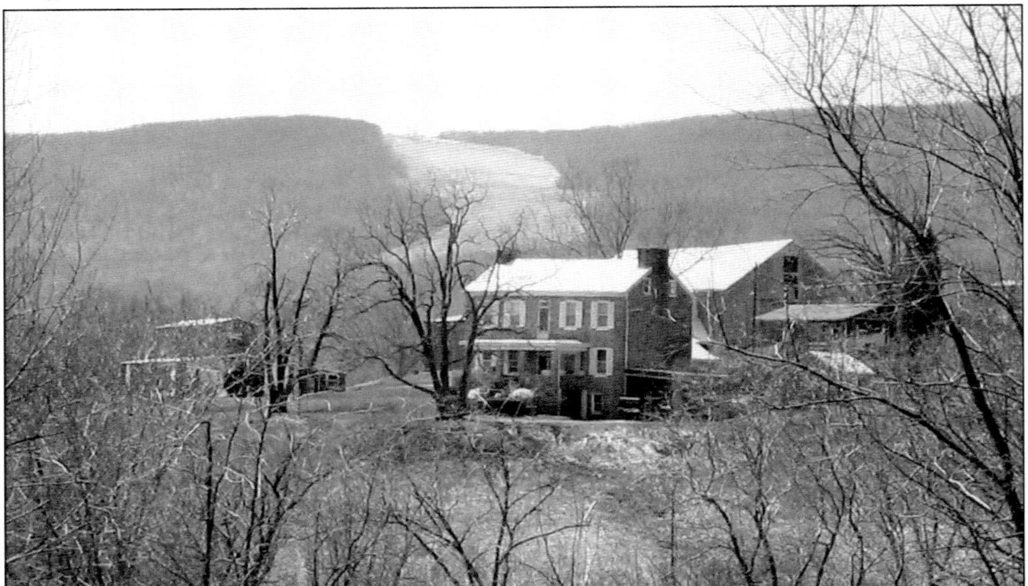

William Logsdon Homestead. The Logsdon family settled around Arnold's Settlement. William built this house in 1858.

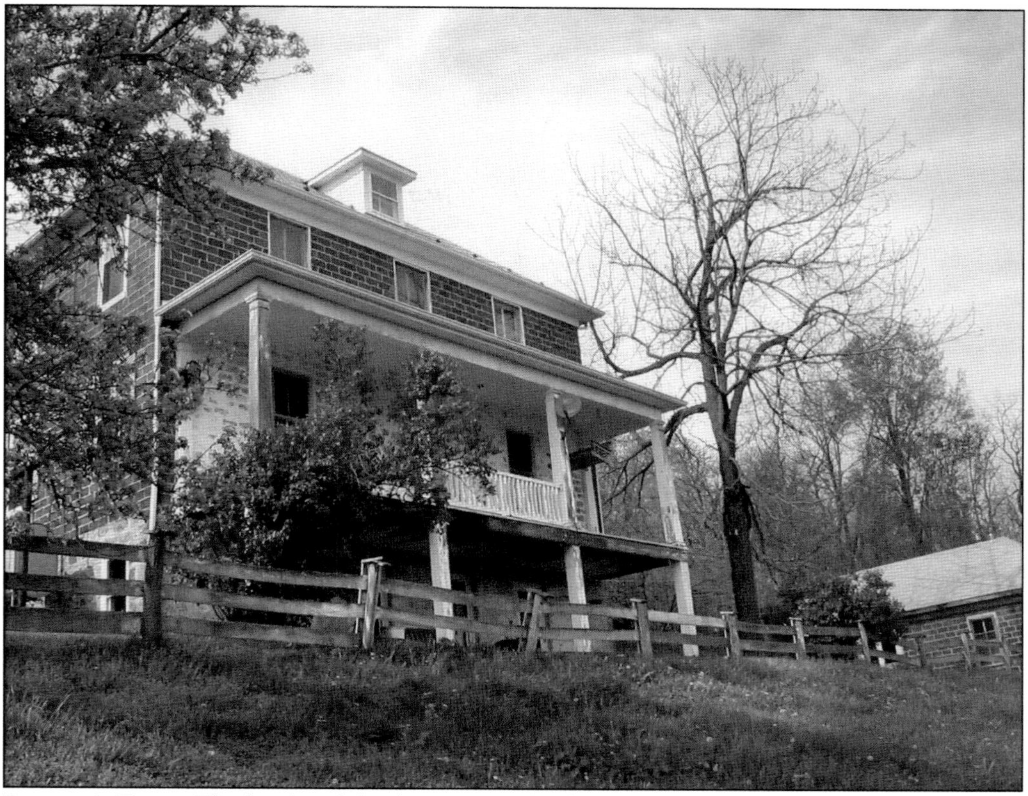

Brailer's Farm. The bricks of this house were fired directly on the property while the house was being built. A makeshift kiln was erected for the production of red brick.

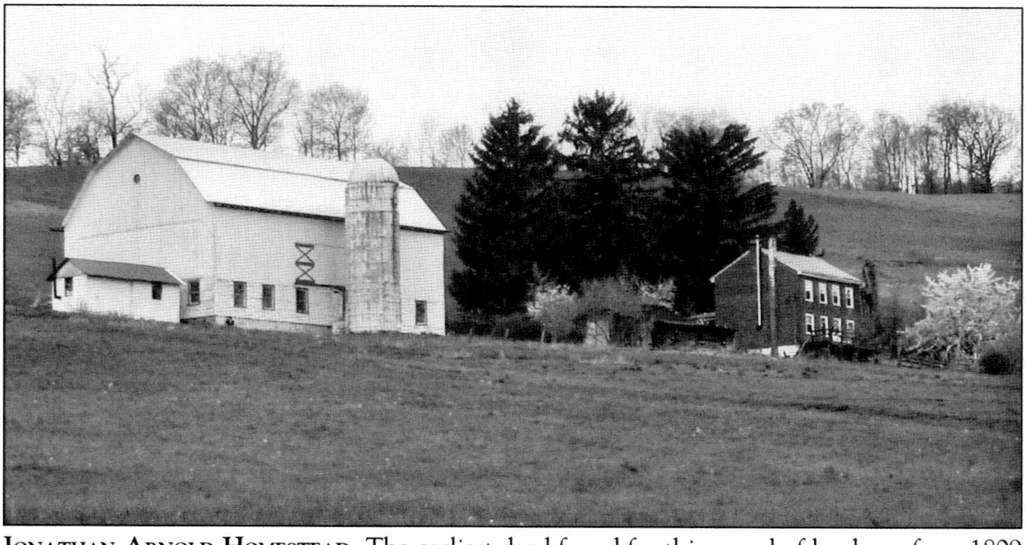

Jonathan Arnold Homestead. The earliest deed found for this parcel of land was from 1809 and was owned by Archibald Arnold and his wife, Fanny. Later, Arnold's son, Jonathan, owned the land and built this house. The Lepley family did not build the current barn until 1943.

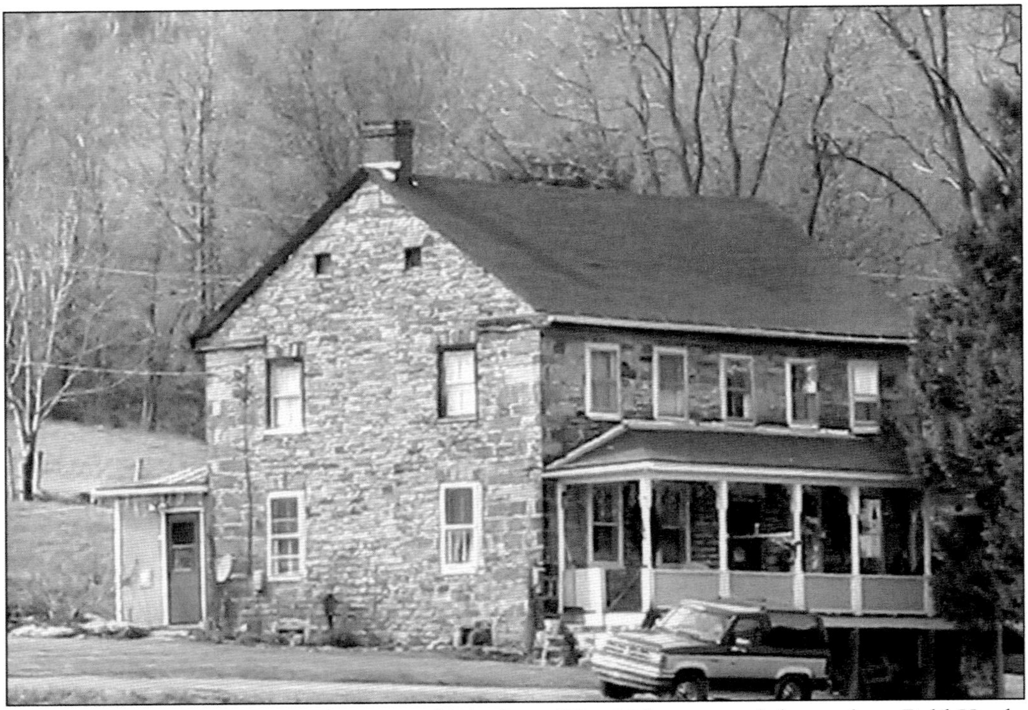

Blank Homestead. This is the original Blank or "Plunk" homestead, located on Bald Knob. Samuel Plunk received this land as a military plot after the Revolutionary War.

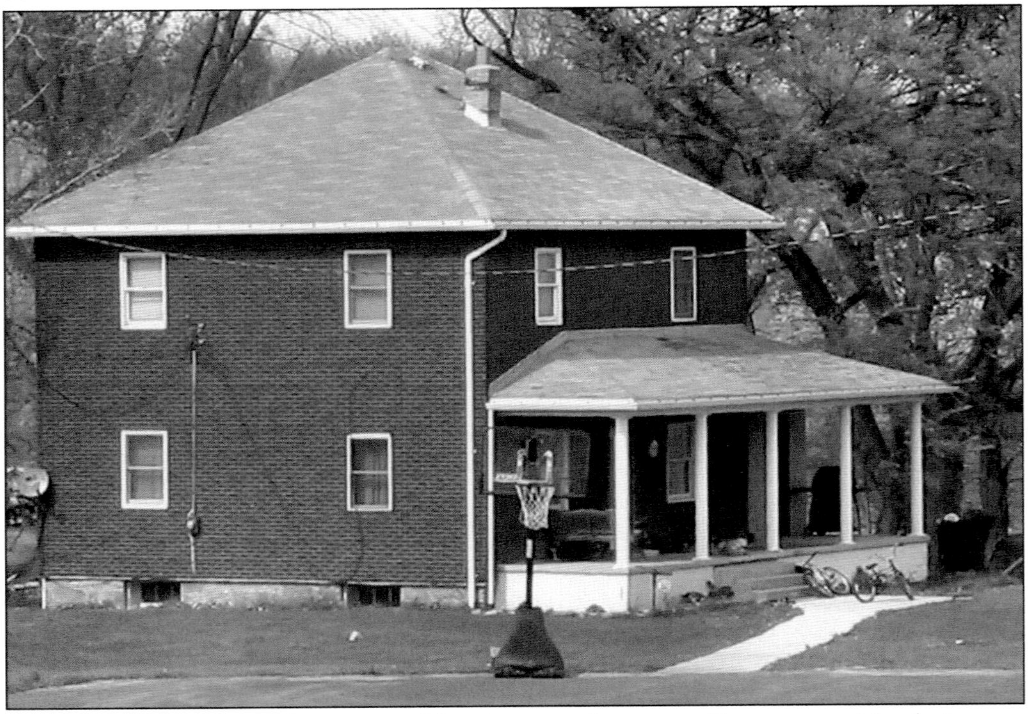

The Albert Logsdon Homestead. This homestead was a military tract of land given to the Logsdon family after the French and Indian War. It stayed in the Logsdon family until the late 1980s.

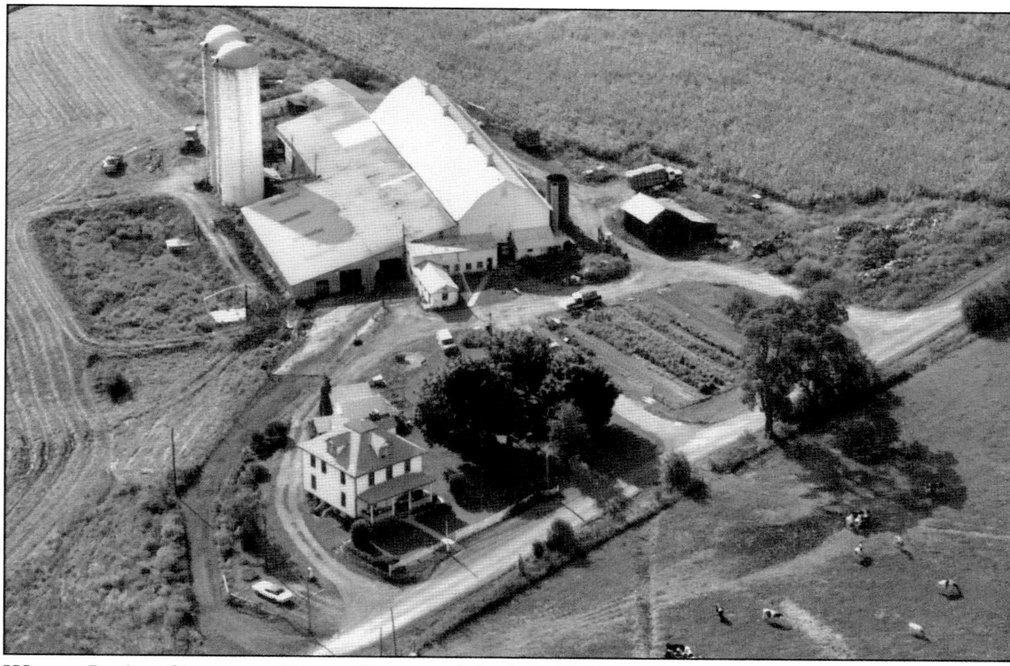

Where It All Started. Originally part of Archibald Arnold's tract of land, this farm consisted of over 1,000 acres of land. A portion of this tract was known as the Tomahawk plot because there were so many arrowheads, tomahawks, and grinding stones found on the land. At one time, the Shawnee Indians had settled here. Next to the current farmhouse (1909), the foundation to Arnold's Hotel can be found. (Courtesy of the James Robison family.)

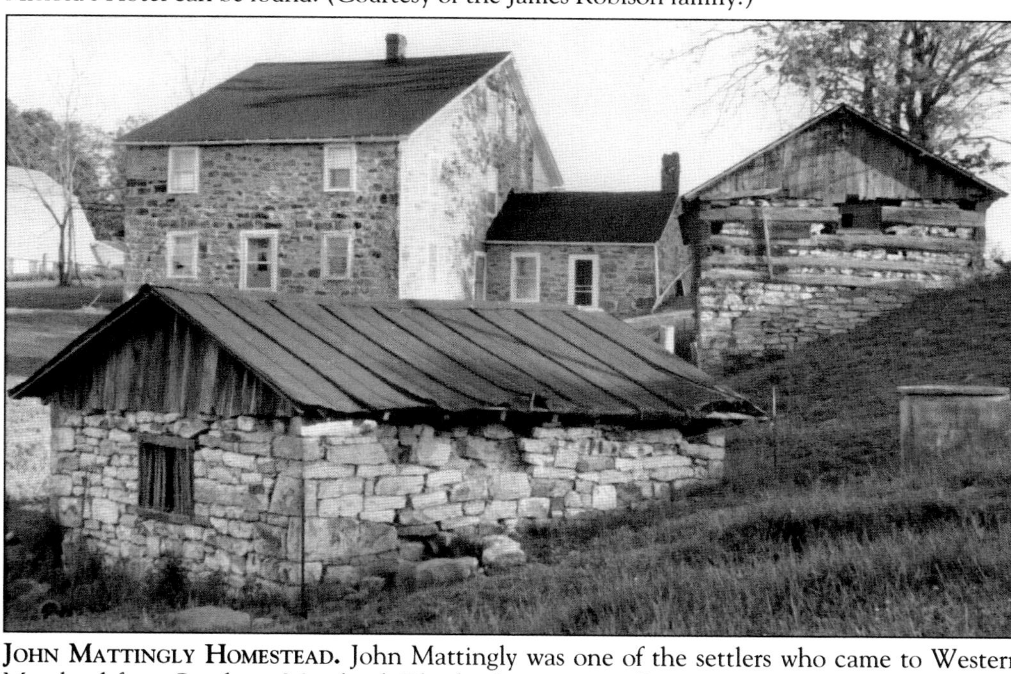

John Mattingly Homestead. John Mattingly was one of the settlers who came to Western Maryland from Southern Maryland. The land was originally given to a man named Ross and consisted of 705 acres from the crown of England. John received the land around 1787 as a military land grant. The Mattinglys referred to the homestead as the "Mansion House."

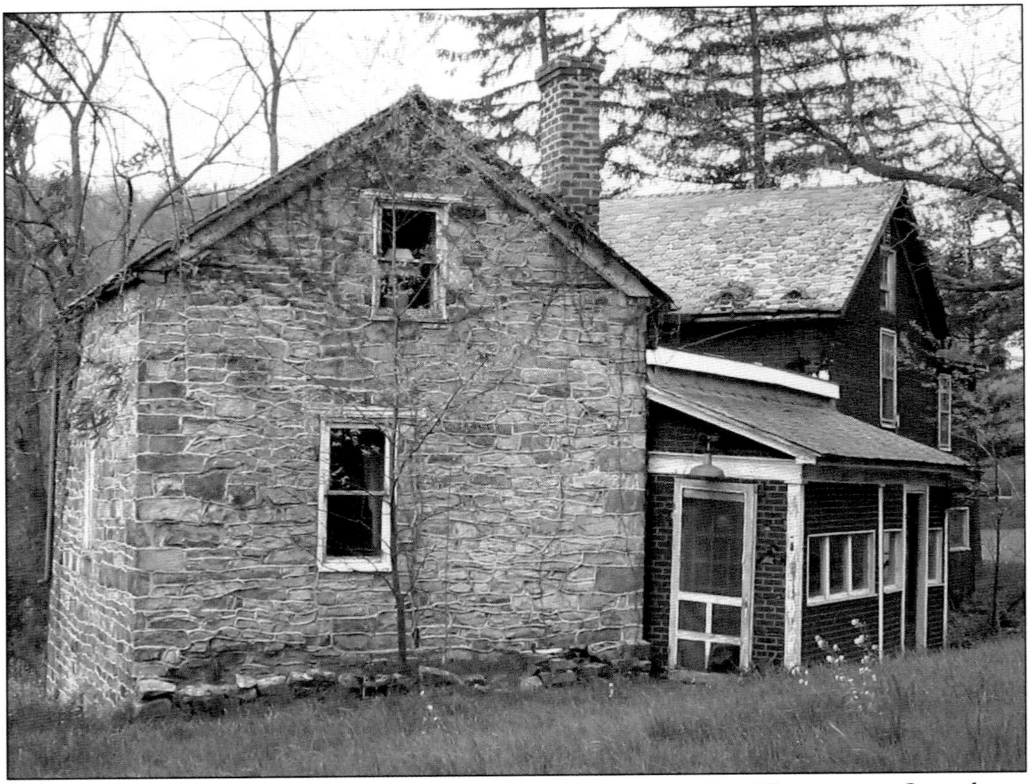

Mattingly Son Homestead. One of the Mattinglys also built this house. It is assumed that the eldest living son of John was given this parcel of land to farm. Later it was sold to the Smith family.

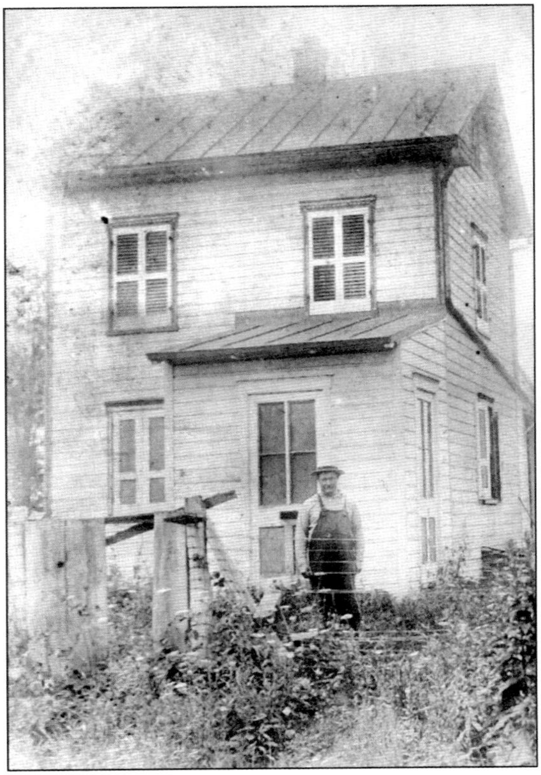

Eli Beal Farm. This farmhouse is built of a combination of stone and log. Many houses that were built early 1800s, like this house, were built in this manner. (Courtesy of the Beal family.)

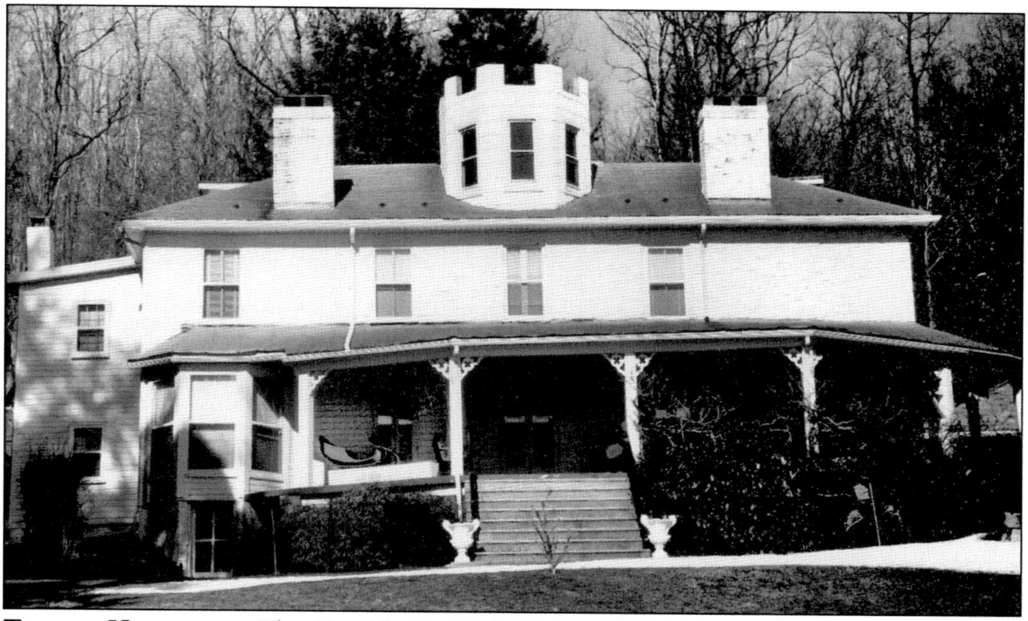

Trimble Homestead. The Trimble family has owned this tract of land since the end of the Revolutionary War. The family named the homestead the Evergreen House. (Courtesy of Cora Carter.)

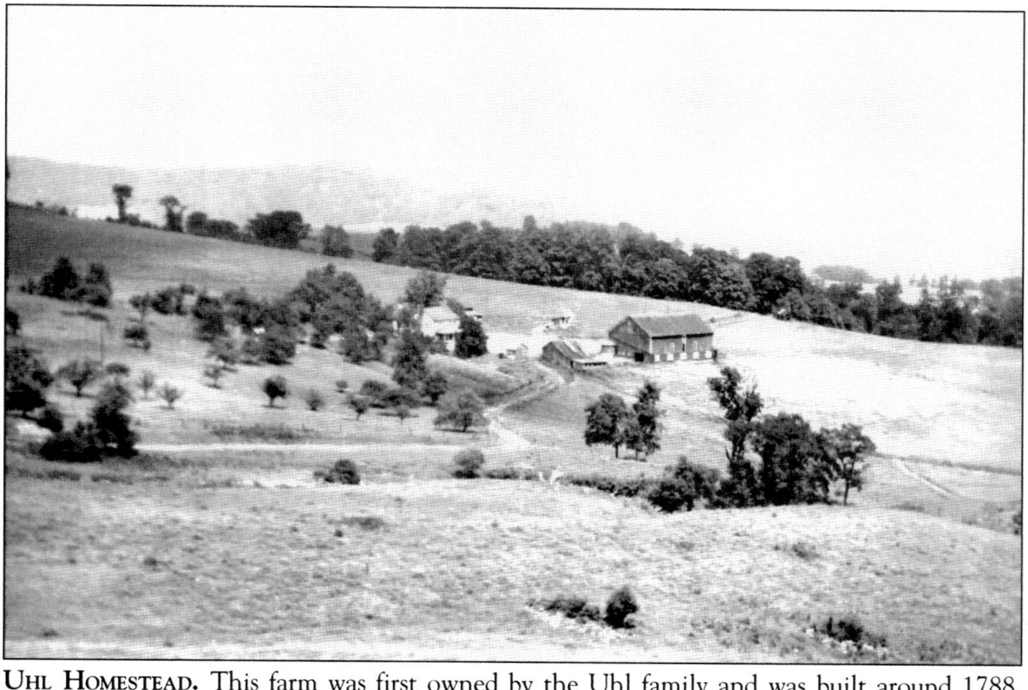

Uhl Homestead. This farm was first owned by the Uhl family and was built around 1788. Around the turn of the 19th century the Delbrook family purchased the farm. (Courtesy of Wilma Delbrook, in memory of Stewart.)

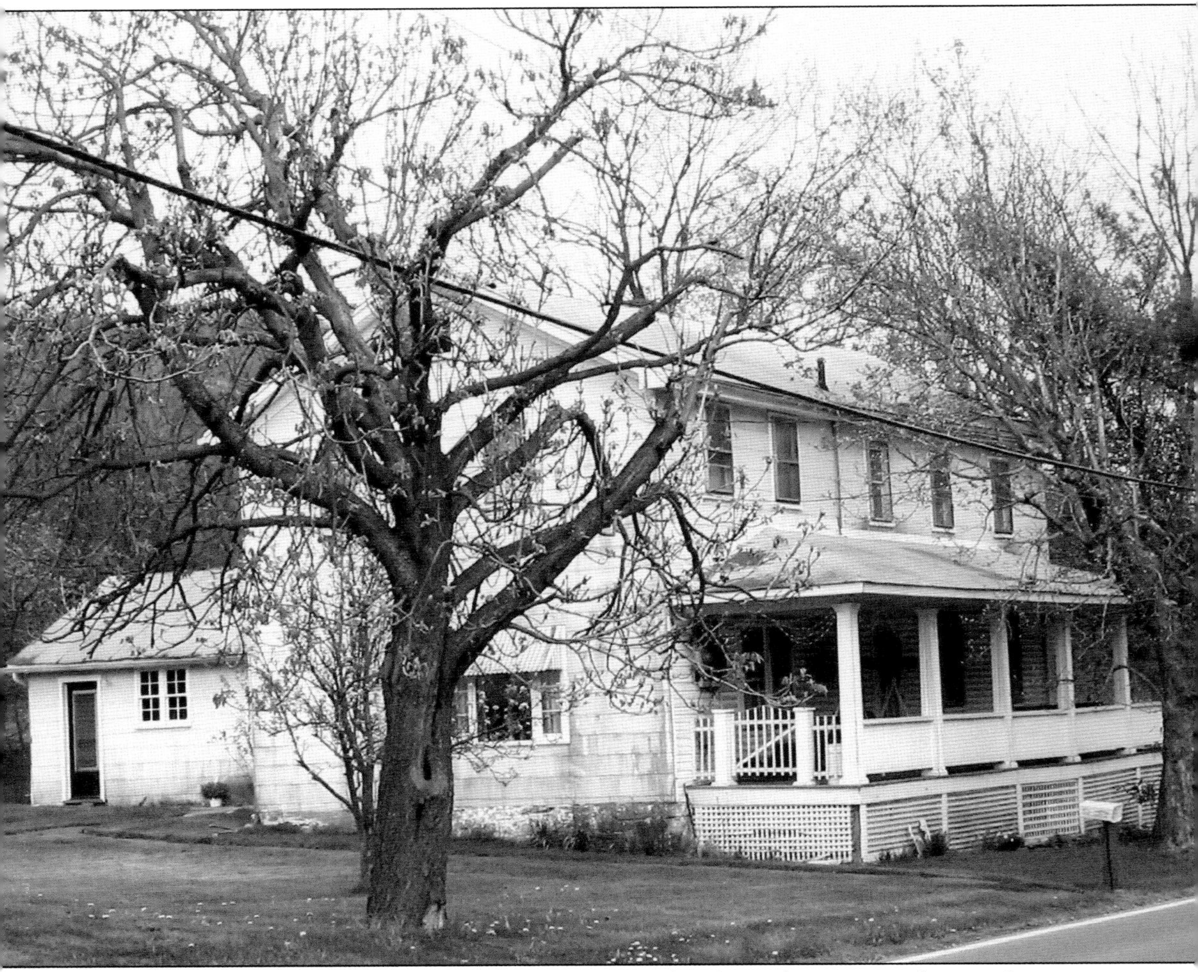

Plank Road Inn. This house was originally an inn that housed weary travelers on their way to and from Pennsylvania. Plank Road was another well-known stagecoach road that led into the North. Today, the road is known as PA Route 160.

Two

The Old Iron Rail Makes History

Just when the farmers of Arnold's Settlement thought the valley below was going to stay a quiet farming community filled with descendants from the Arnold bloodline, Benjamin B. Howell and other Englishmen started the Mount Savage Iron Works in 1837. The New York Iron & Coal Company established the iron works and constructed the furnaces and the rolling mill for the Mount Savage Iron Works.

A road was built from Cumberland to Mount Savage, and the company went into production. The population of the valley grew as German, Welsh, and (mostly) Irish workers poured into the industrial village looking for work and the American dream. This dream became reality in 1842 when the New York Iron & Coal Company began to construct 22 dwellings for their workers. They also built a schoolhouse, a store, and various buildings for manufacturing iron, which included a rolling mill 224 feet wide. The number of buildings that the company constructed increased to 228 buildings in 1847.

In 1844 the first iron rail in the nation was pressed in Mount Savage. When this occurred it changed the railroading system in America. Prior to the production of the iron rail, all rails were made of wood with a thin strip of iron at the top. The reason for this is that the railroads in the United States had to purchase iron from England, and it was very expensive to import full-size rails for track.

By 1845 the iron works was producing approximately 200 tons of iron a week. It was the only company in the United States that was producing vast amounts of iron for the railroad businesses. To supply the blast furnaces, the New York Iron & Coal Company had coalmines in the nearby hills. The furnaces needed 150 tons of coal a day to operate. In addition to supplying the needs of the blast furnaces, the company shipped another 150 tons of coal to the Eastern markets in Baltimore.

In 1847 New York Iron & Coal Company ceased production, only three years after the banner year when the first iron rail was pressed. The property was bought in 1848 and became the Mount Savage Company. The Mount Savage Company returned to producing the iron rails and became the main supplier to the B & O Railroad.

Unfortunately, in 1868 the Mount Savage Company stopped production. Although the iron ore deposits were in several areas, the ore was not of the best quality. Politics also became a factor in the sales of iron products when the protective tariff was reduced and the English undersold the Mount Savage Company.

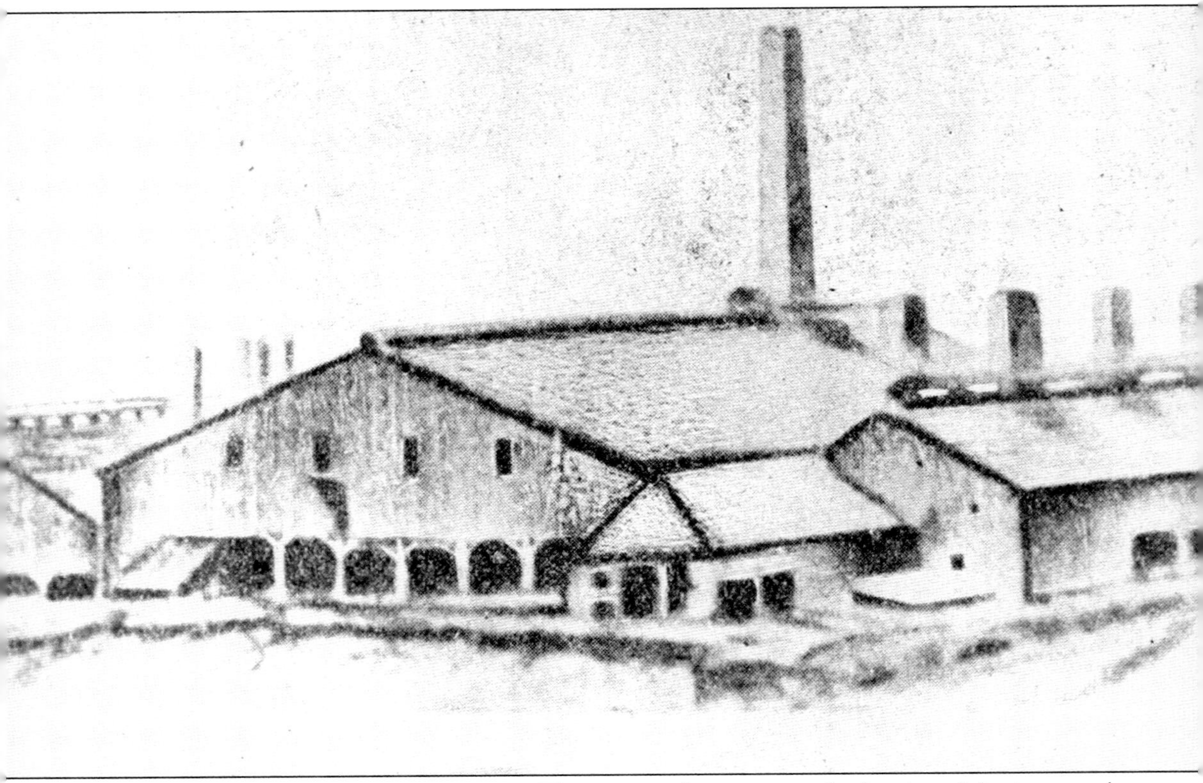

MOUNT SAVAGE IRON WORKS, 1840S. This artistic drawing reveals the size of the iron works that was located in town. (Courtesy of Mount Savage Historical Society.)

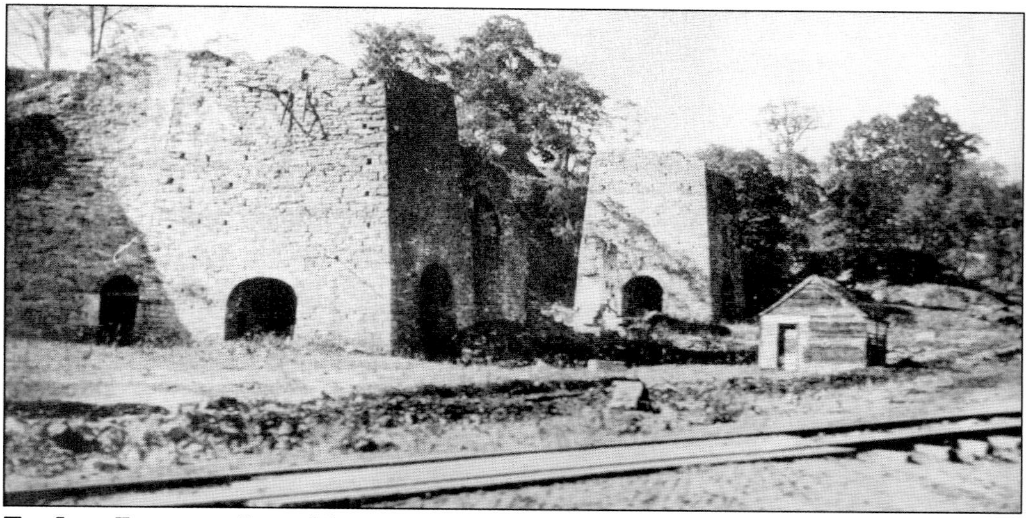

The Iron Furnaces. Several furnaces were active in the manufacturing of iron. Most were torn down after the iron ore deposits were consumed.

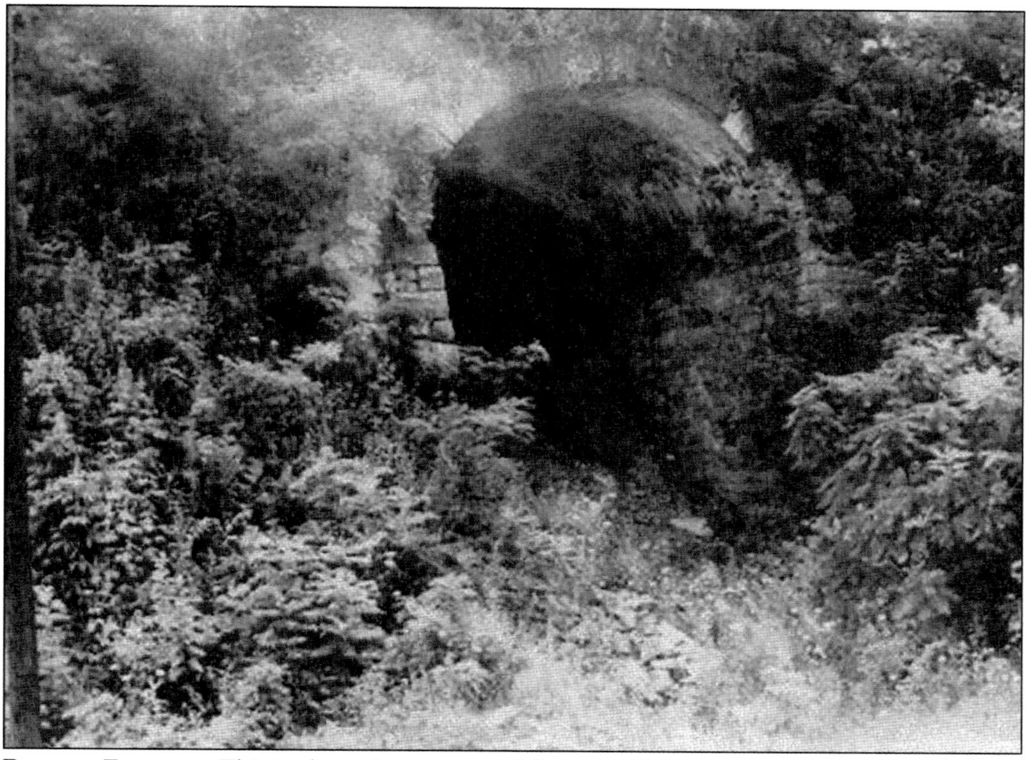

Ruin of Furnace. This is the only remnant of the many furnaces that were used at the iron works. It still stands in the hillside of "Coke Hill," in disarray. This structure was actually two furnaces built beside each other.

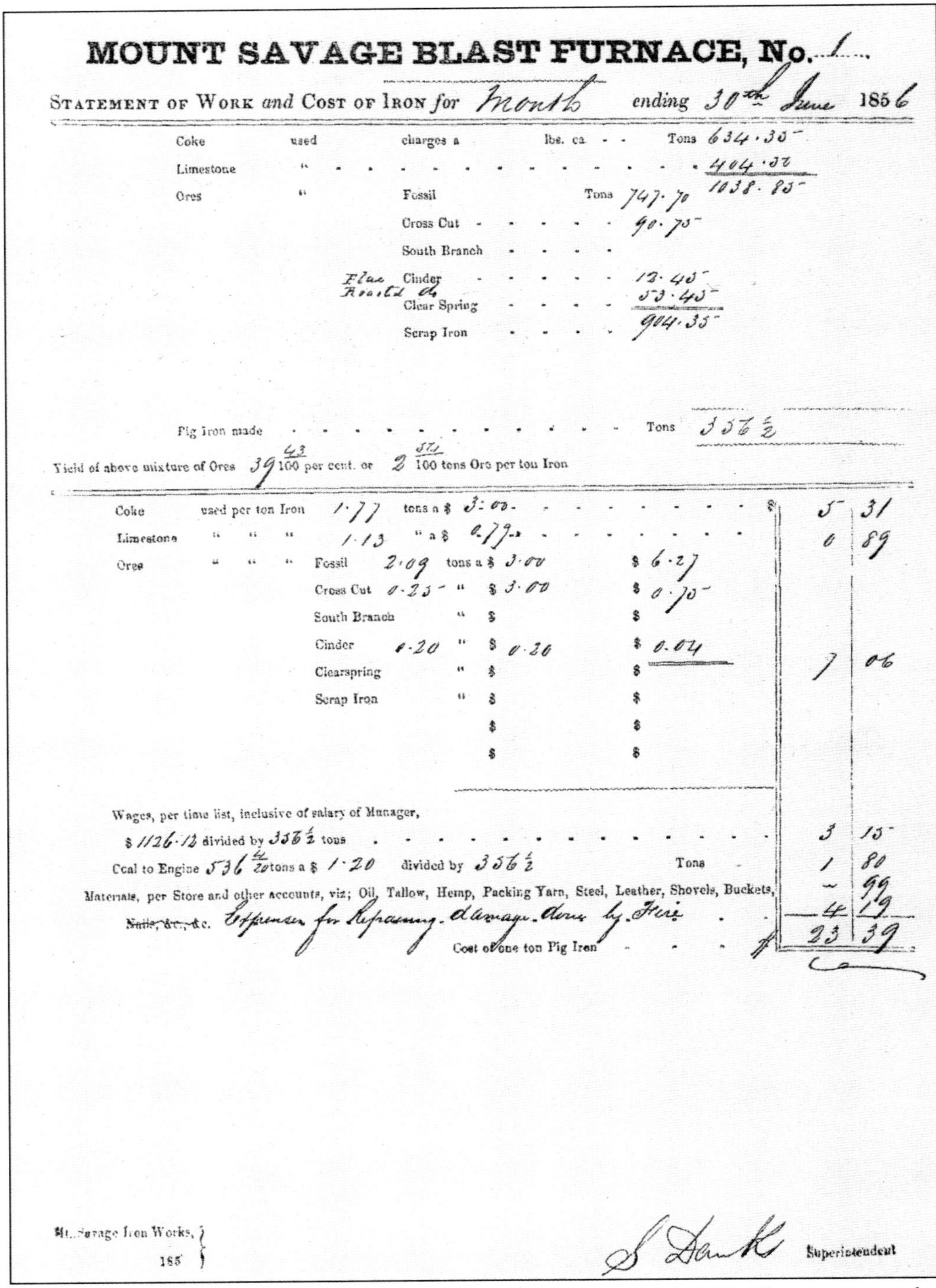

MOUNT SAVAGE BLAST FURNACE, No. 1

STATEMENT OF WORK and COST OF IRON for Month ending 30th June 1856

Coke	used	charges a	lbs. ca	Tons 634.35
Limestone	"			404.32
Ores	"	Fossil	Tons 747.70	1038.85
		Cross Cut	90.75	
		South Branch		
		Flue Cinder	12.45	
		Roasted do	53.45	
		Clear Spring		
		Scrap Iron	904.35	

Pig Iron made . . . . . . Tons 356½

Yield of above mixture of Ores 39 43/100 per cent. or 2 54/100 tons Ore per ton Iron

Coke	used per ton Iron	1.77	tons a $ 3.00		$	5 31
Limestone	" " "	1.13	" a $ 0.79			0 89
Ores	" " "	Fossil 2.09	tons a $ 3.00	$ 6.27		
		Cross Cut 0.25	" $ 3.00	$ 0.75		
		South Branch	" $	$		
		Cinder 0.20	" $ 0.20	$ 0.04		7 06
		Clearspring	" $	$		
		Scrap Iron	" $	$		

Wages, per time list, inclusive of salary of Manager, $ 1126.12 divided by 356½ tons 3 15

Coal to Engine 536 4/20 tons a $ 1.20 divided by 356½ Tons . . 1 80

Materials, per Store and other accounts, viz; Oil, Tallow, Hemp, Packing Yarn, Steel, Leather, Shovels, Buckets, ~~Nails, &c.,~~ &c. . . 99

Expenses for Repairing damage done by Fire . . 4 19

Cost of one ton Pig Iron . . . $ 23 39

Mt. Savage Iron Works, 185

S Danks Superintendent

IRON RAIL SALES RECEIPT. This is a copy of a sales receipt from 1856. There are very few original records remaining from the Mount Savage Blast Furnace, because all other records were destroyed in the Great Baltimore Fire. (Courtesy of Cora Carter.)

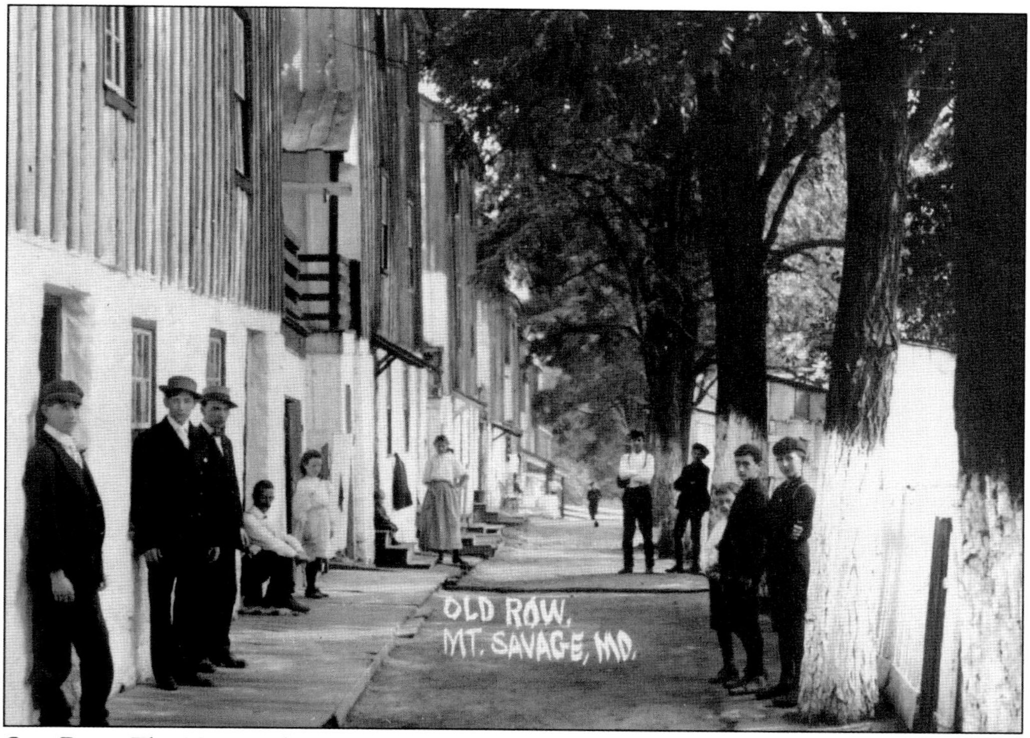

OLD ROW. The New York Iron & Coal Company is responsible for the development of the industrial valley of Mount Savage. It built the factories and many of the houses. Old Row was the first row of houses built to house the company's workers. The workers could rent, lease, or buy these houses from the company. (Courtesy of Mount Savage Historical Society.)

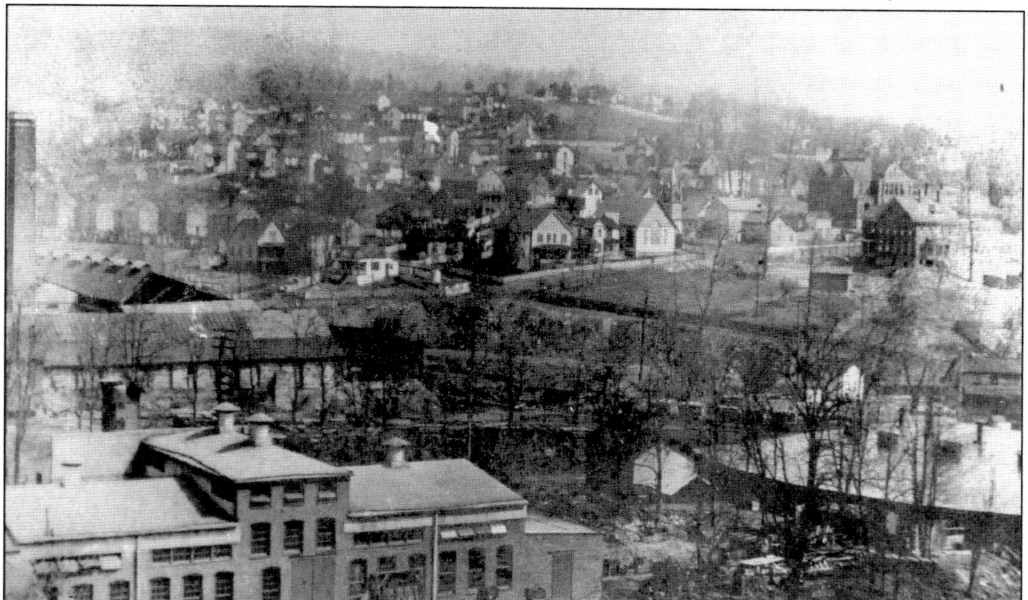

FOUNDRY BIRD'S-EYE VIEW, 1902. Even after the decline of the iron works in town, a foundry was established. It was known for manufacturing tin plates for decorative ceilings. Many of these ornate ceilings can be found throughout Allegany County. (Courtesy of Gary Delaney.)

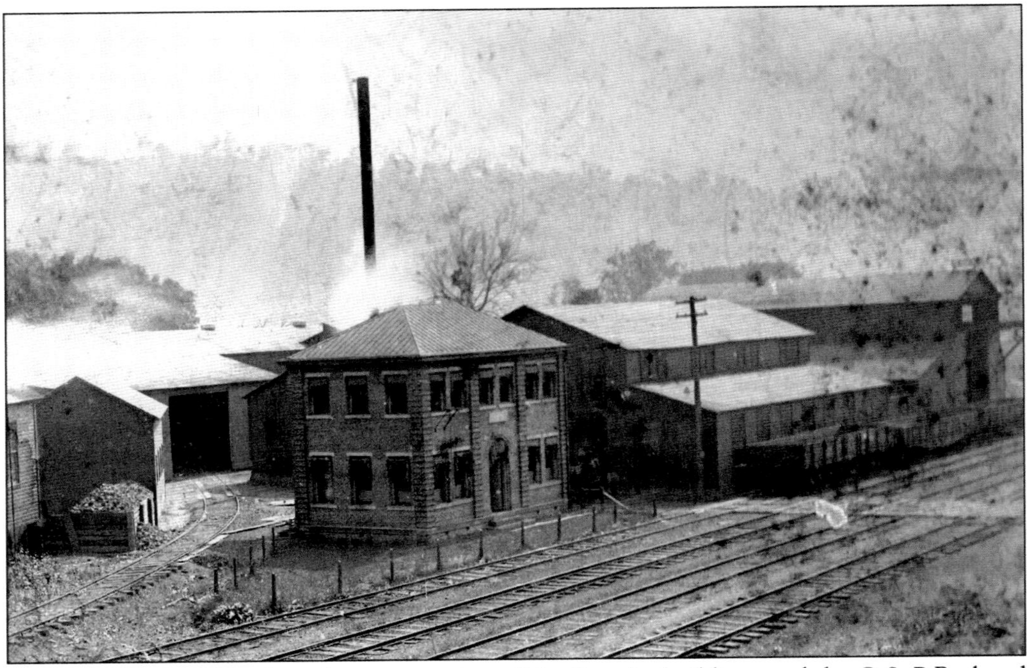

Foundry, 1902. This photo has a great view of the foundry buildings and the C & P Railroad track that went into the plant for freight pickup. (Courtesy of Wilma Delbrook, in memory of Stewart.)

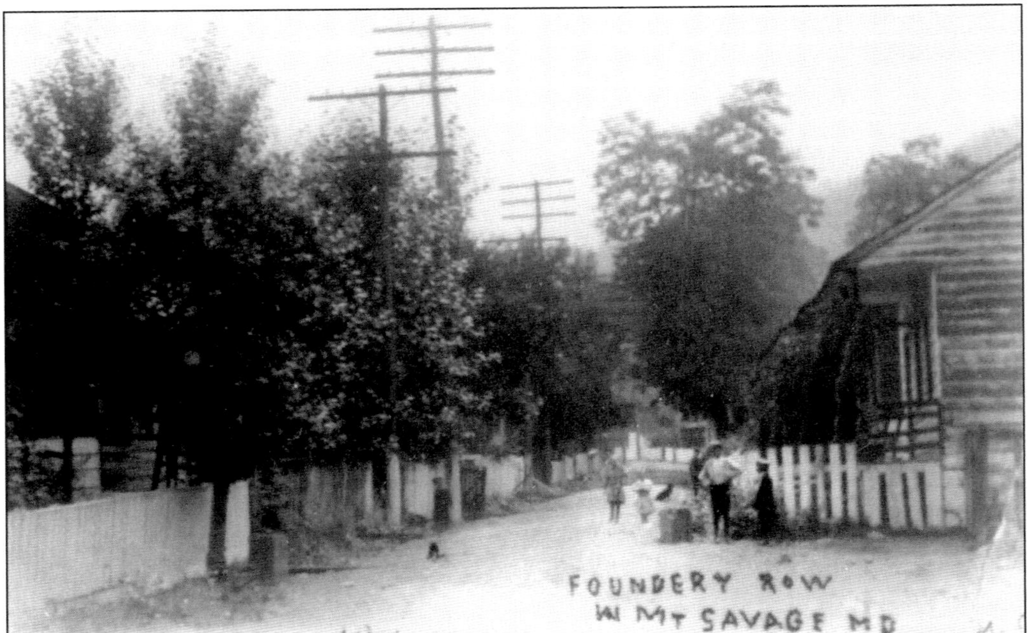

Foundry Row, 1911. The locals named this street after the foundry that was built here. (Courtesy of Paula Fuller.)

Three

THE BRICK YARDS

Around the same time that Mount Savage was experiencing an economic boom from the discovery of iron ore, another mineral deposit—fire clay—was found in the hillsides near the industrial village. In 1839 fire clay was found just a few miles from the production center of the New York Iron & Coal Company. The Union Mining Company stepped in and took control of the fire clay mines.

After testing the clay, the Union Mining Company found that the fire clay was of superior quality. It took several years of experimenting with various types of blast furnaces and heat levels to perfect brick-making in Mount Savage. Finally, in 1861 the brick business was in production on a large scale.

The bricks that were produced by the Union Mining Company were of such high quality that they became in high demand in other industrial areas. The Union Mining Company expanded their yards. The company not only mined fire clay and produced firebrick but also mined coal from its 600 acres of land in and around Mount Savage.

The Union Mining Company was not the only brick producer in Mount Savage. In 1895 Andrew Ramsey, an immigrant from Scotland, and four local men founded the Mount Savage Enamel Brick Company. The four men that Ramsey went into business with were Capt. John Sheridan, who was the general manager of the Union Mining Company; Hugh McMullin, who with his two brothers built the first department store in Cumberland on Baltimore Street; James Findlay, the former superintendent of the clay mines operated by the Union Mining Company; and Warren Delano, the uncle of Franklin Delano Roosevelt and the past superintendent of Union Mining Company operations in Mount Savage.

Ramsey's brick production was unique because he used a one-step process that put enamel glaze on the brick. The bricks were world renowned for their beauty and durability. The brick was used in the building of many of the tunnels in New York City and Pittsburgh. Many cities such as Boston and Buffalo built their post offices with Mount Savage enamel brick.

The Mount Savage Enamel Brick Company was the first of the two brick companies to go out of business. Like many companies, it went bankrupt during the Great Depression, and it was subsequently taken over by the Union Mining Company. The fire clay brickyard went out of business in a downsizing measure in 1987. The workers were laid off or transferred to the Zihlman plant just a few miles to the west of town.

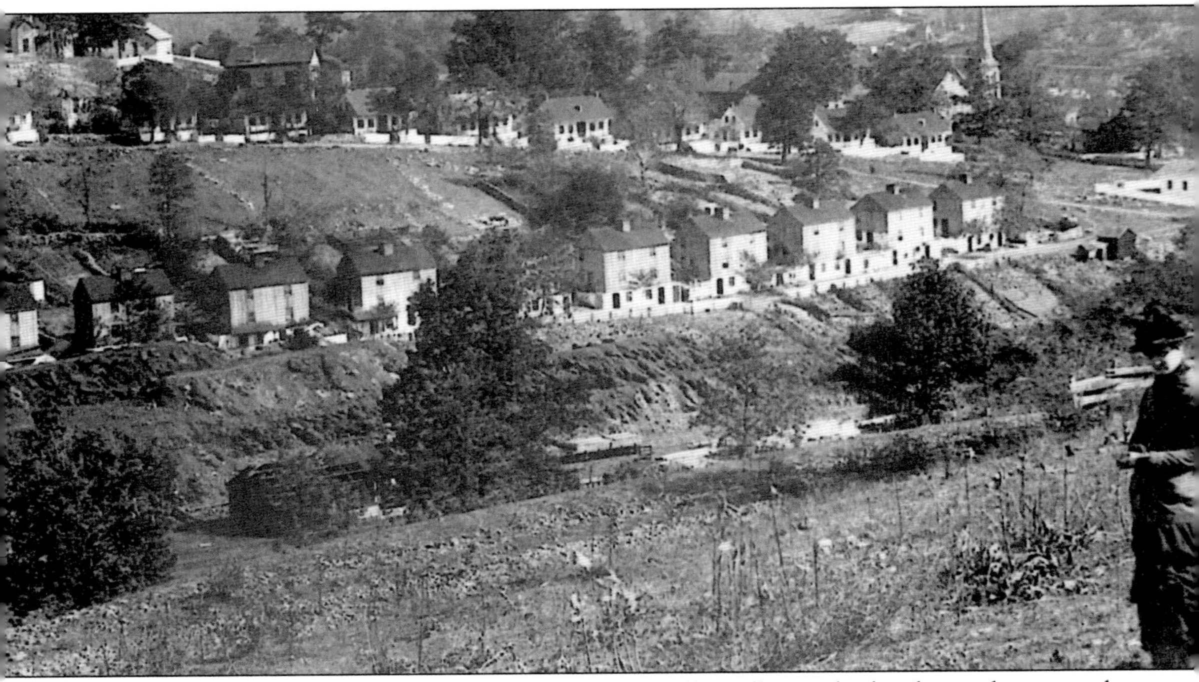

Looking Down at Old Row. This view from Calla Hill reveals the deserted iron works below Old Row. This would become the new location for the Mount Savage Fire Clay Brick Refractory. (Courtesy of Mount Savage Historical Society.)

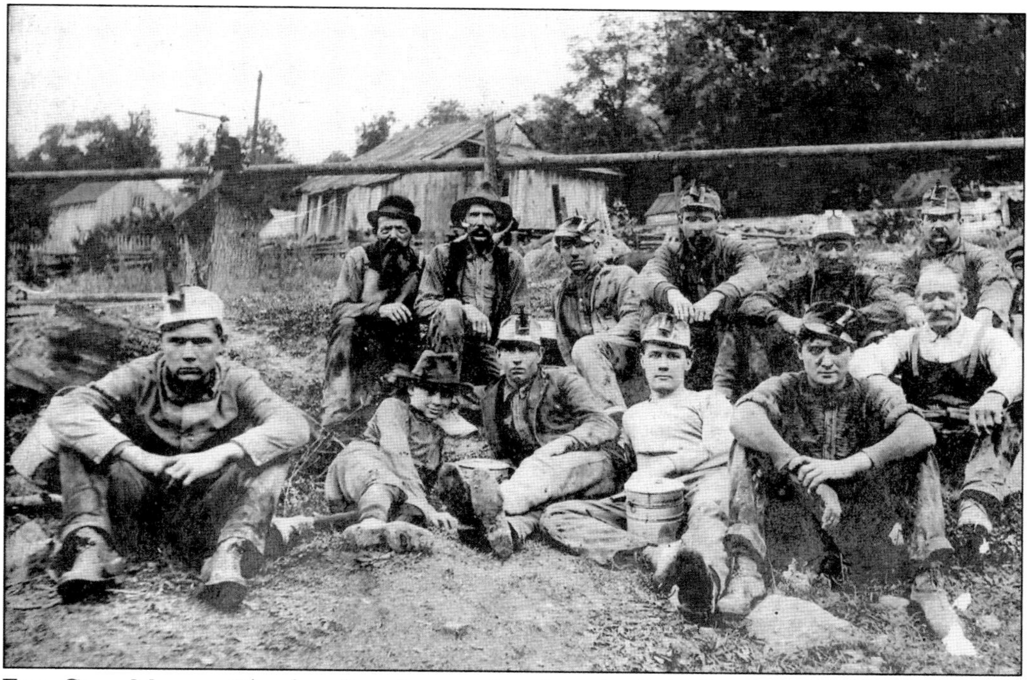

Fire Clay Miners. The first fire clay was found in the Bald Knob area at the foot of Big Savage Mountain. Later, fire clay was found at the foot of Little Allegheny Mountain, just below Barrelville. The miners in the photograph were from the Dutch Hollow area. (Courtesy of Cora Carter.)

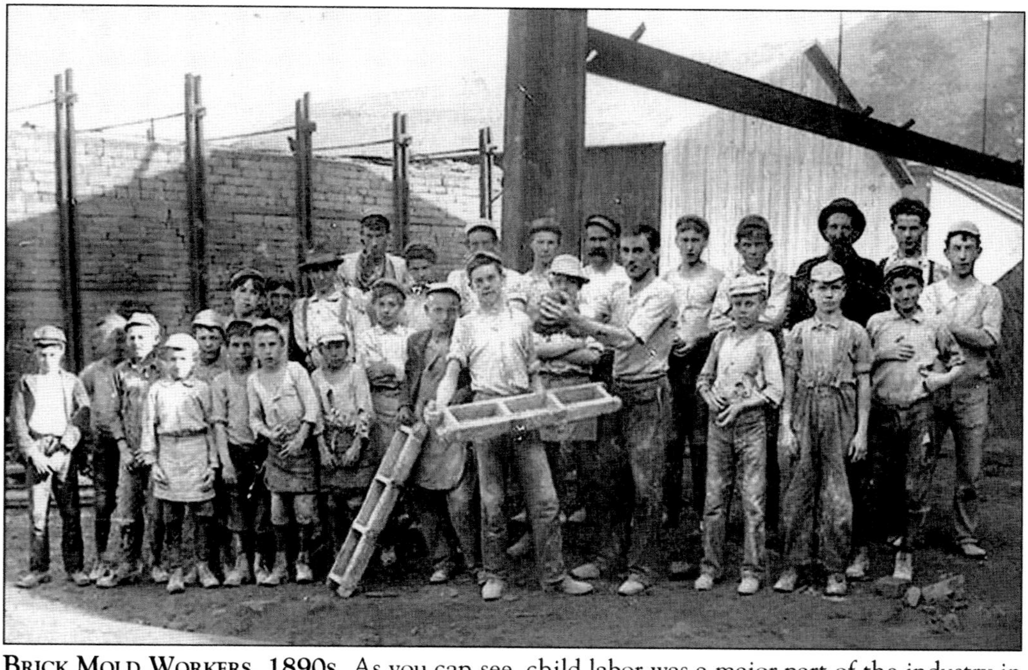

Brick Mold Workers, 1890s. As you can see, child labor was a major part of the industry in Mount Savage. Children were put to work to help support their large families. It was not until after child labor laws were put in place at the turn of the 20th century that the factories and mines stopped using children as workers in the area. (Courtesy of Wilbert Paul.)

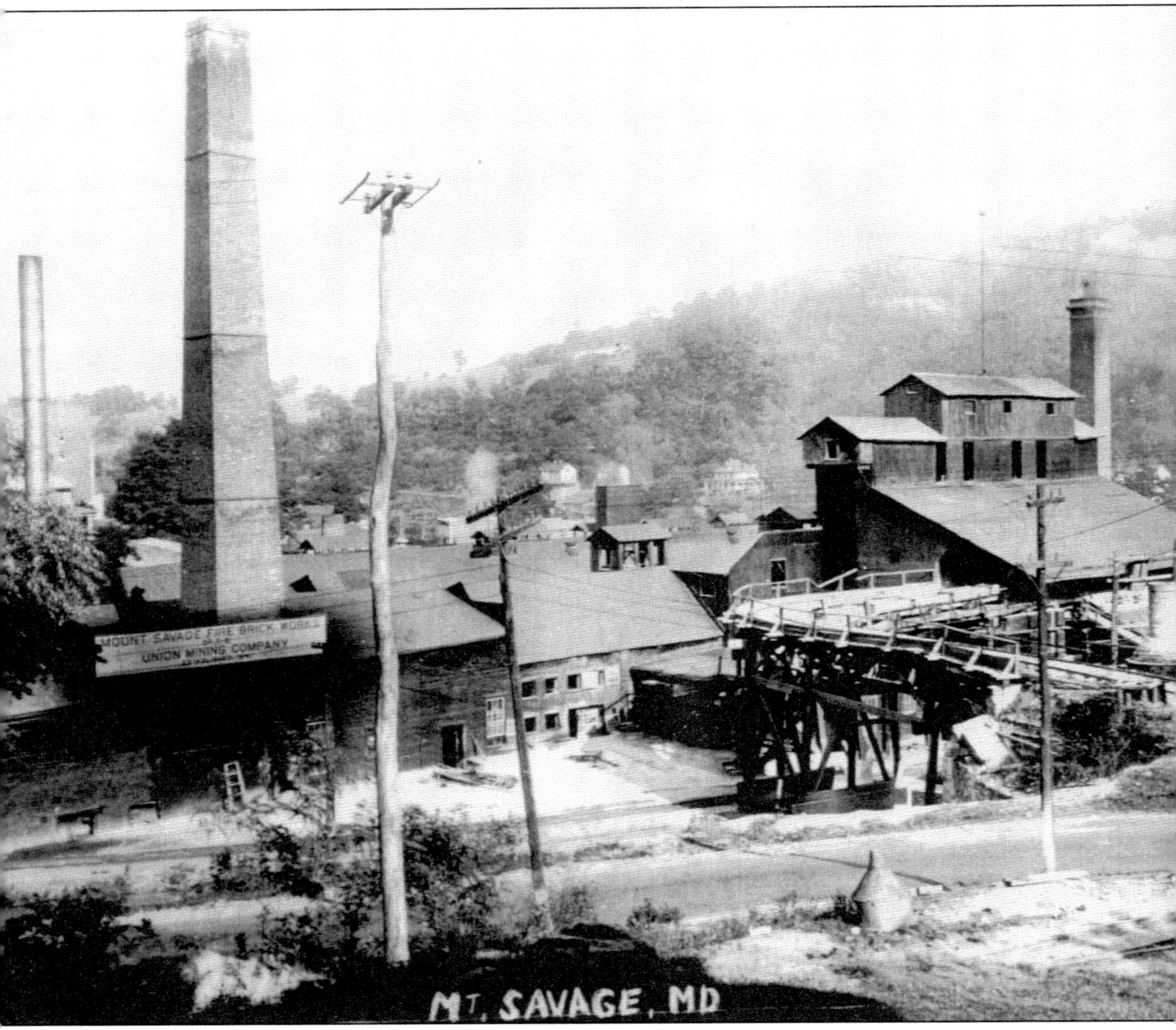

MOUNT SAVAGE FIRE CLAY BRICK REFRACTORY, 1900S. The first brickyard was located near the spot where the C & P passenger depot would later be built in 1839. Then, around 1860 the yard moved to its location near Jennings Run. (Courtesy of Mount Savage Historical Society.)

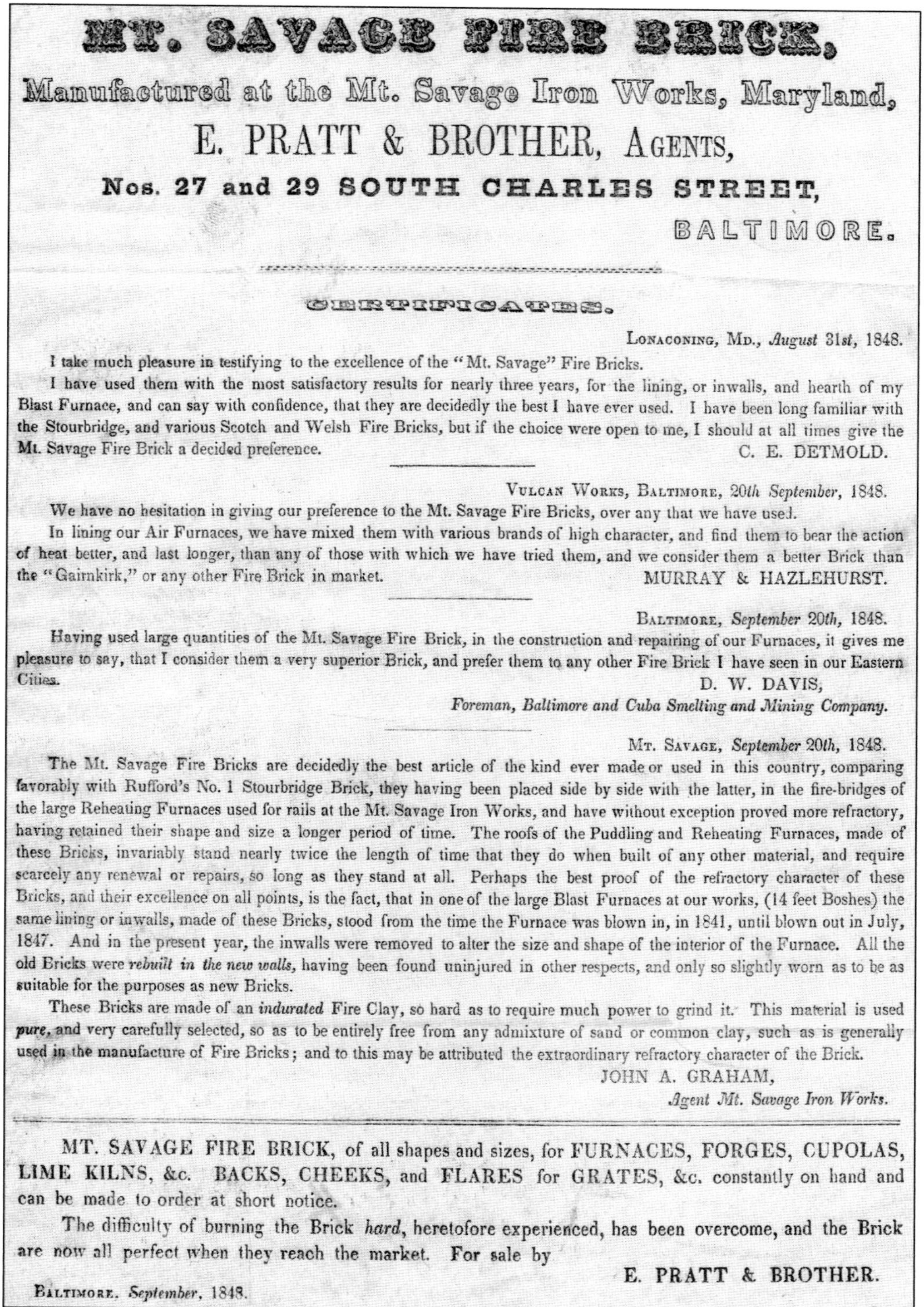

MT. SAVAGE FIRE BRICK,

Manufactured at the Mt. Savage Iron Works, Maryland,

E. PRATT & BROTHER, AGENTS,

Nos. 27 and 29 SOUTH CHARLES STREET,

BALTIMORE.

CERTIFICATES.

LONACONING, MD., *August* 31*st*, 1848.

I take much pleasure in testifying to the excellence of the "Mt. Savage" Fire Bricks.

I have used them with the most satisfactory results for nearly three years, for the lining, or inwalls, and hearth of my Blast Furnace, and can say with confidence, that they are decidedly the best I have ever used. I have been long familiar with the Stourbridge, and various Scotch and Welsh Fire Bricks, but if the choice were open to me, I should at all times give the Mt. Savage Fire Brick a decided preference.

C. E. DETMOLD.

VULCAN WORKS, BALTIMORE, 20*th September*, 1848.

We have no hesitation in giving our preference to the Mt. Savage Fire Bricks, over any that we have used.

In lining our Air Furnaces, we have mixed them with various brands of high character, and find them to bear the action of heat better, and last longer, than any of those with which we have tried them, and we consider them a better Brick than the "Gairnkirk," or any other Fire Brick in market.

MURRAY & HAZLEHURST.

BALTIMORE, *September* 20*th*, 1848.

Having used large quantities of the Mt. Savage Fire Brick, in the construction and repairing of our Furnaces, it gives me pleasure to say, that I consider them a very superior Brick, and prefer them to any other Fire Brick I have seen in our Eastern Cities.

D. W. DAVIS,
Foreman, Baltimore and Cuba Smelting and Mining Company.

MT. SAVAGE, *September* 20*th*, 1848.

The Mt. Savage Fire Bricks are decidedly the best article of the kind ever made or used in this country, comparing favorably with Rufford's No. 1 Stourbridge Brick, they having been placed side by side with the latter, in the fire-bridges of the large Reheating Furnaces used for rails at the Mt. Savage Iron Works, and have without exception proved more refractory, having retained their shape and size a longer period of time. The roofs of the Puddling and Reheating Furnaces, made of these Bricks, invariably stand nearly twice the length of time that they do when built of any other material, and require scarcely any renewal or repairs, so long as they stand at all. Perhaps the best proof of the refractory character of these Bricks, and their excellence on all points, is the fact, that in one of the large Blast Furnaces at our works, (14 feet Boshes) the same lining or inwalls, made of these Bricks, stood from the time the Furnace was blown in, in 1841, until blown out in July, 1847. And in the present year, the inwalls were removed to alter the size and shape of the interior of the Furnace. All the old Bricks were *rebuilt in the new walls*, having been found uninjured in other respects, and only so slightly worn as to be as suitable for the purposes as new Bricks.

These Bricks are made of an *indurated* Fire Clay, so hard as to require much power to grind it. This material is used *pure*, and very carefully selected, so as to be entirely free from any admixture of sand or common clay, such as is generally used in the manufacture of Fire Bricks; and to this may be attributed the extraordinary refractory character of the Brick.

JOHN A. GRAHAM,
Agent Mt. Savage Iron Works.

MT. SAVAGE FIRE BRICK, of all shapes and sizes, for FURNACES, FORGES, CUPOLAS, LIME KILNS, &c. BACKS, CHEEKS, and FLARES for GRATES, &c. constantly on hand and can be made to order at short notice.

The difficulty of burning the Brick *hard*, heretofore experienced, has been overcome, and the Brick are now all perfect when they reach the market. For sale by

E. PRATT & BROTHER.

BALTIMORE, *September*, 1848.

MOUNT SAVAGE FIRE BRICK ADVERTISEMENT, 1848. Agents were sent to cities such as Baltimore and Washington, D.C., to sell bricks from the refractories in town. As seen in the ad, they were sure to have personal accounts by companies and individuals to prove that the brick was "superior brick." (Courtesy of Mount Savage Historical Society.)

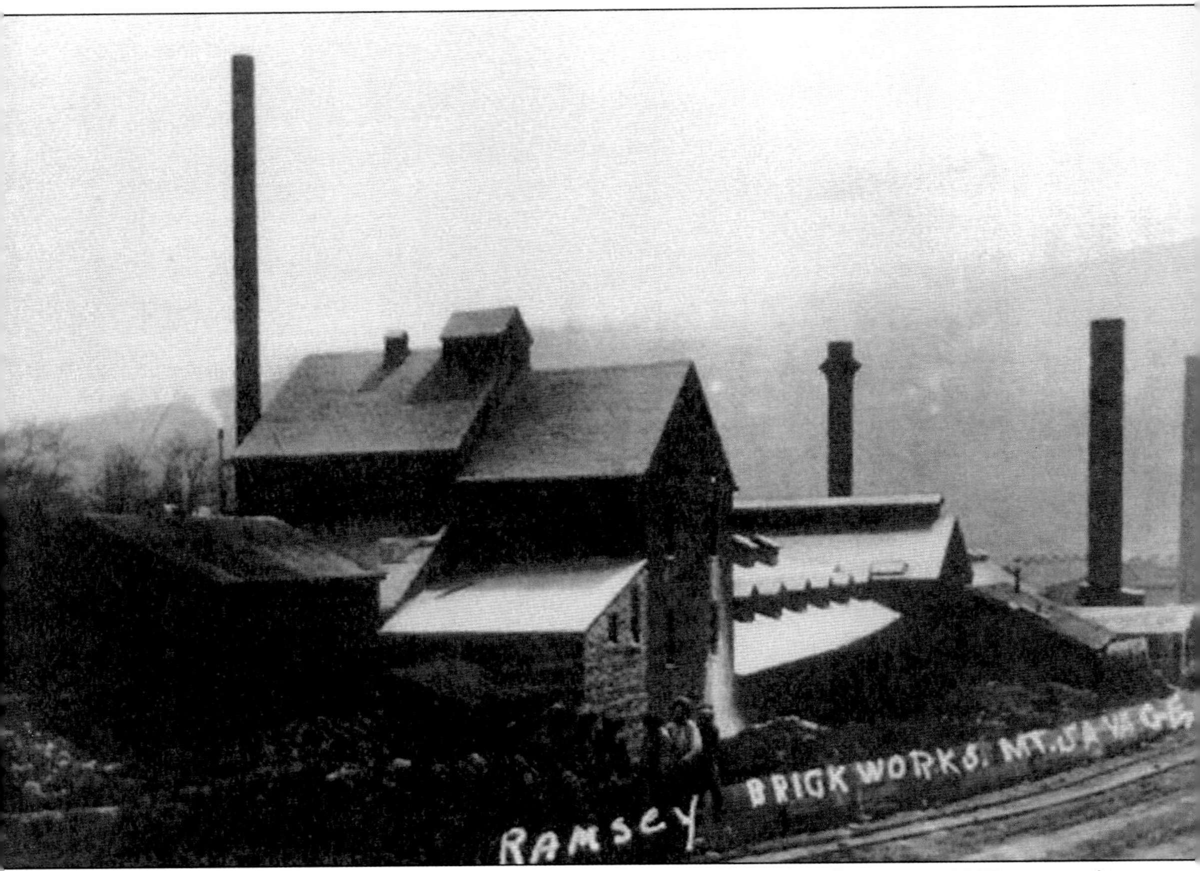

Ramsey Glazed Brick Works. Andrew Ramsey came to Mount Savage in 1895 to start his own specialized brick manufacturing. With help from Capt. John Sheridan, the foreman who left the fire clay refractory, he started a glazed brick works. (Courtesy of Cora Carter.)

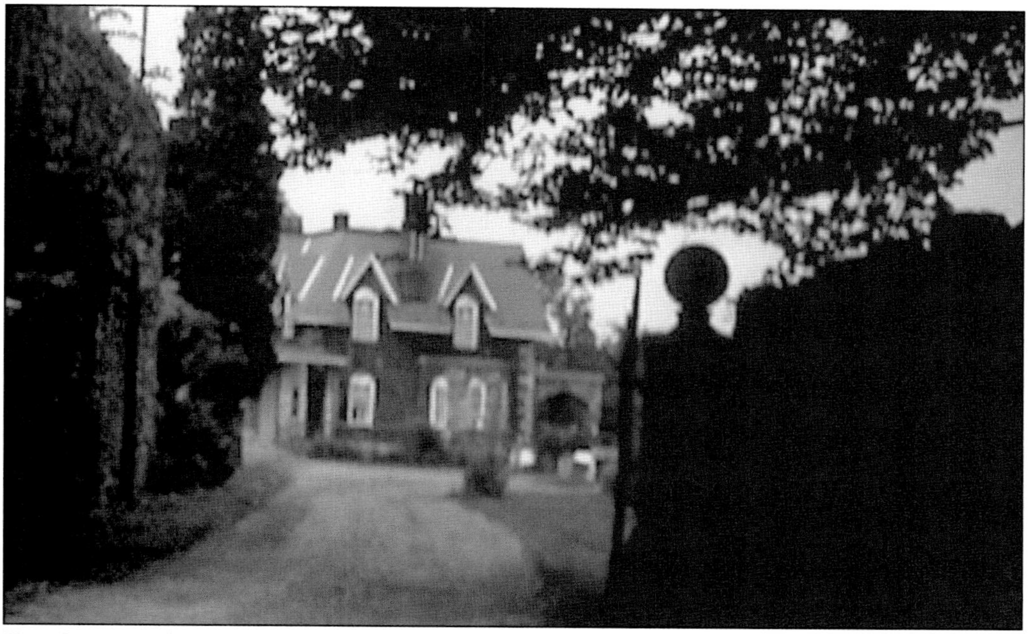

The Castle. This house was actually built by the Union Mining Company to entice a doctor to move to the town and work for the company. The Union Mining Company later sold the house to Andrew Ramsey. Ramsey renovated the structure to resemble Castle Craig in his homeland, Scotland. He lived here until the Great Depression hit, and at that point he and his company went bankrupt. (Courtesy of Carol Barry.)

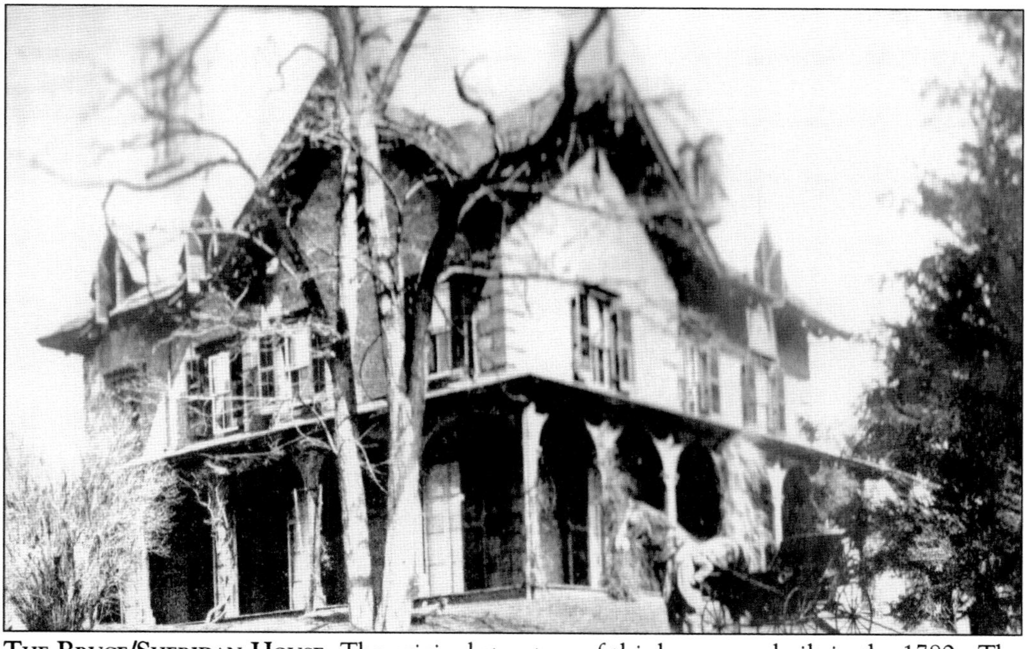

The Bruce/Sheridan House. The original structure of this house was built in the 1780s. The house was enlarged during the post–Civil War industrial boom when John Sheridan purchased the house after becoming president of the Union Mining Company and owner of the fire clay brick refractory. Later, in the late 19th century, Warren Delano, F.D.R.'s uncle, took up residence at the estate while he oversaw the Union Mining Company. (Courtesy of Cora Carter.)

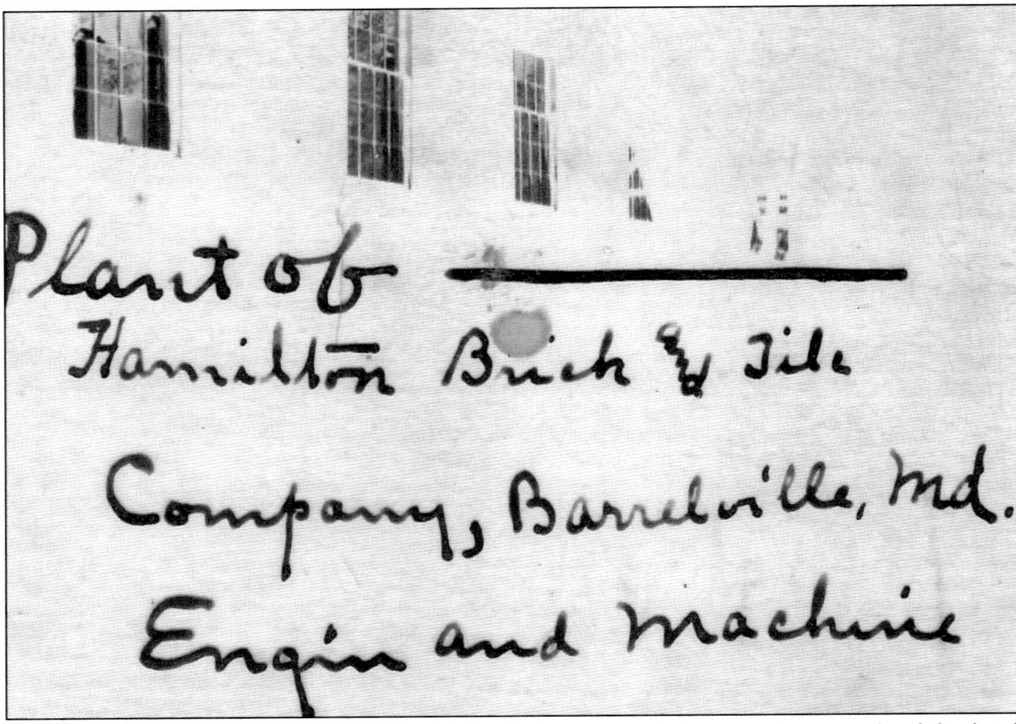

HAMILTON BRICK AND TILE FACTORY, 1915. This is the only known photograph of the brick refractory that was located at Prince Albert's Square (Barrelville). The photo is very faded, but you can make out the windows of the office.

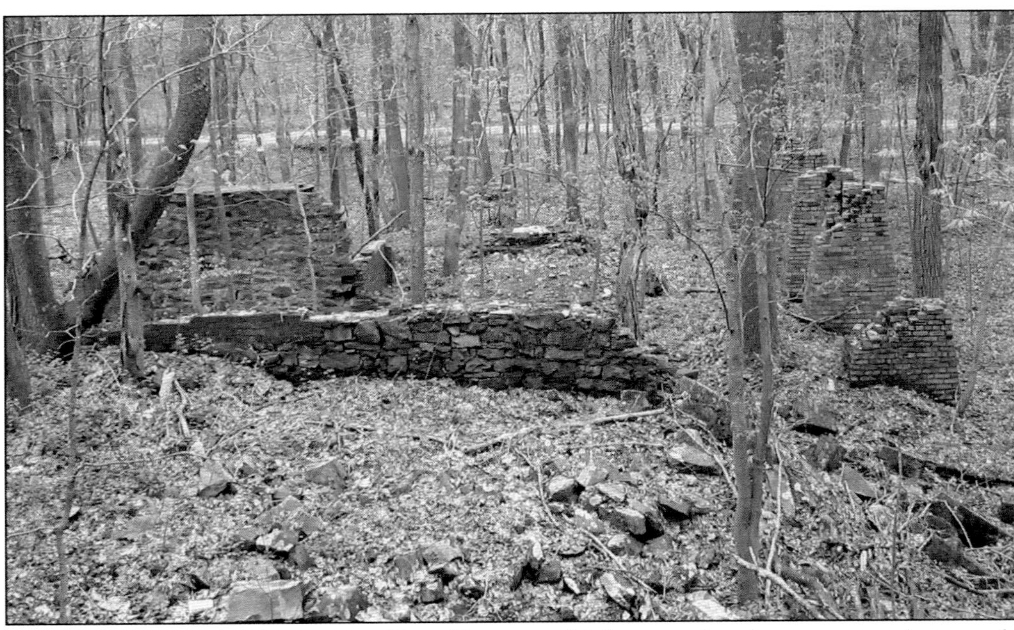

RUINS OF HAMILTON BRICK AND TILE FACTORY. Unfortunately, there are no photographs of this brick factory while it was in use. It produced sandy brown brick that was used for a few houses and chimneys in the Mount Savage area. It went out of business shortly after World War I.

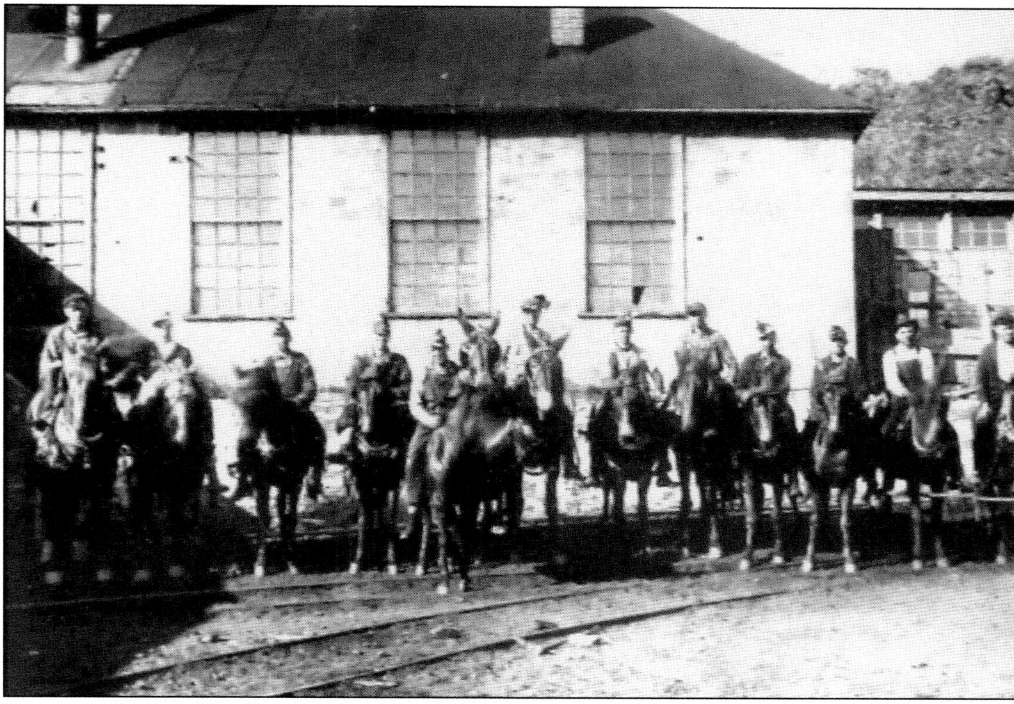

BRAILER MINING. The Brailer family owned and operated coal and clay mines in Dutch Hollow. They sold much of the coal and used some to fire their own brick kilns on their property. It seems they had a pretty good business, judging by the workers and their mules. (Courtesy of the Folks.)

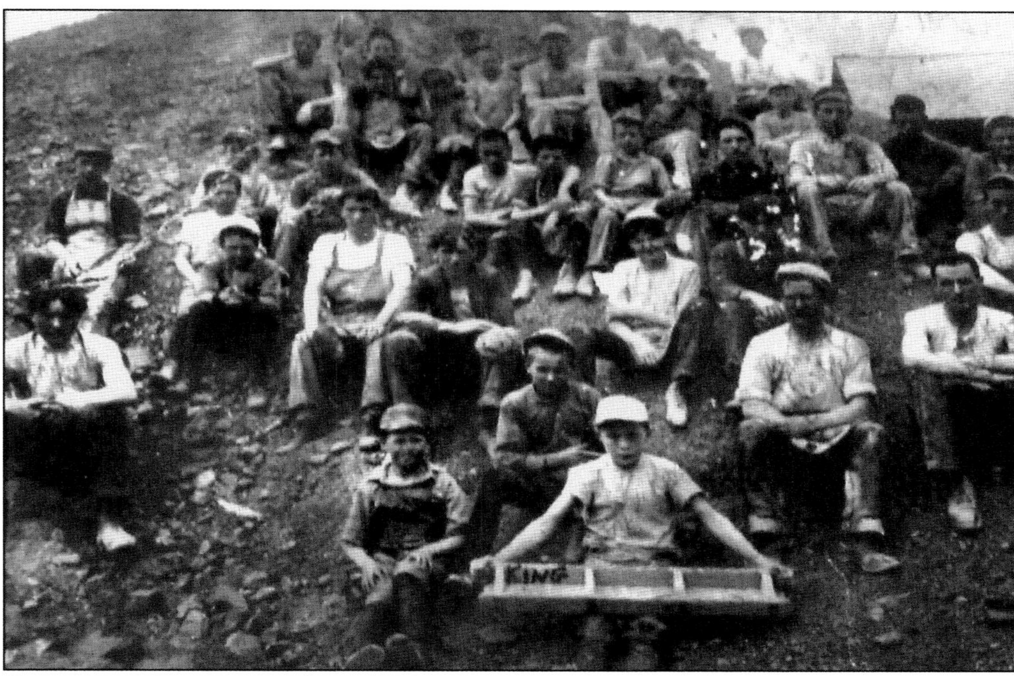

KIDS ON THE SLATE PILE. These children worked for the Brailer family brick refractory. Many children at the time worked at brickyards molding brick. (Courtesy of the Folk's.)

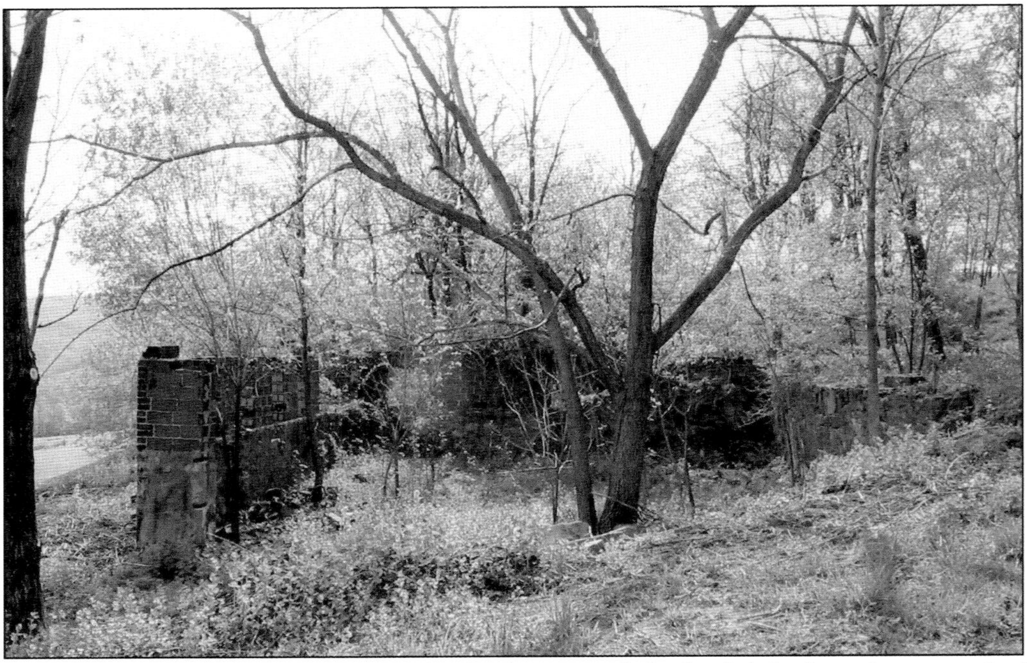

Ruins of the Brailer Brickyard. The family operated the brick kiln for a short period of time. They mined coal from the Dutch Hollow area until the 1930s. (Courtesy of the Folks)

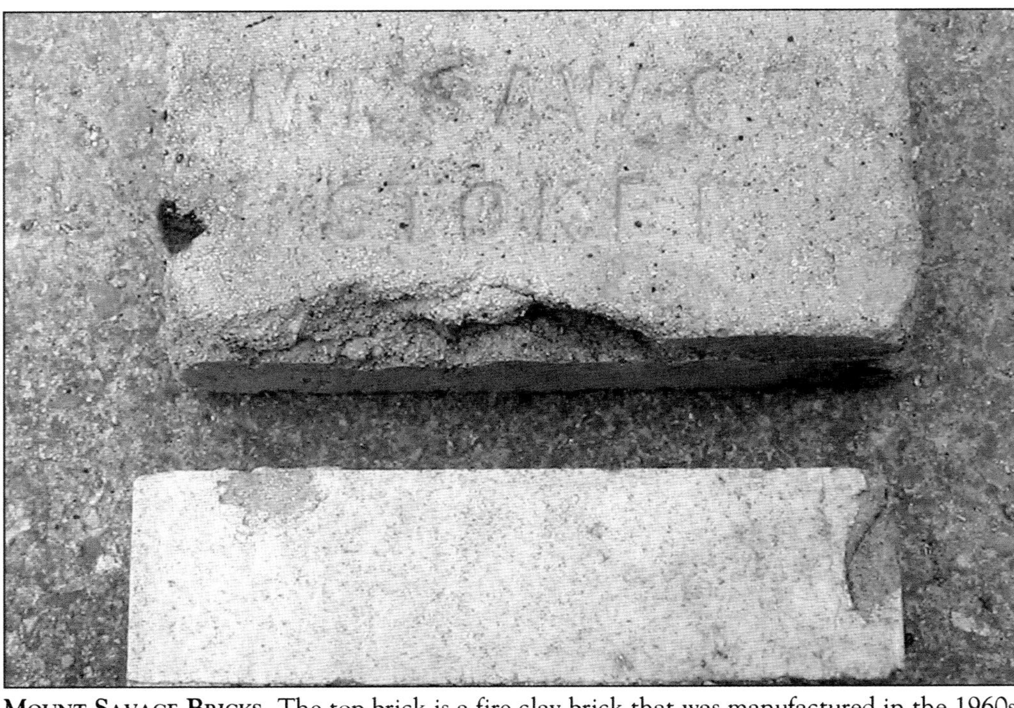

Mount Savage Bricks. The top brick is a fire clay brick that was manufactured in the 1960s. At one time, the quality of Mount Savage fire clay brick was so sought after that some other companies started printing "Mt. Savage" on their bricks in hopes of selling more. The bottom brick is a Ramsey glazed brick, another well-known brick.

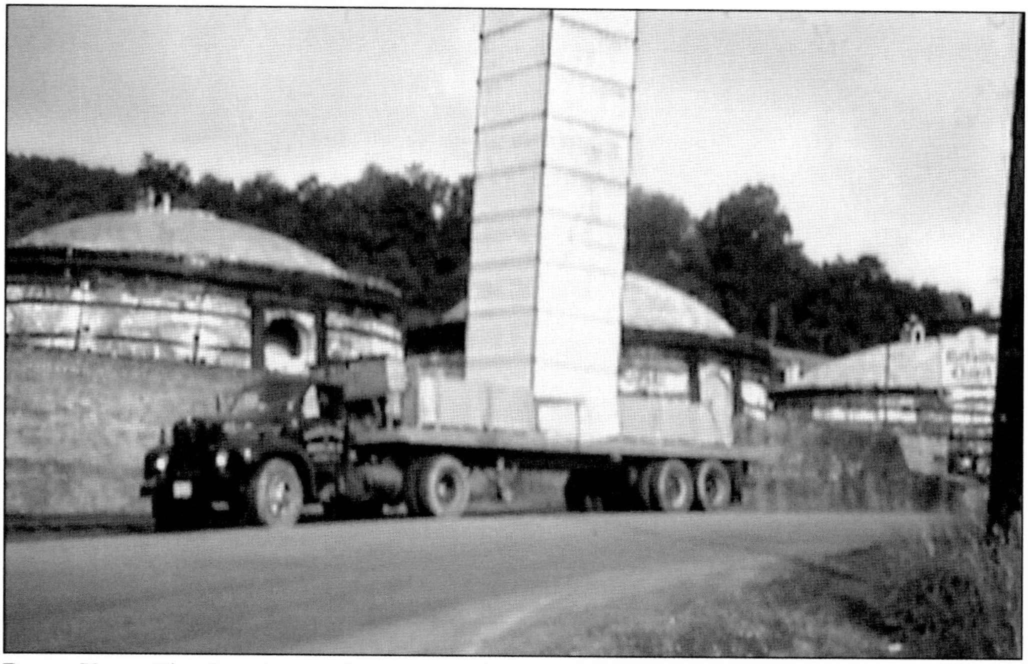

Brick Kiln. The fire clay yard overcame the economic depression in the 1930s. It steadily produced brick for the nation. (Courtesy of Carol Barry.)

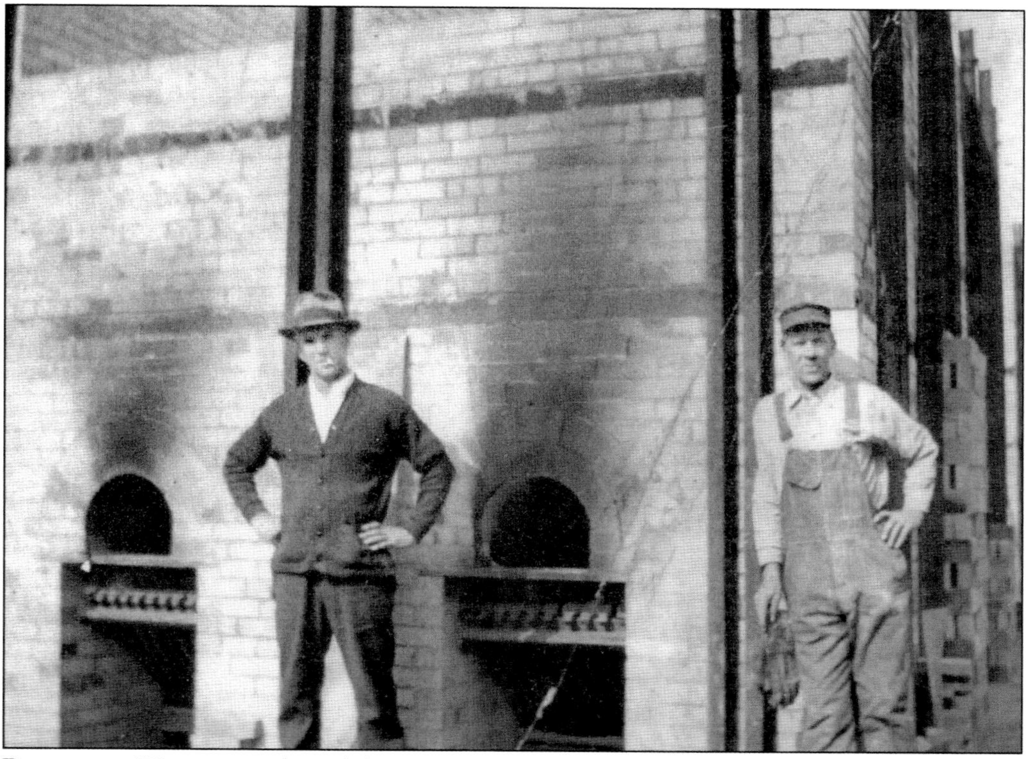

Brickyard Workers. These kiln workers stopped their work briefly for a picture. This photograph is one of very few taken of workers on the job. (Courtesy of Cora Carter.)

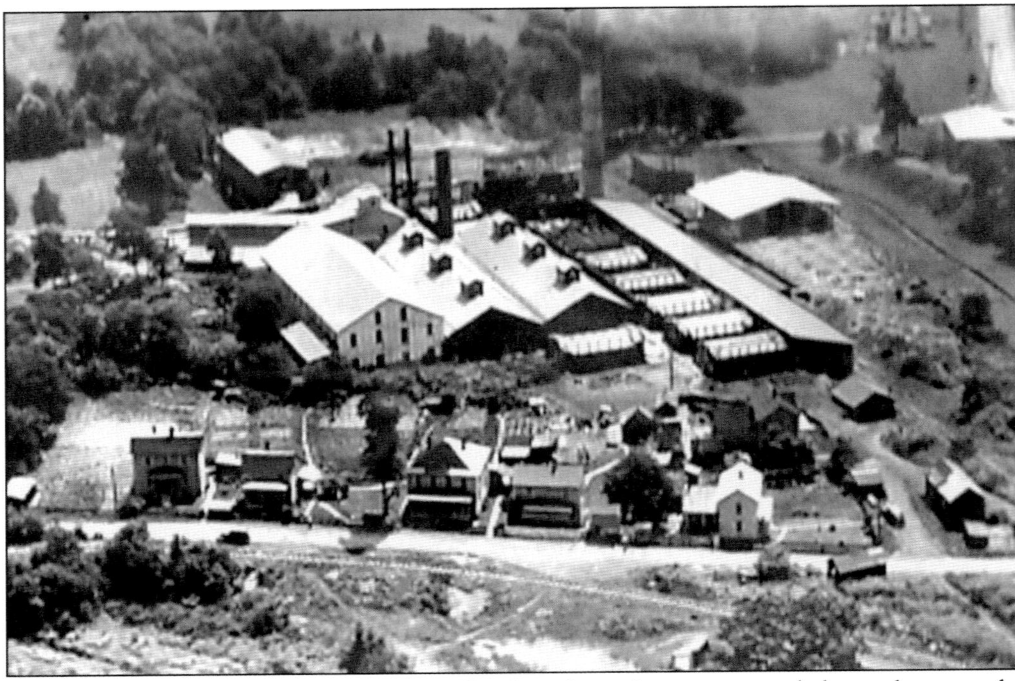

The Expanding Fire Clay Business. The fire clay refractory expanded to take over the location of the Enamel Brick Refractory area along with the area where the iron blast furnaces were located. This aerial view of the yard allows a bird's-eye view of the business. (Courtesy of Carol Barry.)

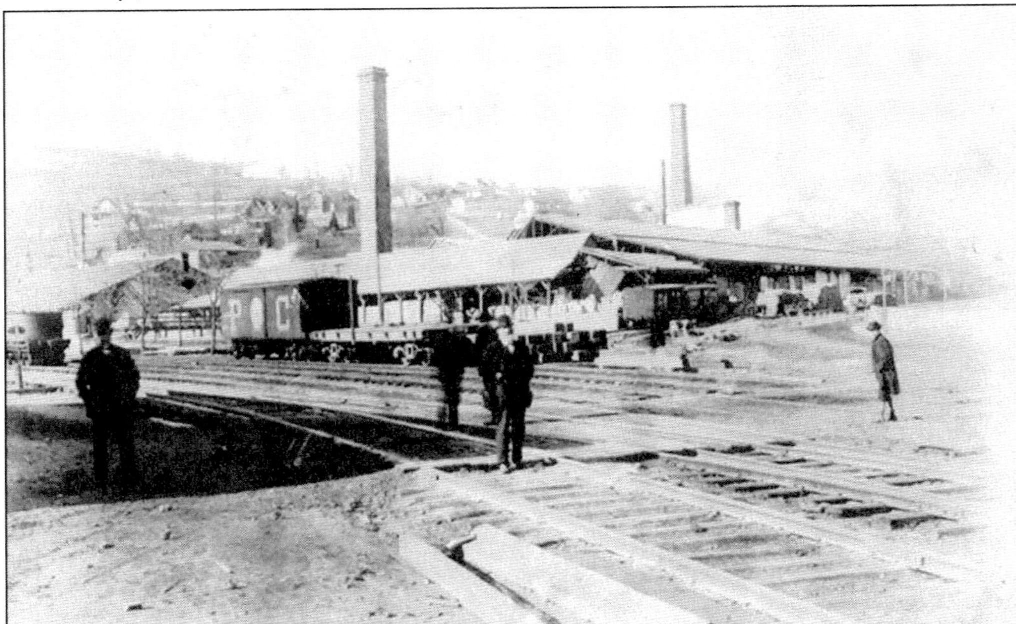

C & P Railroad at Loading Brick. The brickyard and the C & P Railroad worked closely together as businesses. The C & P was used to transport the bricks to larger train systems so they could be sold at market. Before the railroad was in operation, the bricks were shipped via freight wagon. (Courtesy of J.G. Farrell Collection.)

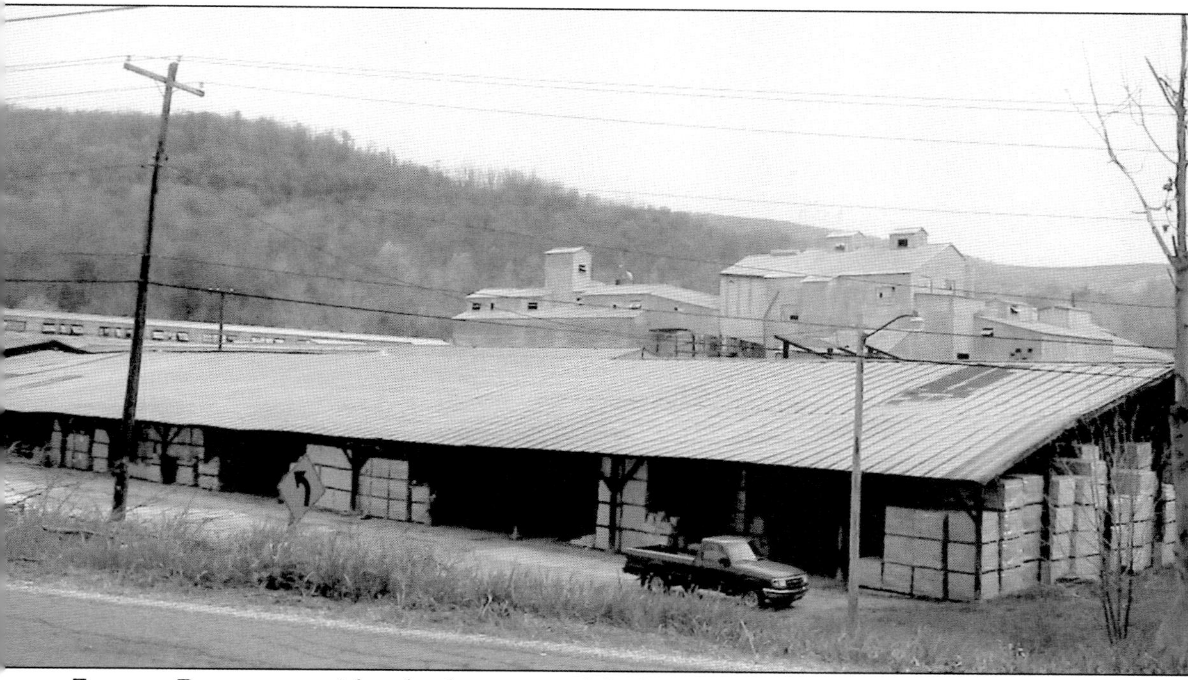

ZIHLMAN REFRACTORY. After the downsizing of the Rost Company, the brick production was moved to Zihlman, just five miles west of Mount Savage. Brick is still produced there today.

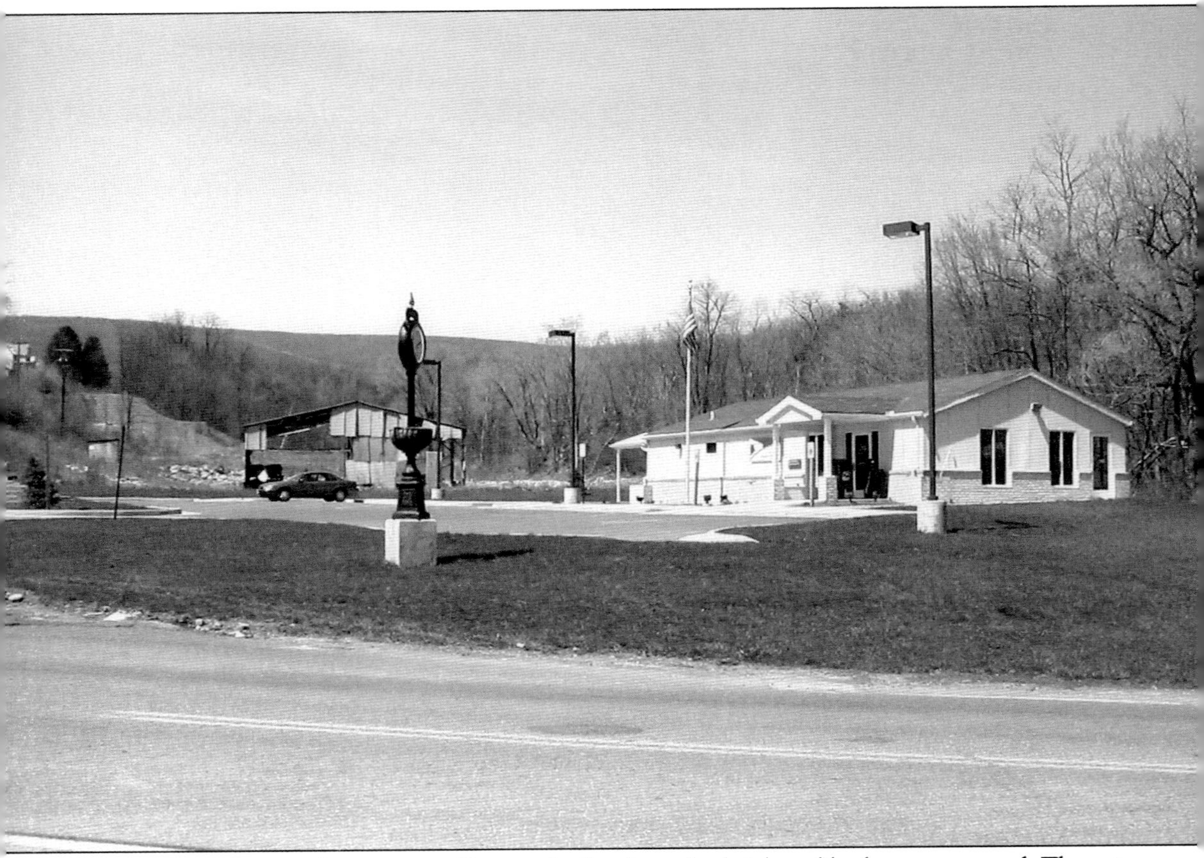

The Post Office. A new post office was built where the brickyard had once operated. There is only a shell of a storage building that remains at the rear of the post office.

Four

Cumberland and Pennsylvania Railroads

After the Baltimore and Ohio Railroad broke ground in 1828 and became prominent in the lives of people in the nation, many other railroads began to pop up and develop across the country. Many of these railroad lines worked in conjunction with the B & O Railroad as trunk railroad lines. These trunk railroad lines were short lines that were used to deliver goods to larger railroads and, many times, canals that were in the vicinity of the trunk line.

The Cumberland and Pennsylvania Railroad was one of these trunk lines that emerged in Allegany County after the B & O Railroad and the C & O Canal made their way to Western Maryland. The C & P Railroad was developed at first to accommodate the Union Mining Company. The mining company used the railroad to transport coal and bricks along with other goods that the nearby towns would have to haul.

Freight was not the only purpose of the C & P Railroad. It also had a very popular passenger service that lasted for almost 100 years. Eight times a day trains arrived and departed from Mount Savage to Cumberland and Piedmont. This schedule of passenger trains was cut back in the 1930s and stopped altogether in the mid-1940s.

The C & P Railroad line ran from Cumberland to Piedmont, West Virginia. Its shops, roundhouse, and certain offices were built in Mount Savage. Depots were built in Mount Savage, Frostburg, and Piedmont. Spur lines were also extended to Barrelville, Ellerslie, Eckhart, and Wellersburg, Pennsylvania. Mount Savage remained the heart of the operation with the shops, roundhouse, and offices.

In 1844 the shops were built in town, and the company was incorporated in 1850. The shops employed approximately 600 men. The railroad began building locomotives in 1868. In 1901 the office building was constructed in Mount Savage.

Locomotives were manufactured and repaired in Mount Savage until 1944. At this point, the Western Maryland Railway purchased the C & P Railroad and closed the shops. Then, in 1953 the C & P merged with the Western Maryland Railway. The last train to go through Mount Savage departed town in 1983, after Chessie Rail System purchased Western Maryland Railway.

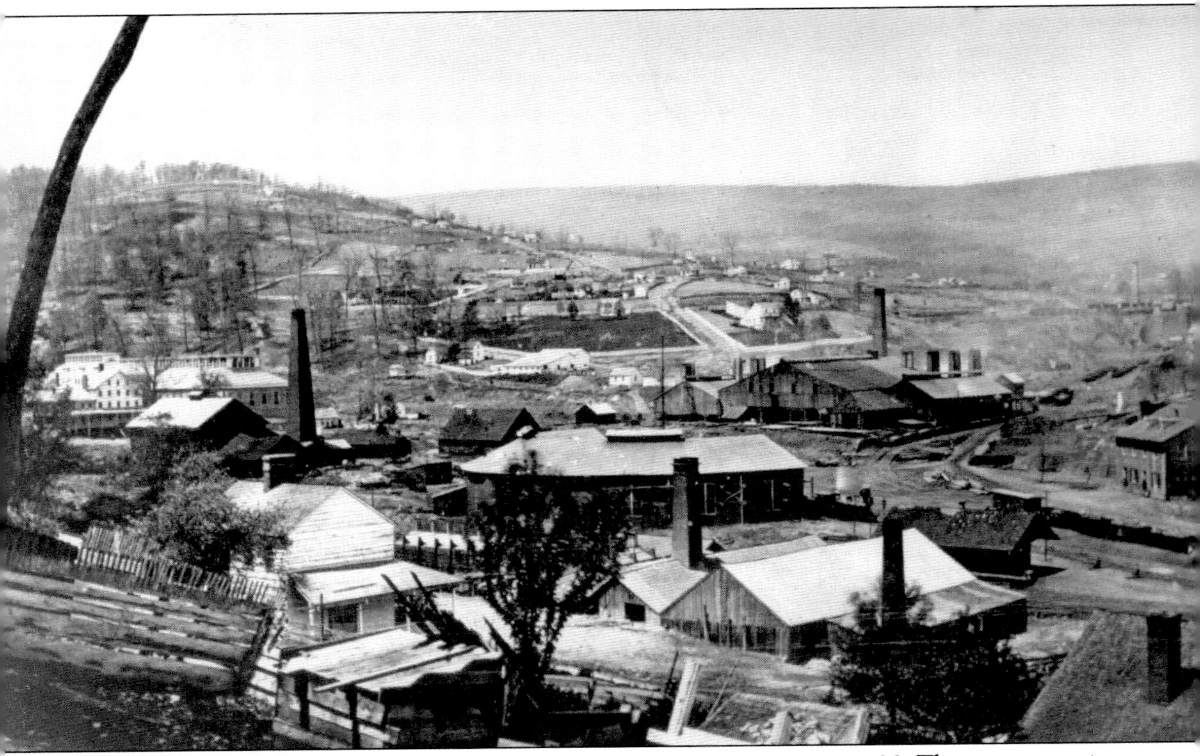

The Cumberland & Pennsylvania Railroad Shops and Yards, 1866. This is a great view of the C & P yards and the neighboring industry in town. In the center of the picture is the roundhouse and passenger depot. To the right is the fire clay brick refractory and to the left is the Ramsey Glazed Brick Works. (Courtesy of the Mount Savage Historical Society.)

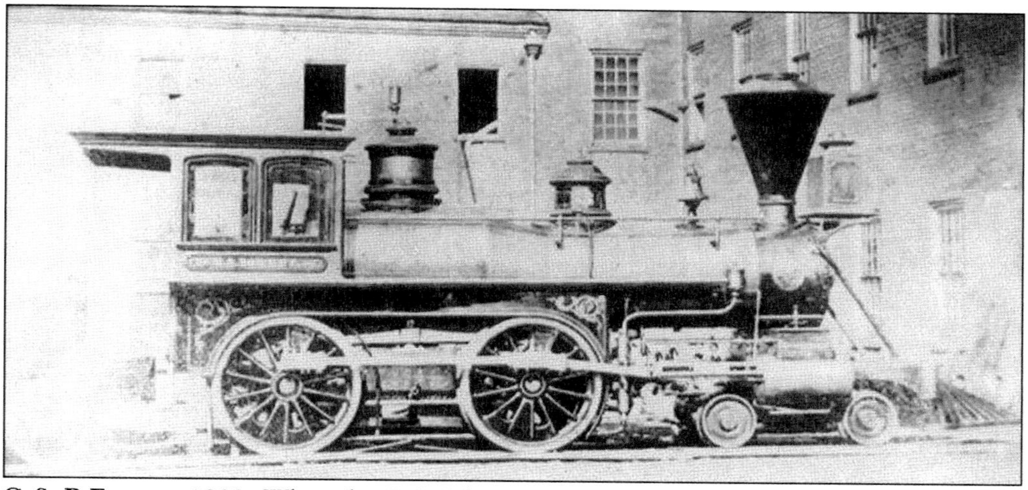

C & P Engine, 1882. When the C & P began, it was in the business to build and refurbish locomotive engines. Later, the company expanded its services to hauling goods and transporting passengers. (Courtesy of J.G. Farrell Collection.)

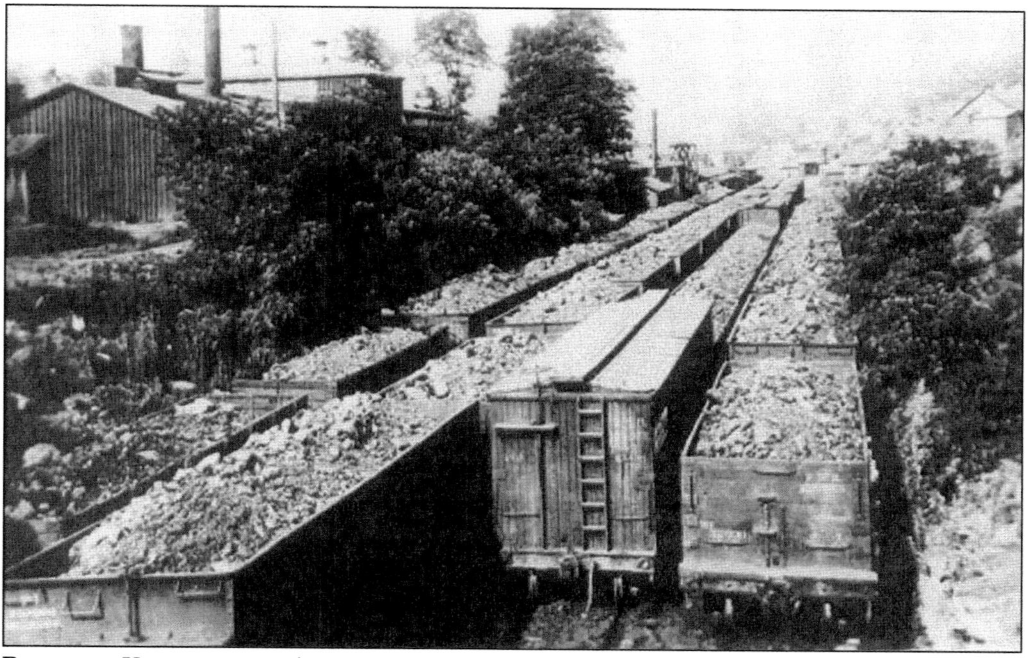

Railroad Yard, 1902. The C & P was a busy trunk-line railroad. It carried coal from the Georges Creek Valley to Cumberland, in addition to the bricks that it carried from the brickyards in town. (Courtesy of J.G. Farrell Collection.)

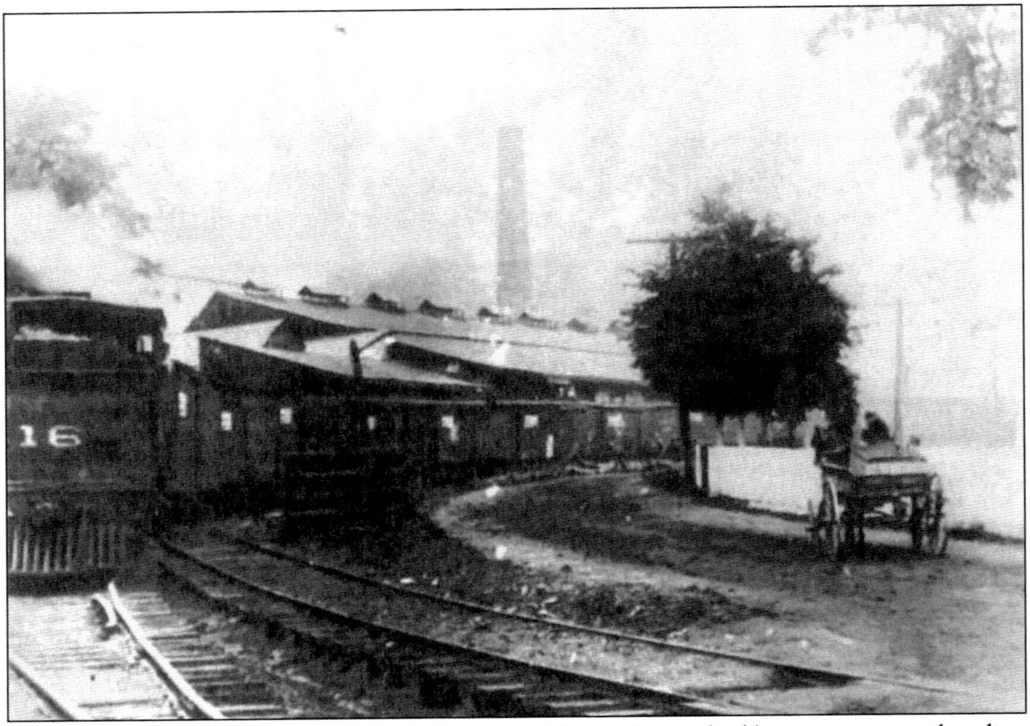

Railroad Town. By the turn of the 20th century Mount Savage had become a true railroading town. Its people functioned with the timing of the train whistle blowing as the trains moved in and out of town in a regular fashion. (Courtesy of Cora Carter.)

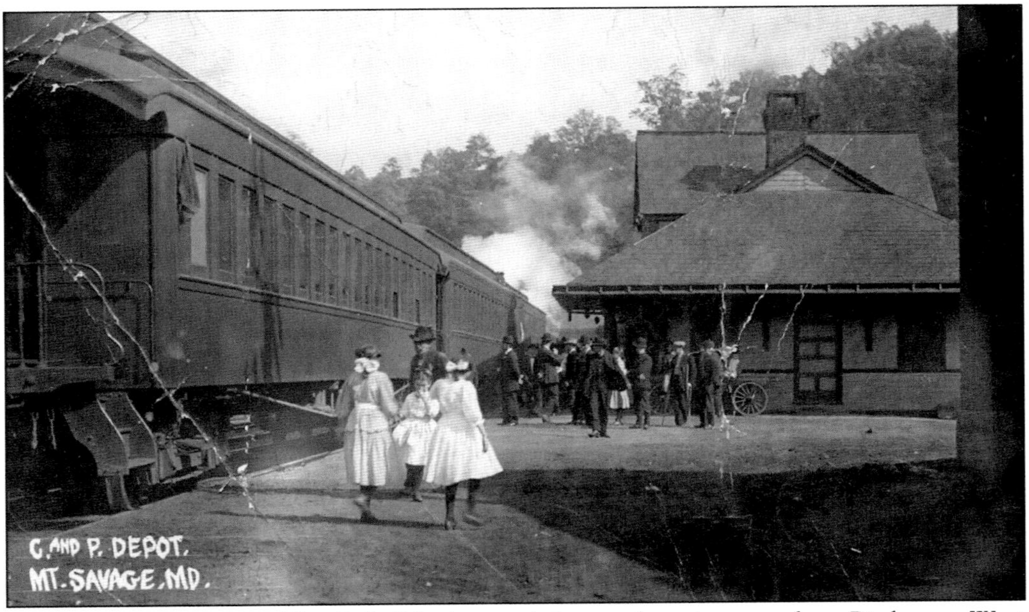

Mount Savage Depot. The C & P had several depots along its route from Piedmont, West Virginia, to Cumberland, Maryland. (Courtesy of Gary Delaney.)

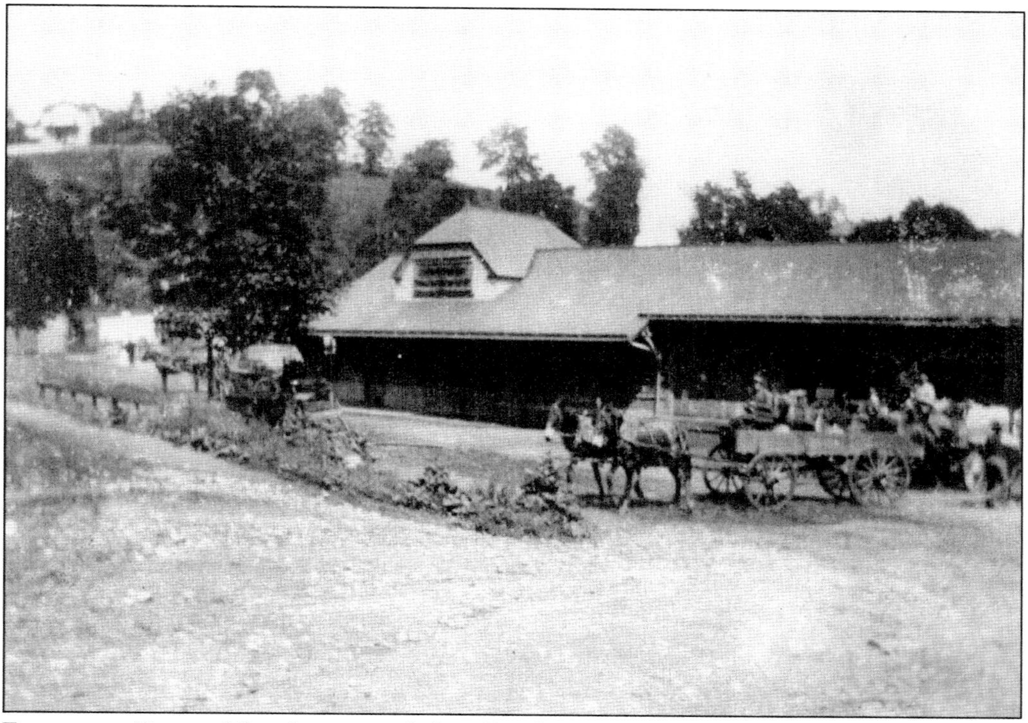

Frostburg Depot. This depot, just below Frostburg's Main Street, was quite a busy station because the C & P made daily deliveries to the merchants of Frostburg. In addition to the depot, the Tunnel Hotel was also located here.

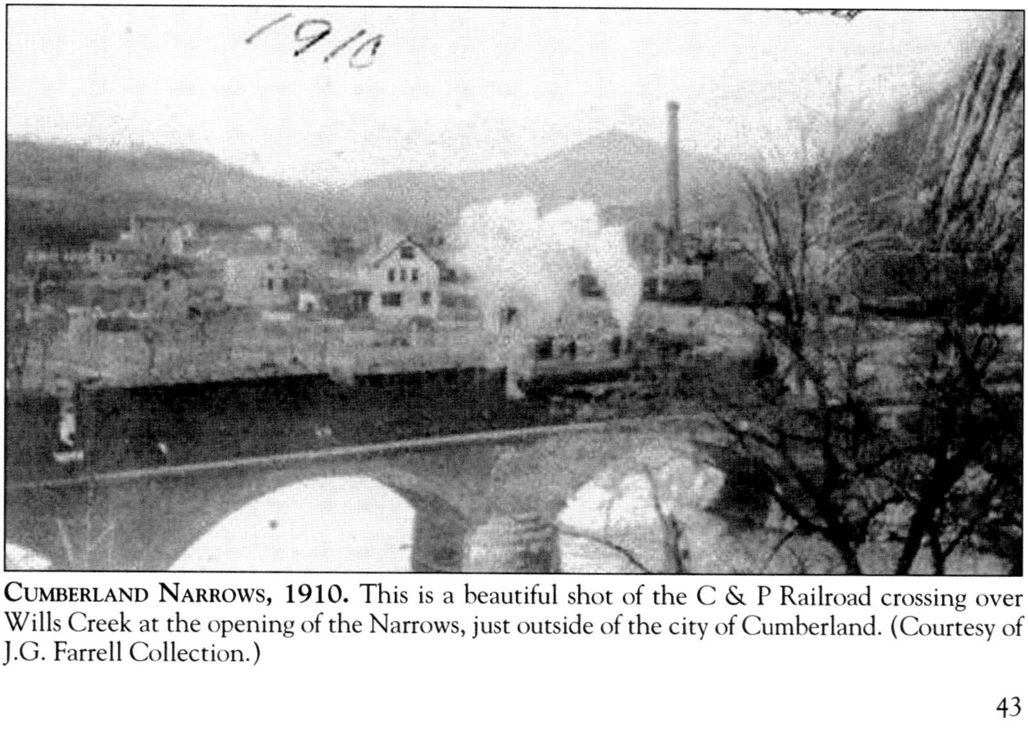

Cumberland Narrows, 1910. This is a beautiful shot of the C & P Railroad crossing over Wills Creek at the opening of the Narrows, just outside of the city of Cumberland. (Courtesy of J.G. Farrell Collection.)

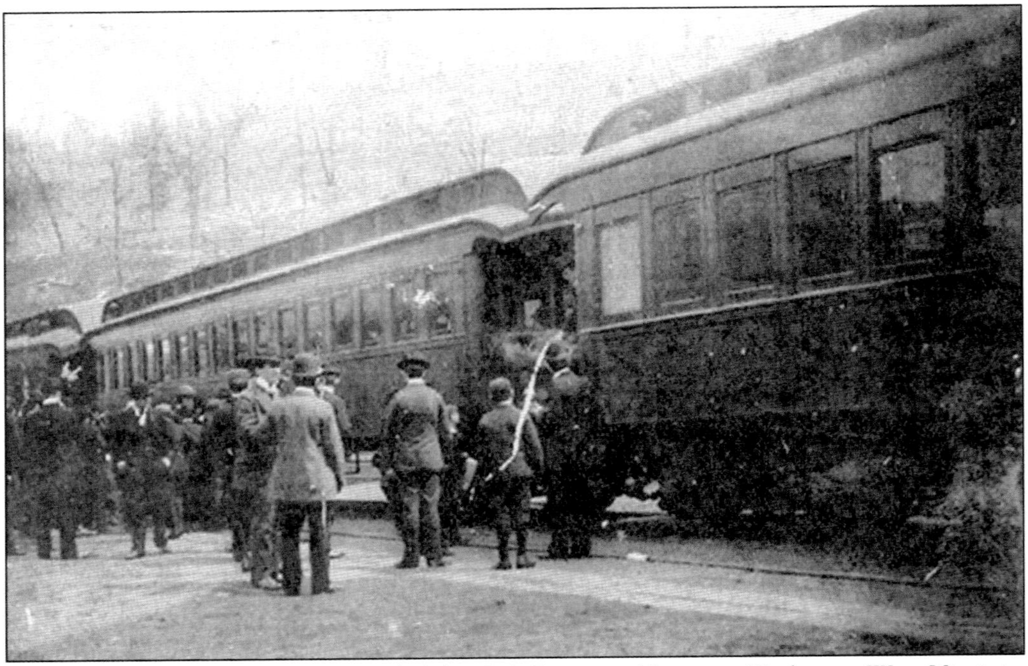

PASSENGERS, 1908. Passengers boarded the C & P to travel between Piedmont, West Virginia, and Cumberland, Maryland. There were depots in various towns along the route where people could purchase a ticket to travel on the line. (Courtesy of J.G. Farrell Collection.)

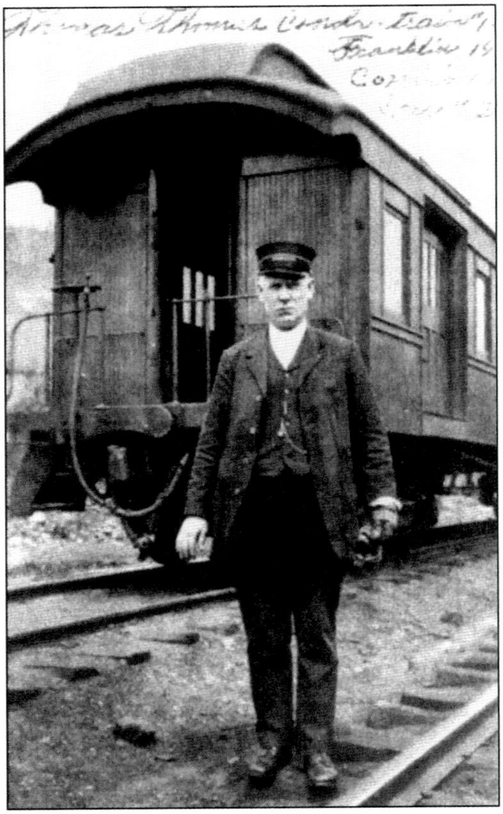

CONDUCTOR. These men of the railroad were the princes and the bulls of the line. As soon as the train pulled away from the station or depot, the conductor had complete control of the train. He told the engineer to slow down or speed up, in addition to collecting tickets from the passengers. (Courtesy of J.G. Farrell Collection.)

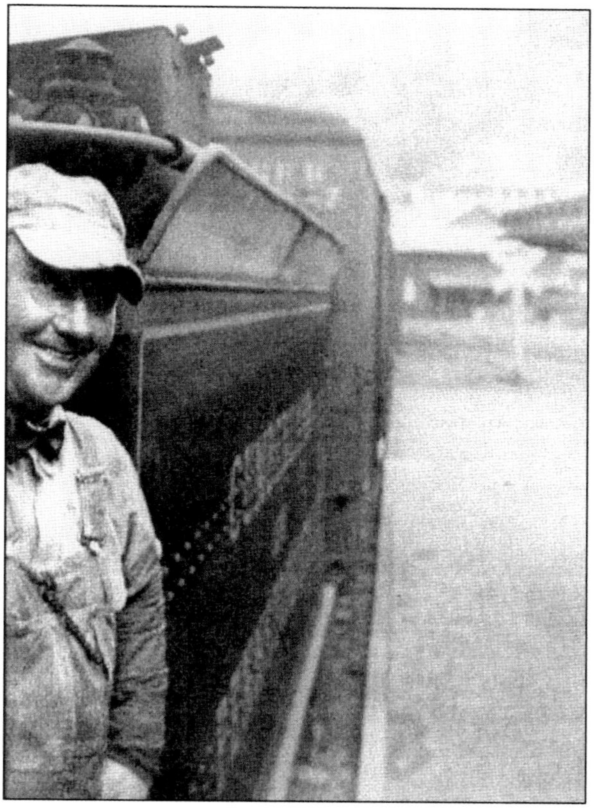

ENGINEER. This photo taken in the 1940s is of J.G. Farrell. He worked on the C & P Railroad as an engineer. He loved trains so much that he started a very large collection of local train scenes. (Courtesy of J.G. Farrell Collection.)

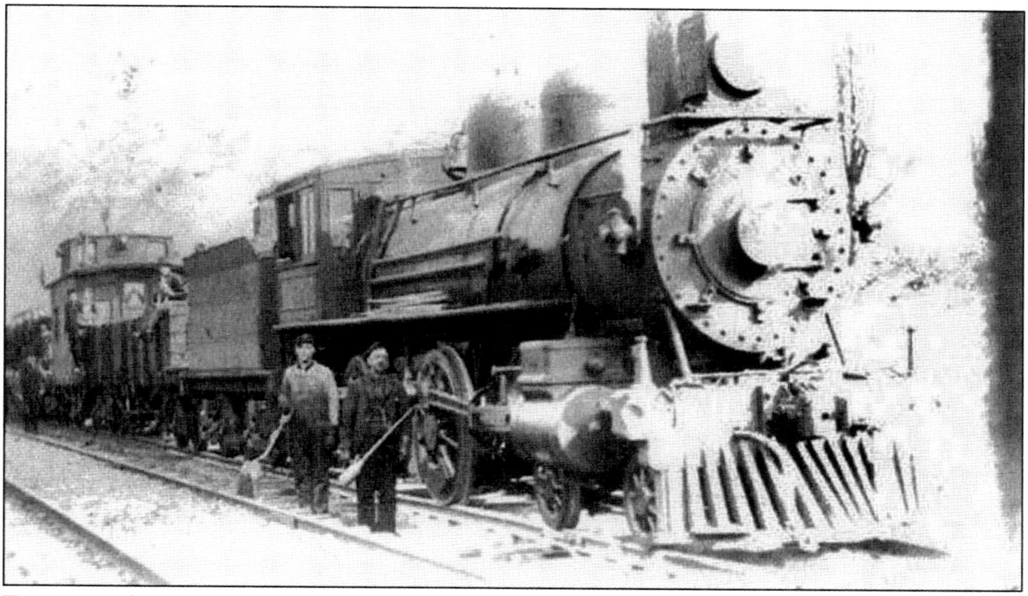

FIREMEN. These men had the backbreaking job of keeping the firebox hot so that the steam engine's boiler would produce steam. They would shovel coal from the tender into the firebox, almost non-stop, to keep the train running. (Courtesy of J.G. Farrell Collection.)

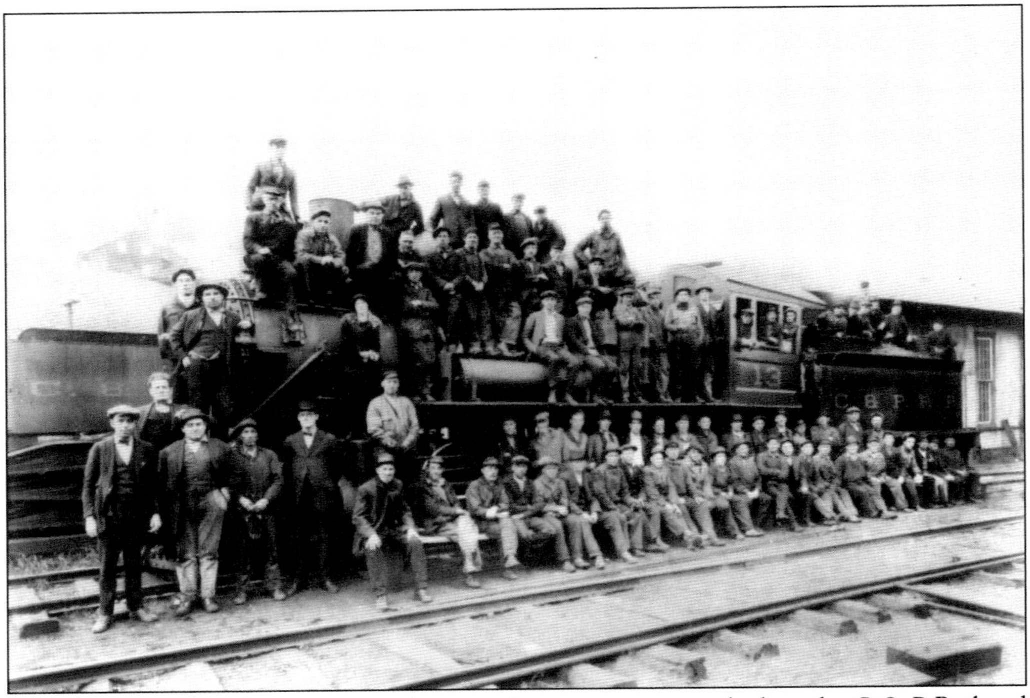

C & P CREW. This photo gives an idea as to how many men worked on the C & P Railroad during a shift. (Courtesy of Cora Carter.)

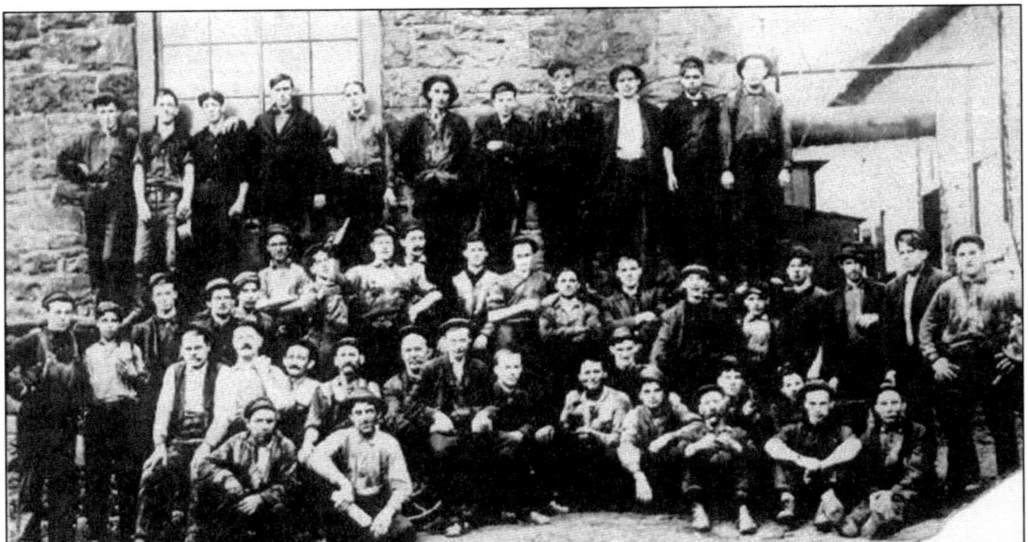

SHOP EMPLOYEES, 1914. This group of hard-working men stopped to pose for a group shot. Look closely and you will find that there were young boys around the age of 13 working alongside grown men. (Courtesy of J.G. Farrell Collection.)

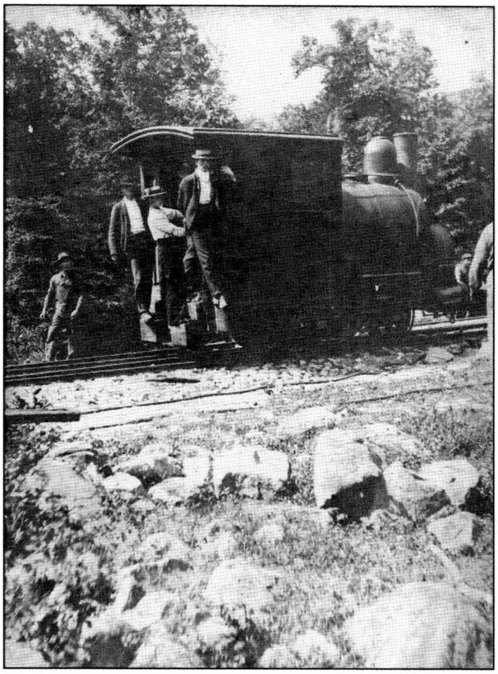

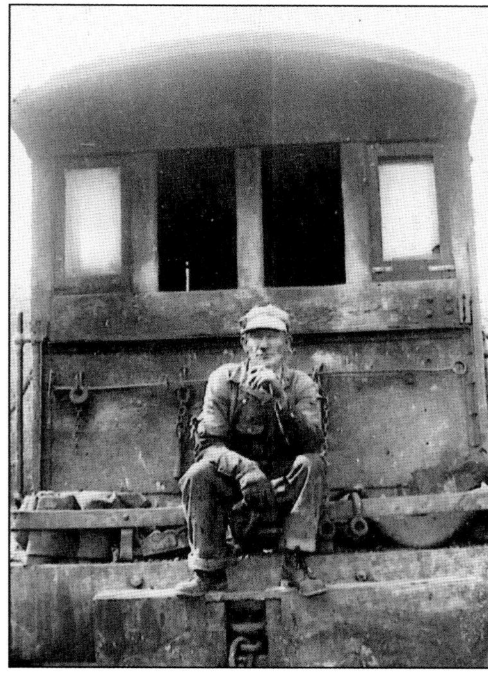

(Above left) **"THE DINKY."** This small engine was built and worked on the C & P line. It was a favorite of all whom it passed. (Courtesy of Cora Carter.)
(Above right) **THE DINKY ENGINEER.** This back view of the Dinky shows Howard Crow. He operated the Dinky for much of his life. (Courtesy of Cora Carter.)

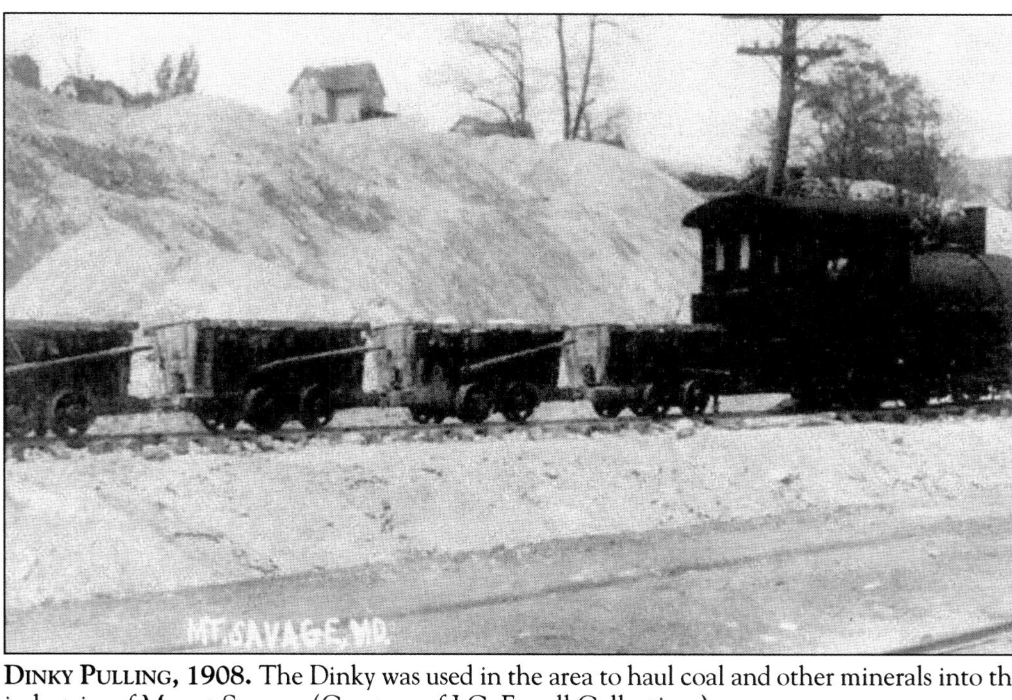

DINKY PULLING, 1908. The Dinky was used in the area to haul coal and other minerals into the industries of Mount Savage. (Courtesy of J.G. Farrell Collection.)

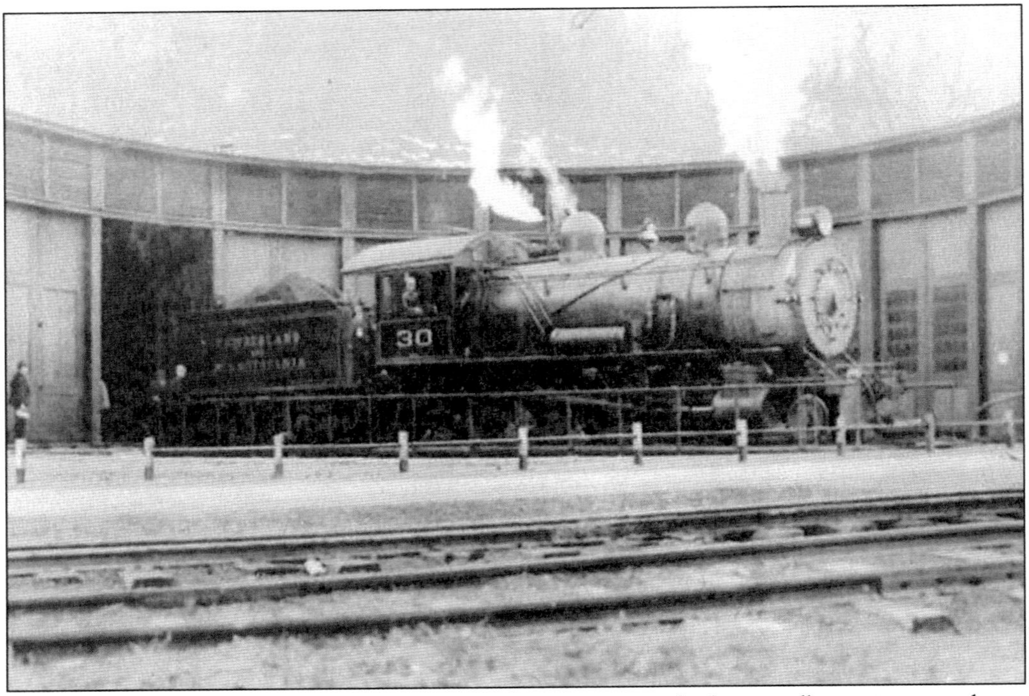

NUMBER 62 TRAIN IN ROUNDHOUSE. An uncommon view inside the roundhouse in town shows an engine being turned around. (Collection of J.G. Farrell.)

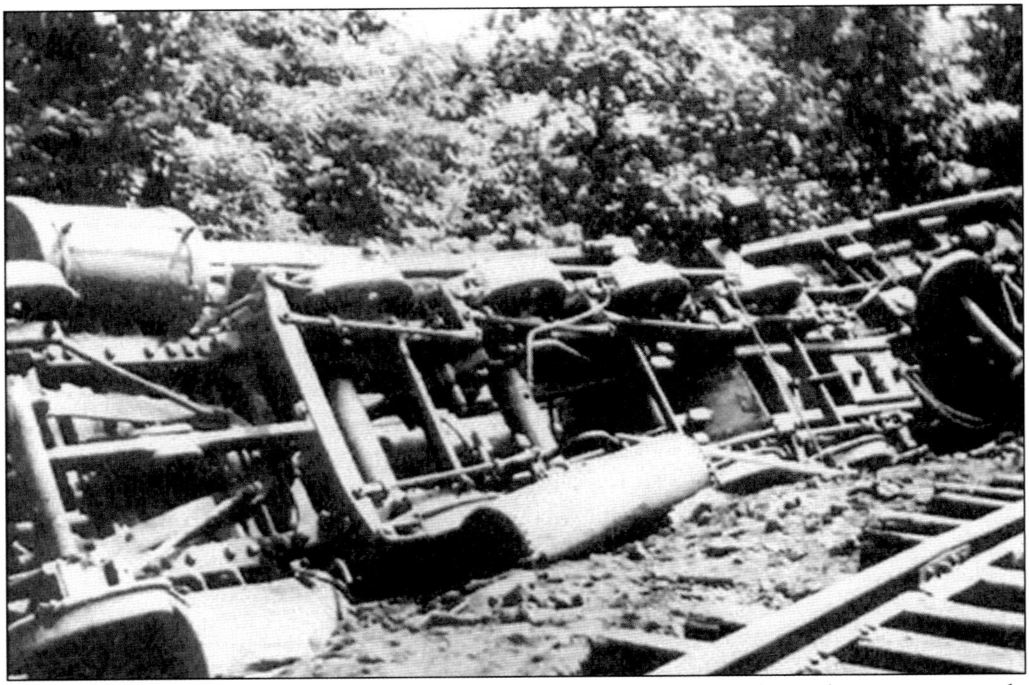

TRAIN WRECK, 1917. The C & P Railroad did not always have glory days. There were a couple of minor derailments and train wrecks. (Courtesy of J.G. Farrell Collection.)

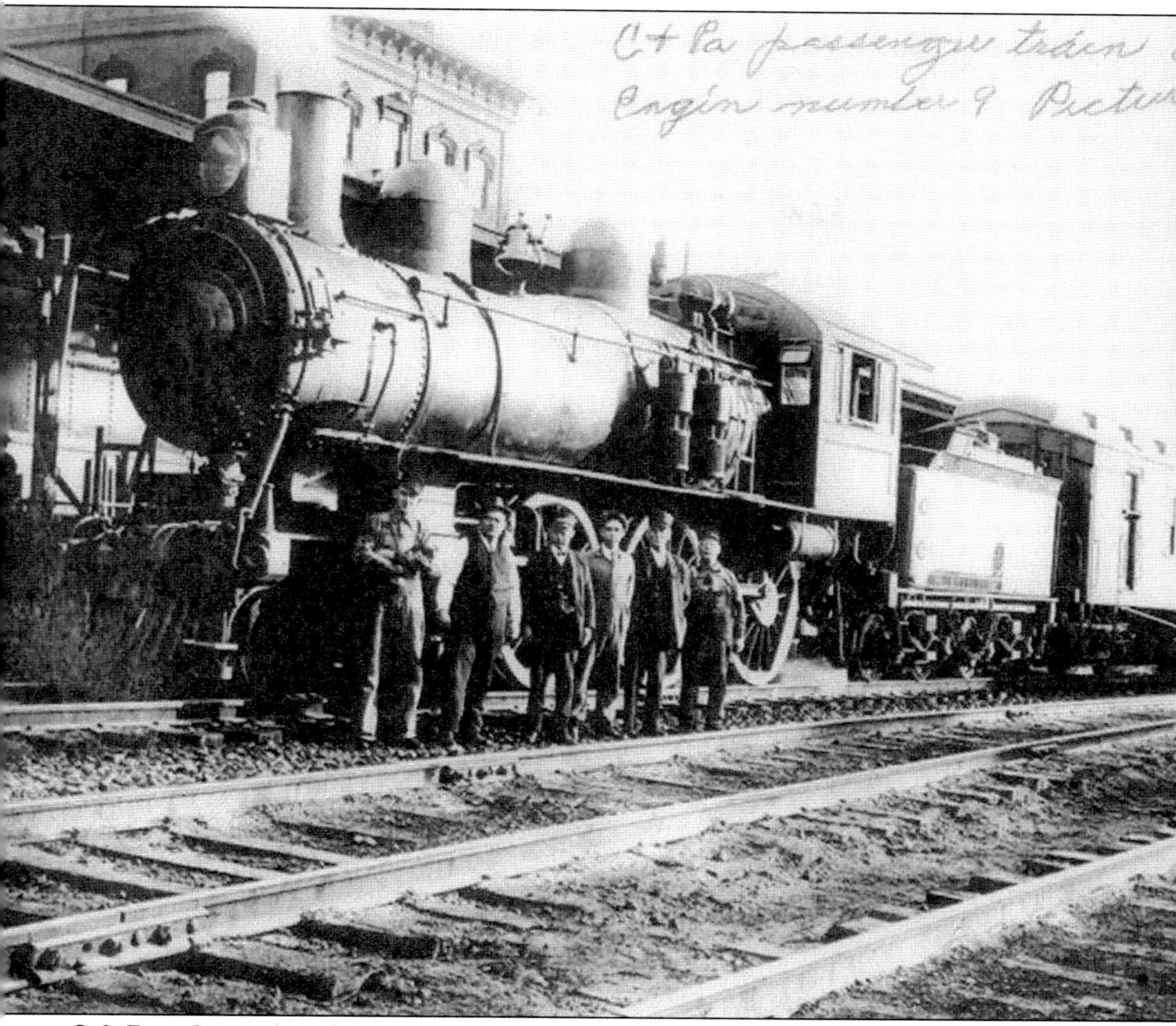

C & P AT QUEEN CITY STATION. The passenger service on the C & P would often take people into the Baltimore and Ohio Stations in Cumberland, where the passenger could transfer to the main rail and travel east or west. (Collection of J.G. Farrell.)

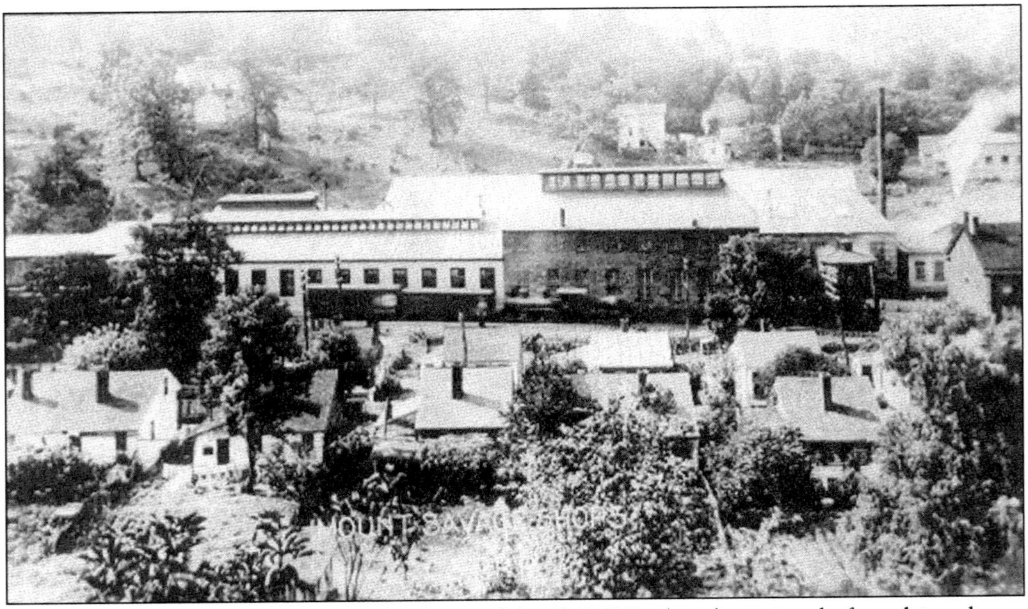

C & P Shops. By the early 1900s the shops of the C & P Railroad consisted of machine shops, blacksmith shops, passenger car sheds, and other buildings, including the head office for the operation. (Courtesy of J.G. Farrell Collection.)

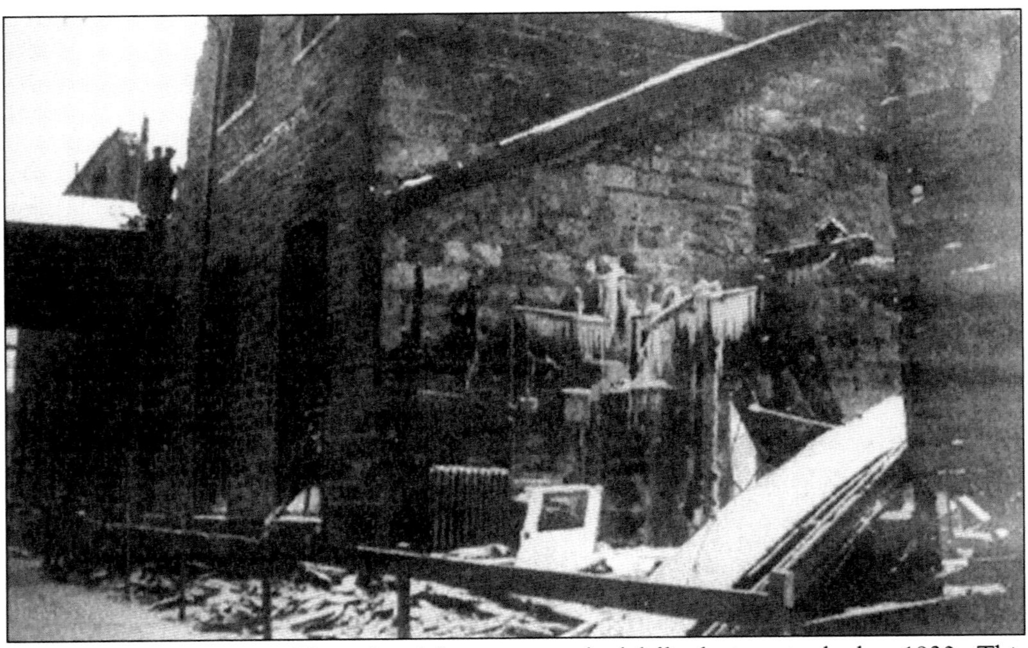

Shop Fire, March 1937. The railroad shops in town had difficult times in the late 1930s. This is a shot of the fire that destroyed a shop building. (Courtesy of J.G. Farrell Collection.)

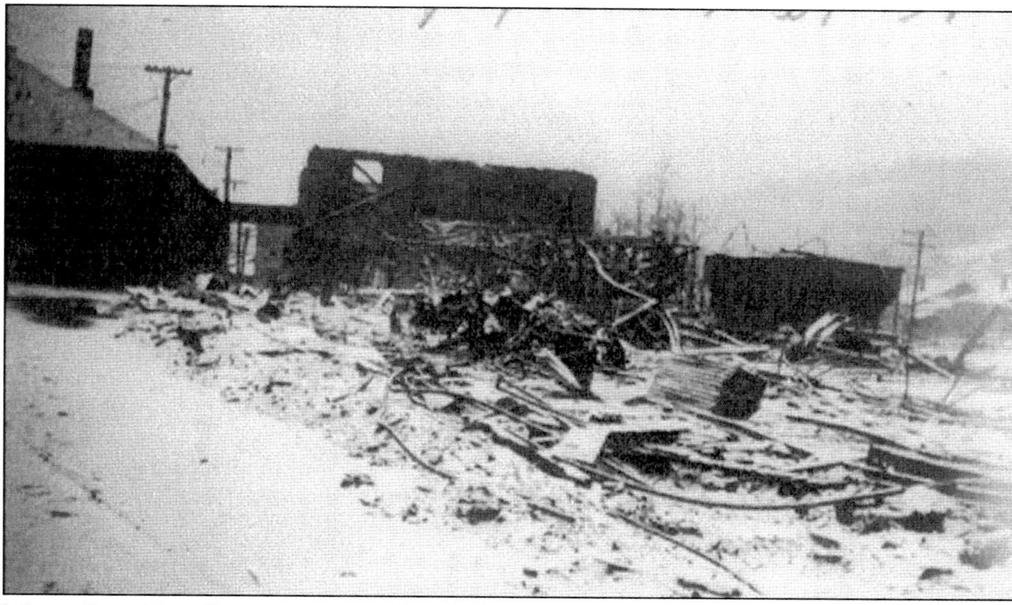

Major Shop Fire, January 1939. This fire leveled several buildings and caused major damage to others. (Courtesy of J.G. Farrell Collection.)

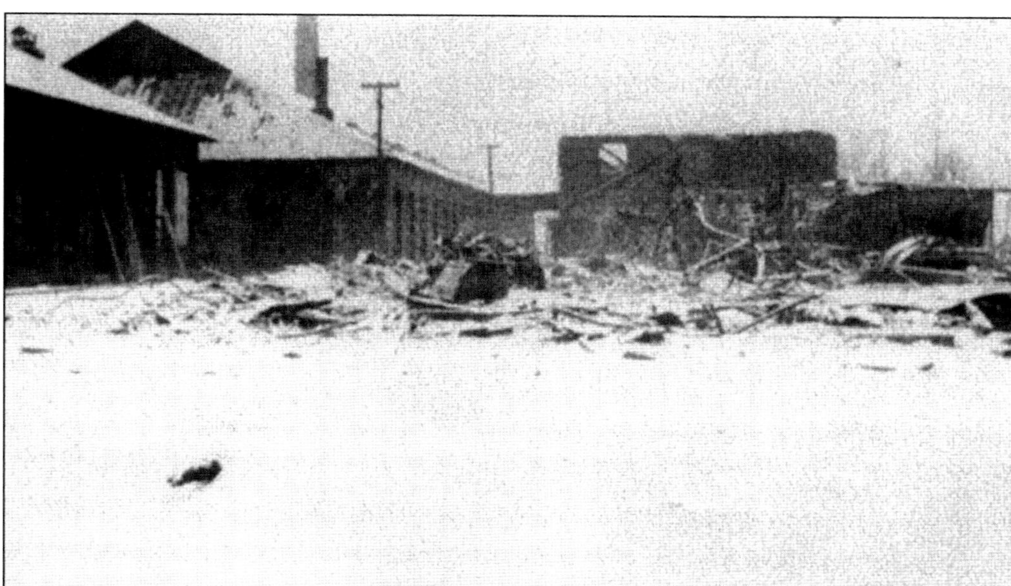

Blacksmith Shop and Machine Shop Fire Damage. To the left of the photo is the gutted blacksmith shop and to the right is the machine shop falling in on itself. (Courtesy of J.G. Farrell Collection.)

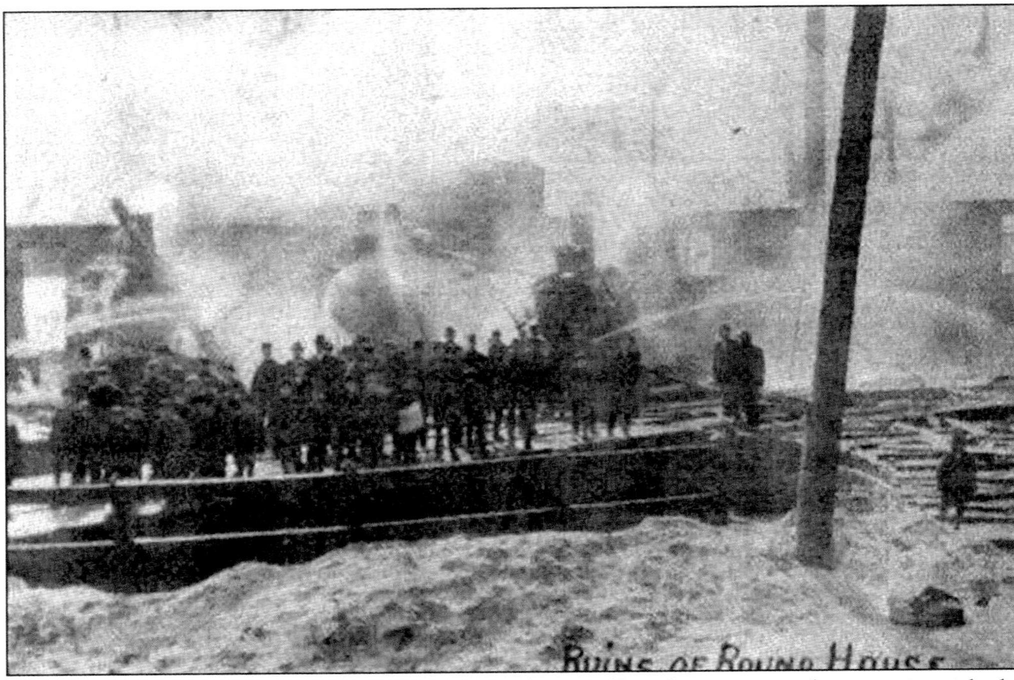

Ruins of Roundhouse. The Mount Savage Volunteer Fire Company works to extinguish the fire that swept through the roundhouse in 1907. (Courtesy of J.G. Farrell Collection.)

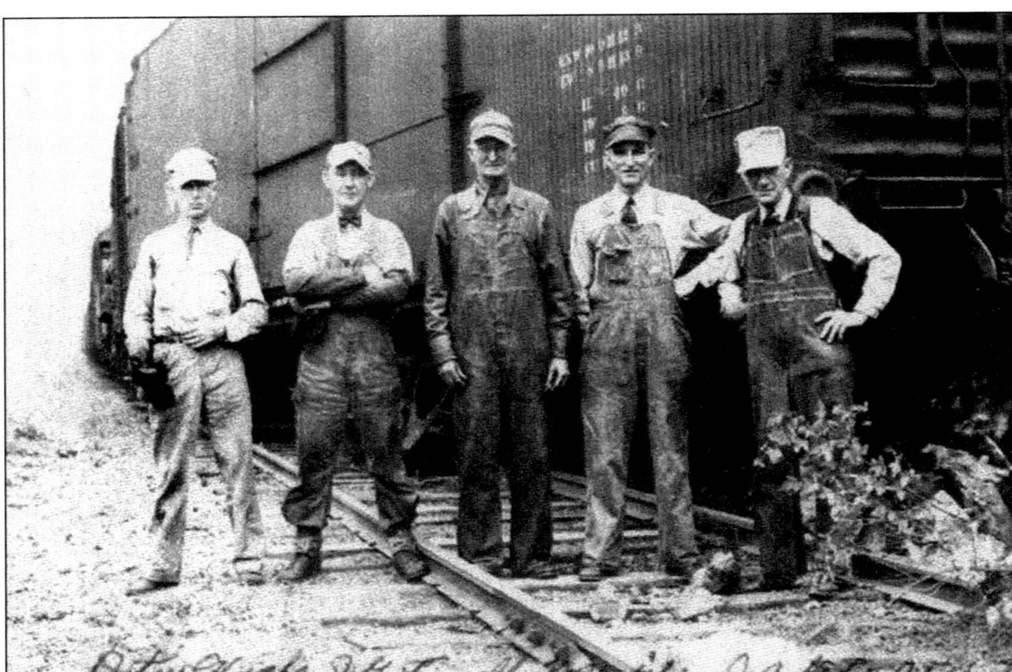

Workers in 1943. In the 1940s the C & P Railroad was starting to have financial problems and began to downsize their operation; they eliminated passenger service and only hauled freight. (Courtesy of Theresa Swanson.)

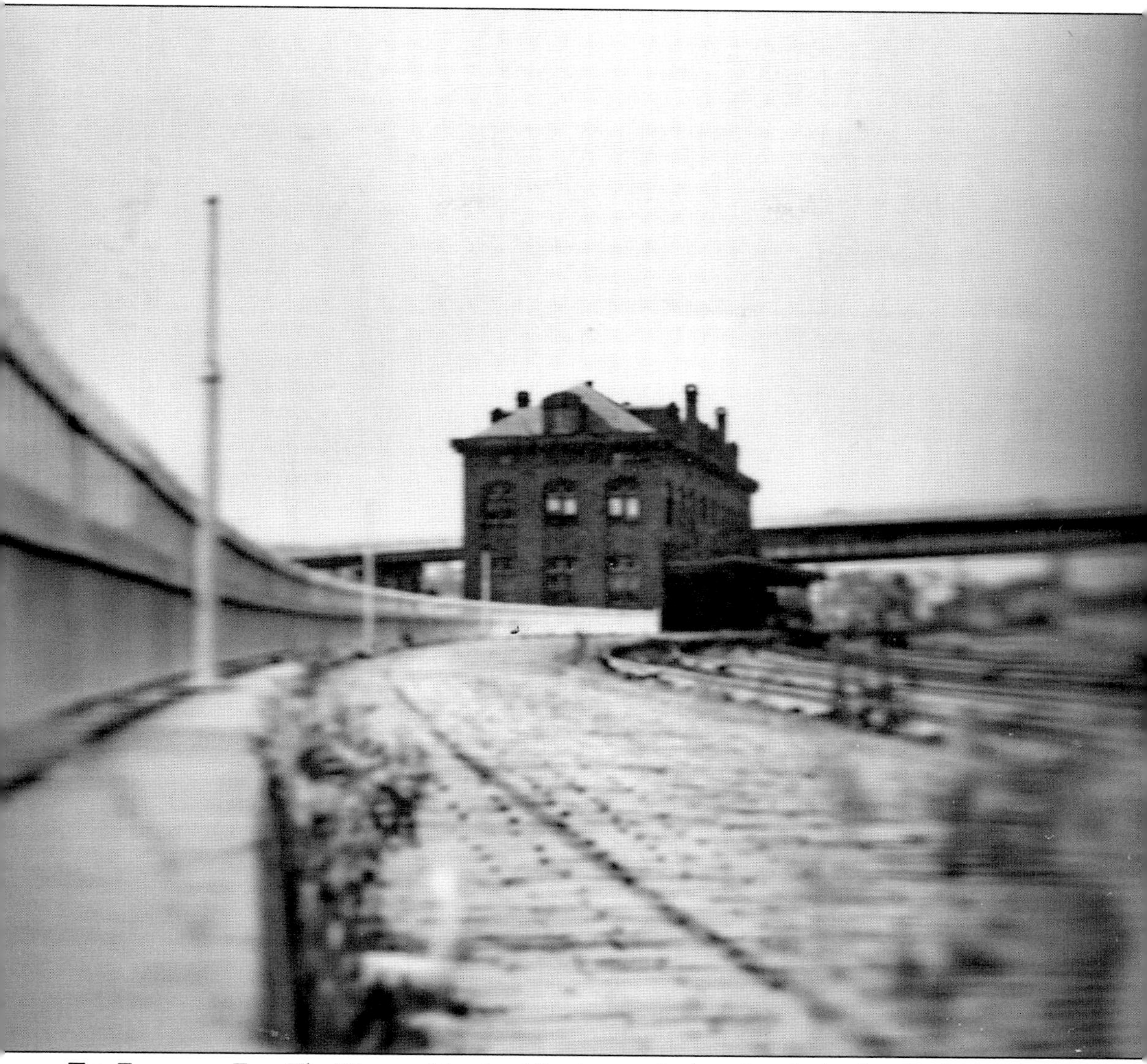

The End of an Era. The Western Maryland Station was built in Cumberland in 1913 after the rail system came to the area in 1910. In 1953 the C & P Railroad was purchased by the Western Maryland Railway. Under the new management the train schedule was cut back.

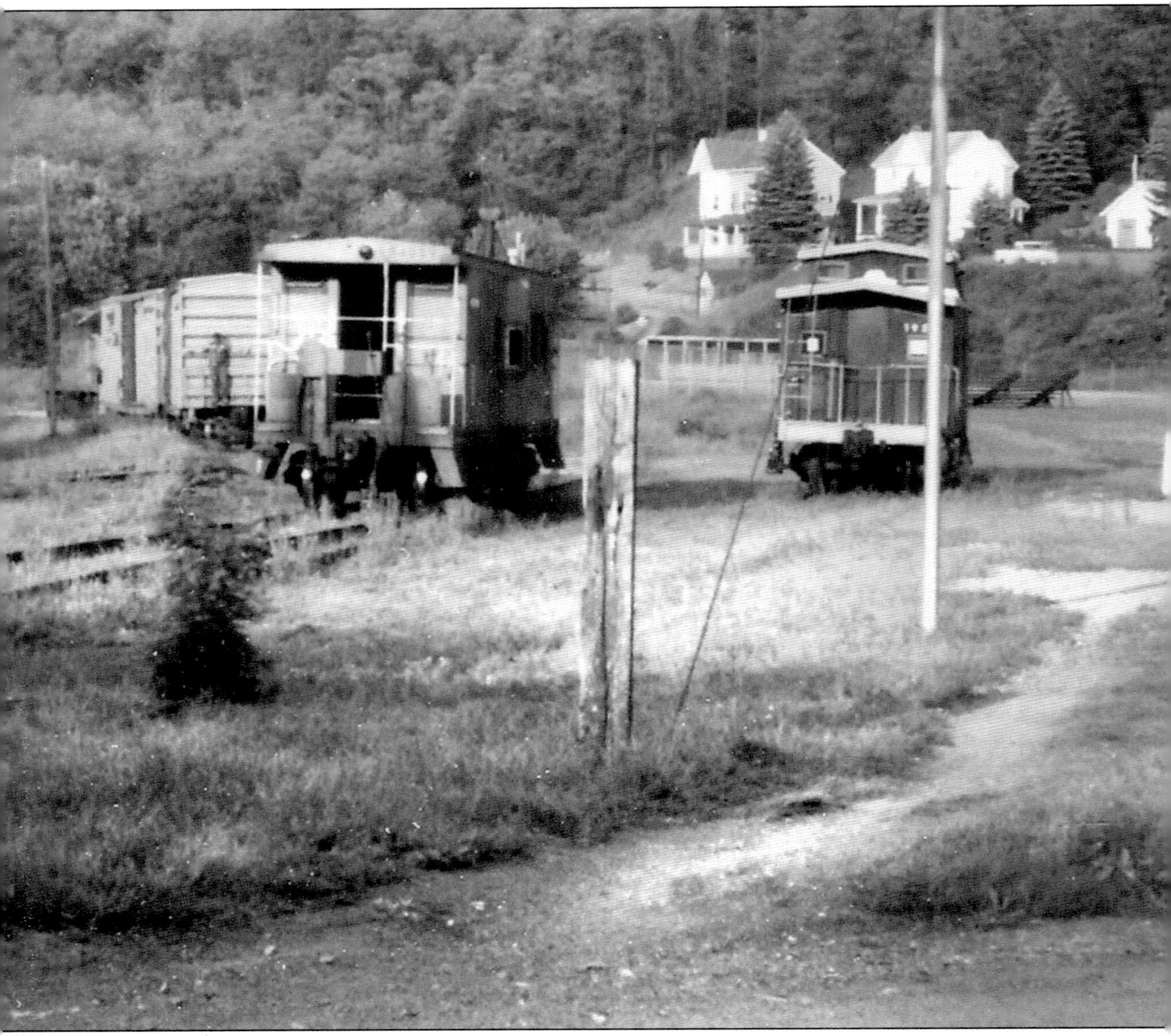

The Last Train Out of Town. The Western Maryland Railway used the small trunk line to haul freight from the small town that it served until 1983, when the new management stopped using the old line. This is a photo of the last train that left Mount Savage. (Courtesy of Jon Stark.)

Five

Church Hill

The Mount Savage area started with a community of devout Christians at Arnold's Settlement. This devotion spread from a small Catholic church on Mile Lane to the industrial valley of the town. The townspeople were so closely linked to religion that their employers donated the land that would become worship centers for the town.

The first church built in town was St. Patricks Church. Prior to it, the church congregation attended St. Ignatious Church on Mile Lane, built in 1825 in the vicinity of St. Patricks. Once the Catholic community grew in the mid-19th century with the influx of Irish Catholics working in the mines, brickyards, blast furnaces, and railroad, it was apparent that a new and larger church was needed to accommodate the congregation.

The Mount Savage Iron Company donated a half-acre of land for the church to be built in town. The dedication of the church took place on October 5, 1873. In 1896 the church purchased land behind and in front of the church for the development of a lawn, a school, and a convent. St. Patricks Catholic Church became the first church located on Church Hill.

In 1876 the Union Mining Company donated a parcel of land for the building of Methodist Episcopal Church on Jealous Row. After that church's congregation grew, the Union Mining Company donated another piece of land so that the members of the Methodist congregation could also build a new church on Church Hill. In 1901 the church was built and became Methodist Church.

Another Episcopal church was started in Mount Savage in 1844 one block from Church Hill on Zig-Zag Street. The membership there also increased, and in 1903 St. George's Episcopal Church was constructed. This church is a beautiful edifice of stone and native brick. The first service did not take place until June 5, 1904.

Just down the road a few miles from Church Hill in Barrelville is First Presbyterian Church, which stands at the foot of Little Allegheny Mountain. This small mining town started the church so they did not have to travel to Mount Savage or to Wellersburg, Pennsylvania.

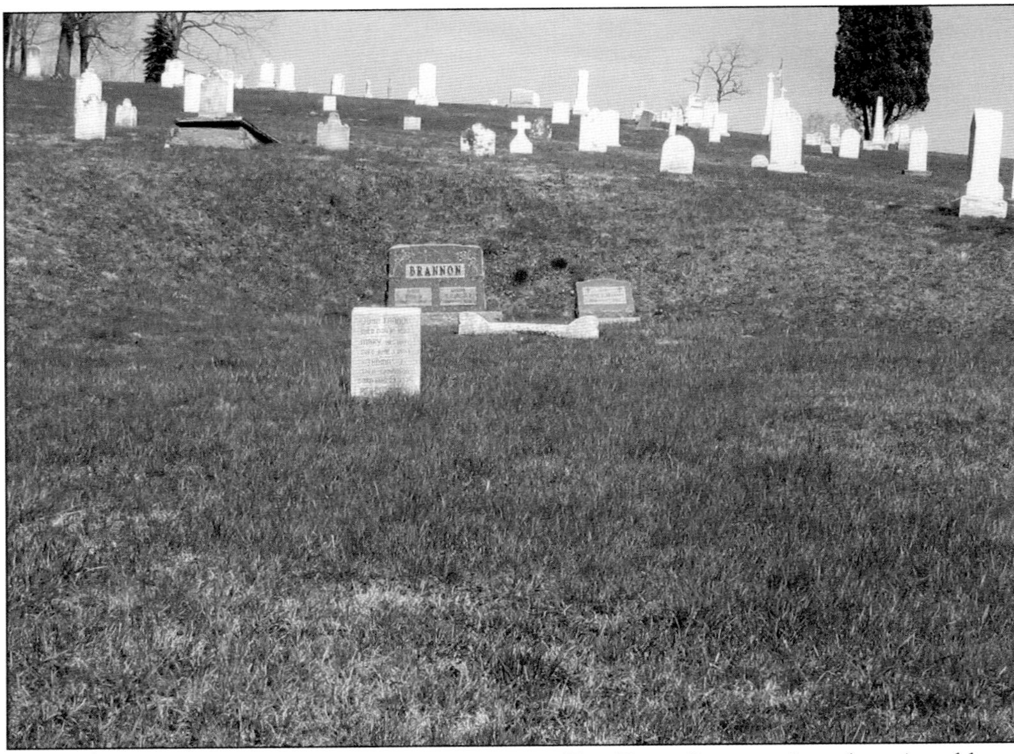

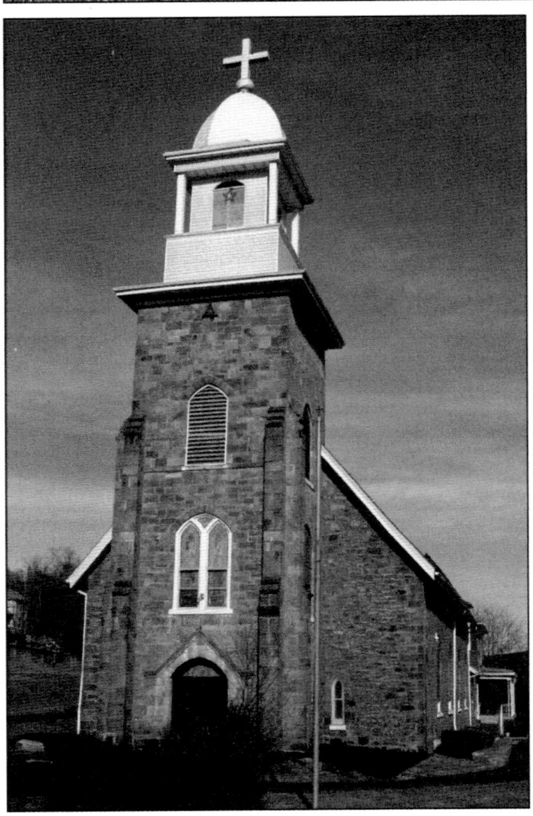

THE FIRST CHURCH. Jonathan Arnold gave the lot for the first church to be built in the community of Mount Savage. The large sunken area in the cemetery is where St. Ignatius Church once stood. It was a small one-room church.

ST. PATRICKS CHURCH. In 1873 this church was built to seat 600 people. Today, the church is still a worship center for the devoted Catholics in the area. (Courtesy of Cora Carter.)

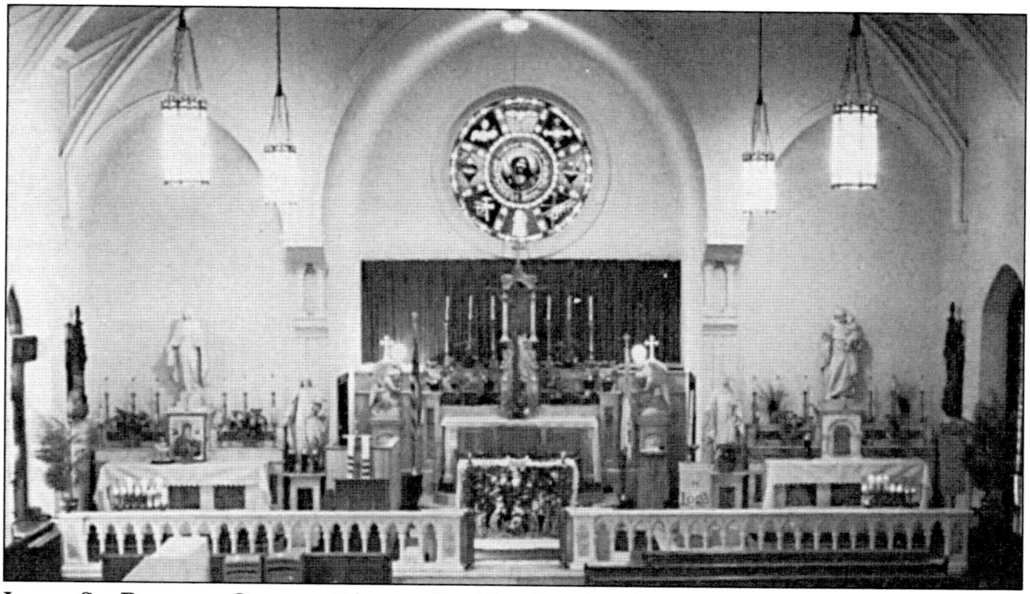

Inside St. Patricks Church. The inside of the church is decorated in a beautiful Gothic style, which was overseen by Fr. Richard Brown, the architect of the church and first clergy to lead the parish after the construction of the church.

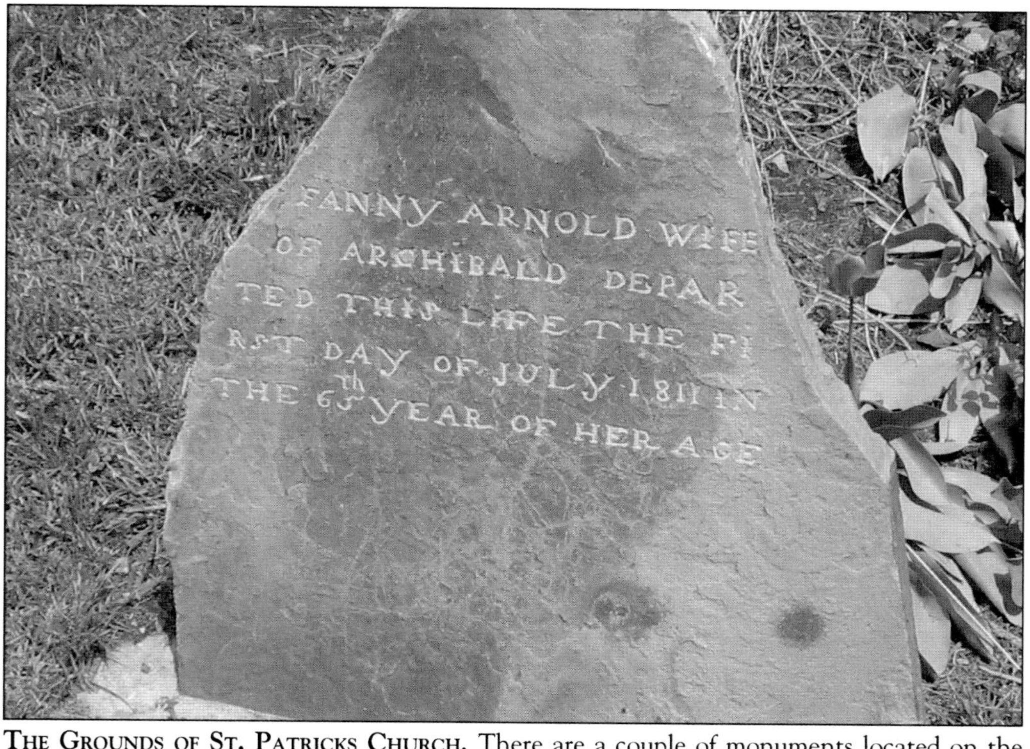

The Grounds of St. Patricks Church. There are a couple of monuments located on the grounds of the church. One monument is a gravestone of Fanny Arnold, who was the wife of Archibald Arnold, the founder of Mount Savage.

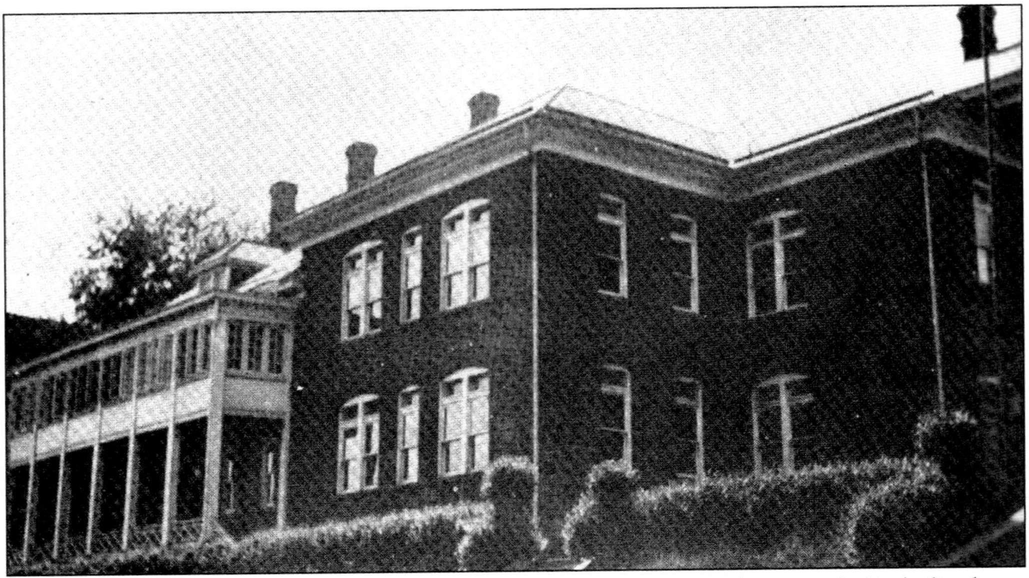

The Convent and School. At one time Mount Savage was so predominantly Catholic that a convent for nuns was built in 1900. A Catholic school was also connected to the convent. The school and convent was in use until 1970, and the school was razed in 2001.

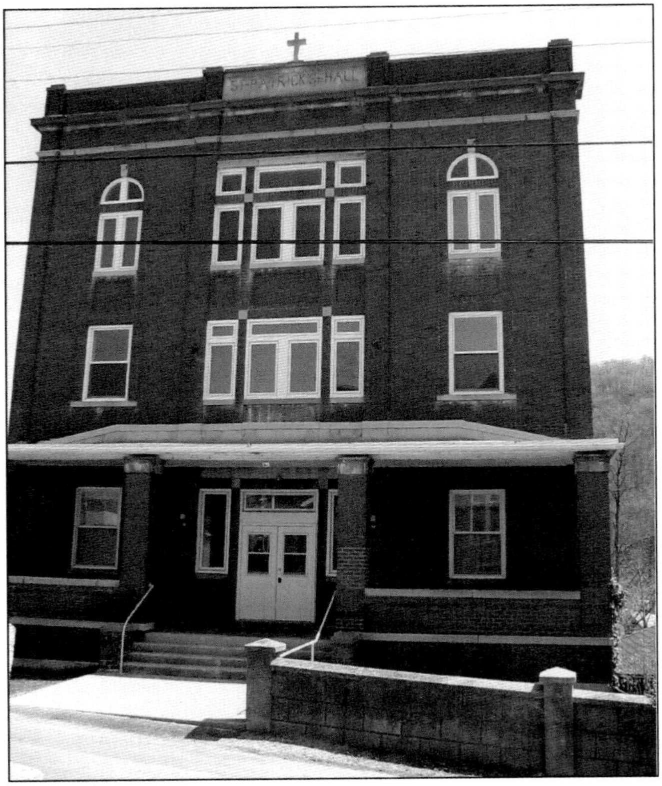

St. Patricks Hall. This three-story social hall was built in 1921, replacing the former hall after it was destroyed by fire in 1914. The building has been used for basketball leagues, social events, bingo, and dances for the community.

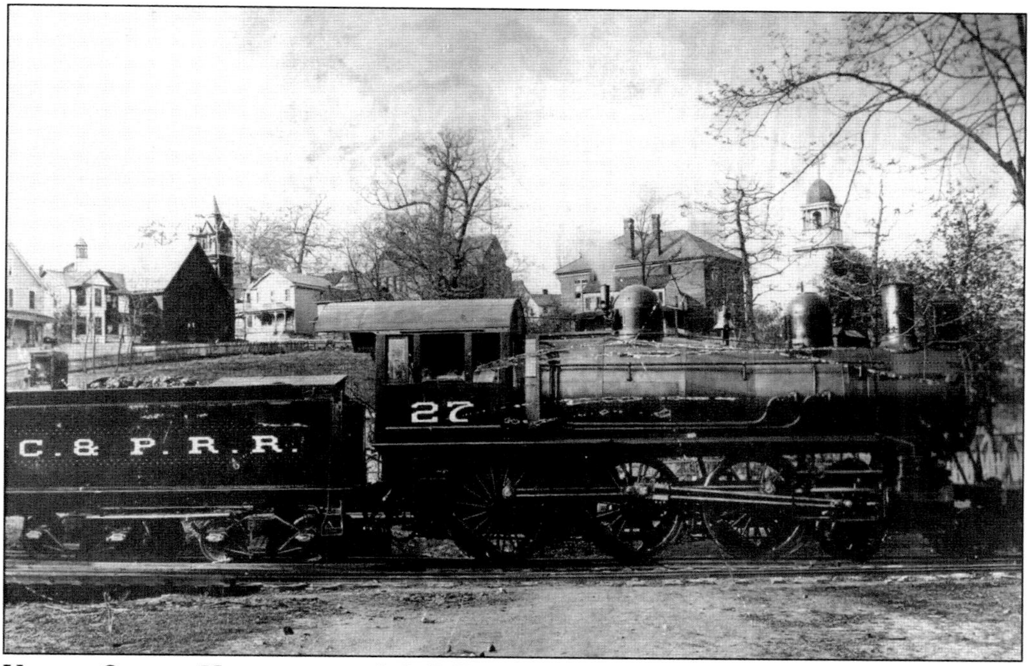

VIEW OF CHURCH HILL FROM THE C & P TRACK, 1900. Above the steam engine in this photo is a wonderful view of Church Hill. St. Patricks Church is the focal point of the view, but there is the new Methodist church being built down the street from the Catholic church. (Courtesy of Mount Savage United Methodist Church.)

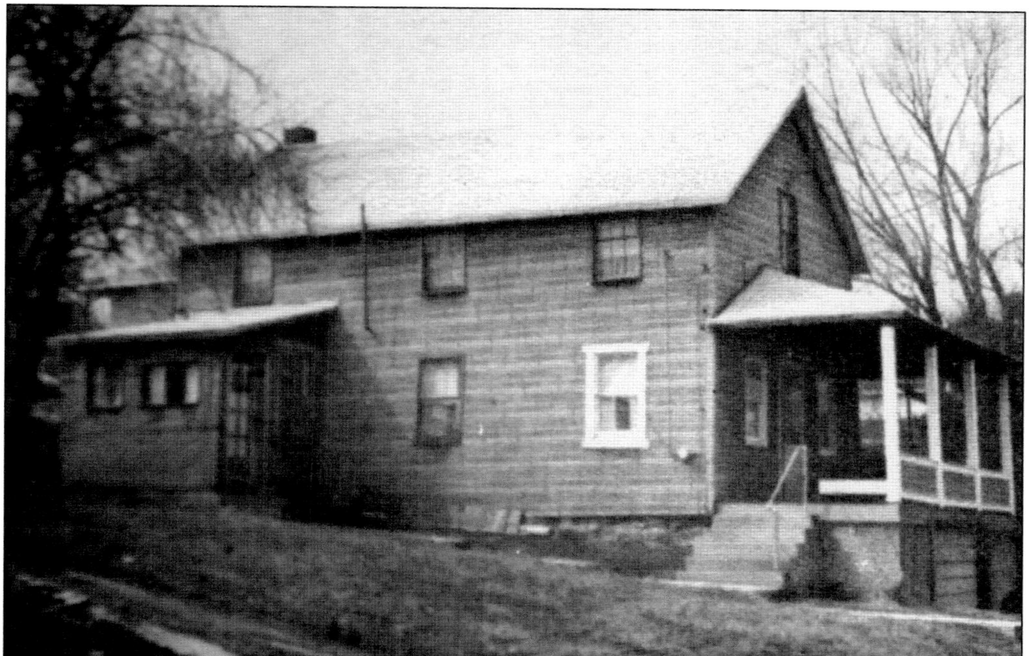

FIRST METHODIST CHURCH. The first church was located on Calla Hill at the head of Jealous Row (Jelly's Row at the time), and the congregation started in 1870. The church was known as the Methodist Episcopal Church and has now been converted into a private residence.

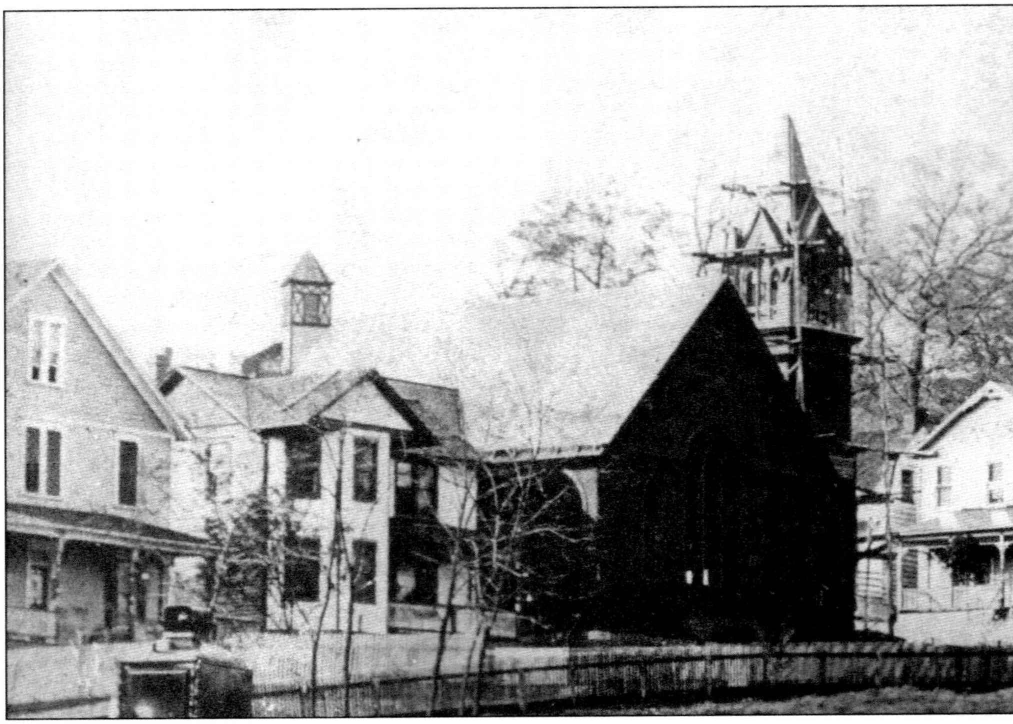

BUILDING OF THE METHODIST CHURCH, 1900. This is a rare photograph of the construction of the United Methodist Church. The scaffolding is still on the bell tower. (Courtesy of Mount Savage United Methodist Church.)

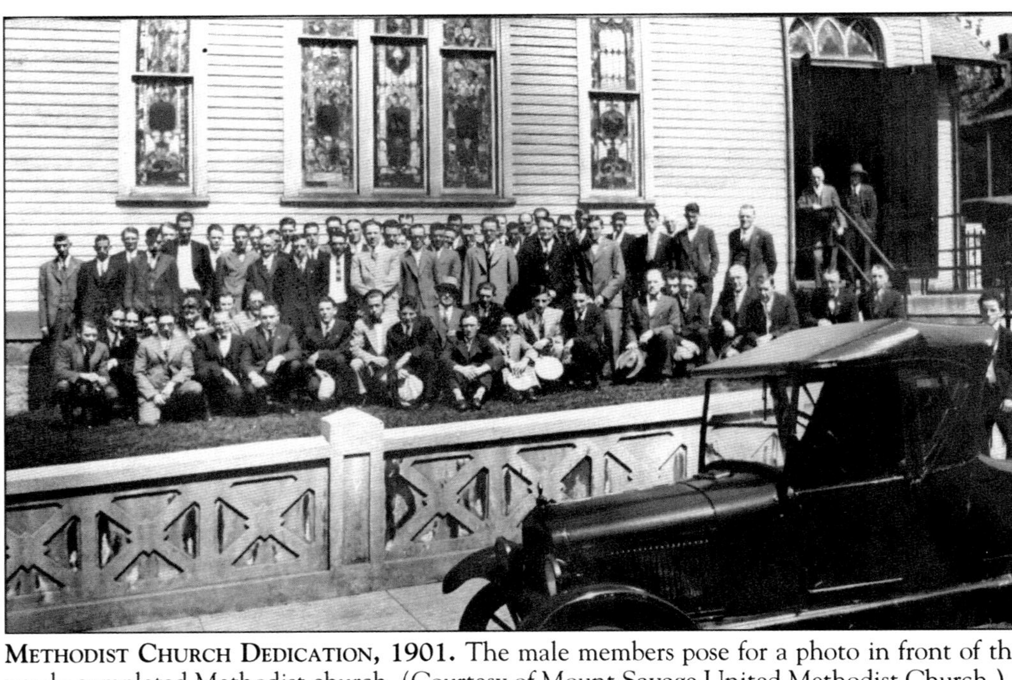

METHODIST CHURCH DEDICATION, 1901. The male members pose for a photo in front of the newly completed Methodist church. (Courtesy of Mount Savage United Methodist Church.)

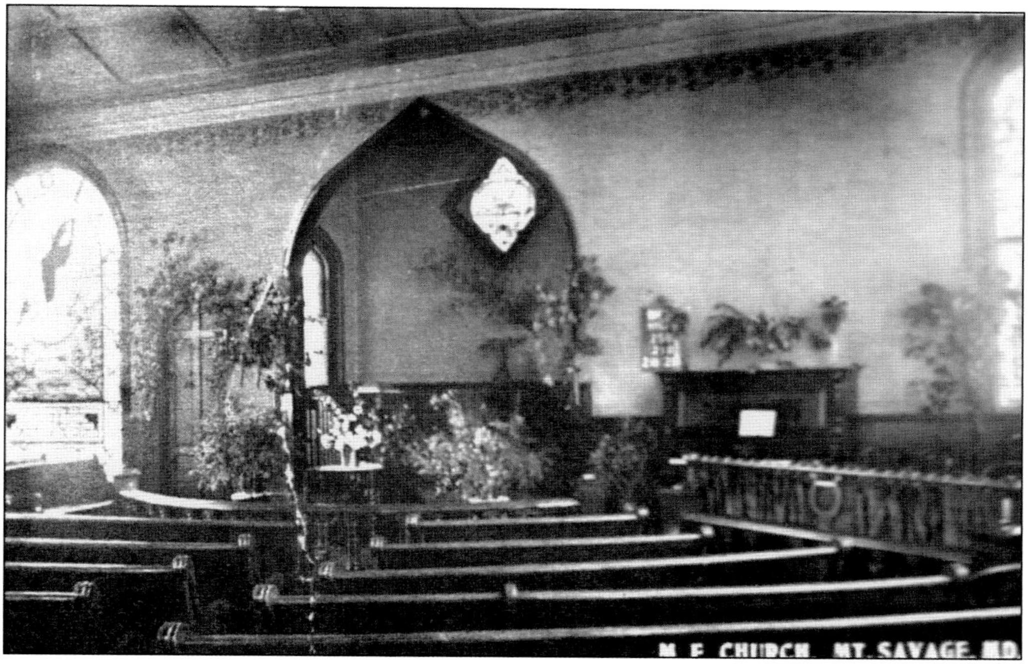

INSIDE THE METHODIST CHURCH. This quaint little church has a beautiful stained glass window, pictured on the far left, depicting Christ's resurrection.

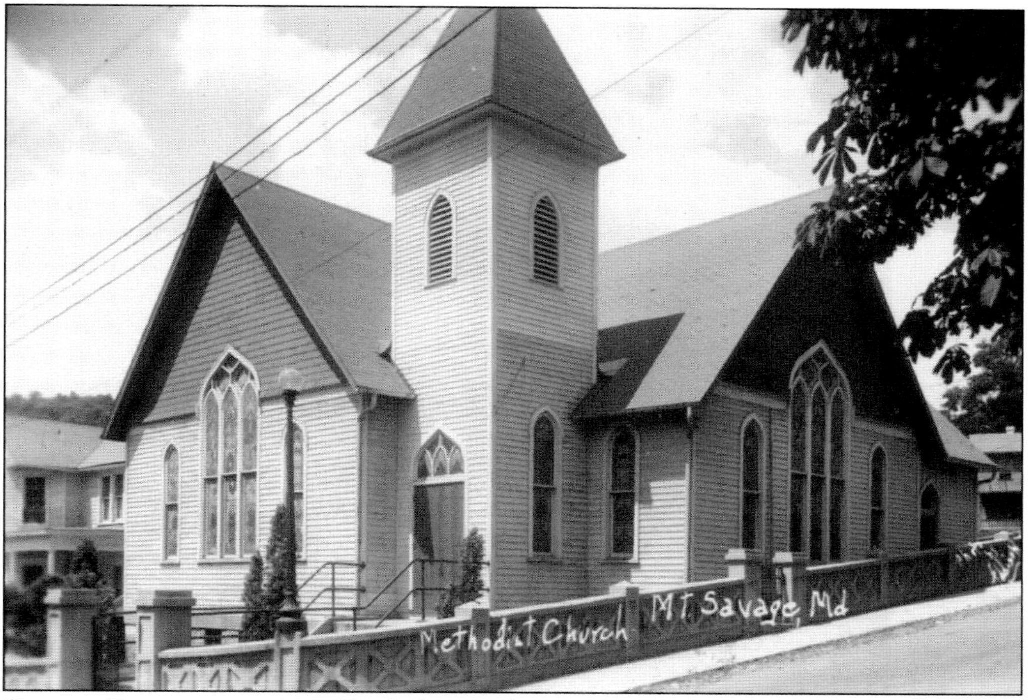

OUTSIDE RENOVATION 1948. The bell tower became structurally unsafe, and the tower was reconstructed into the present-day bell tower.

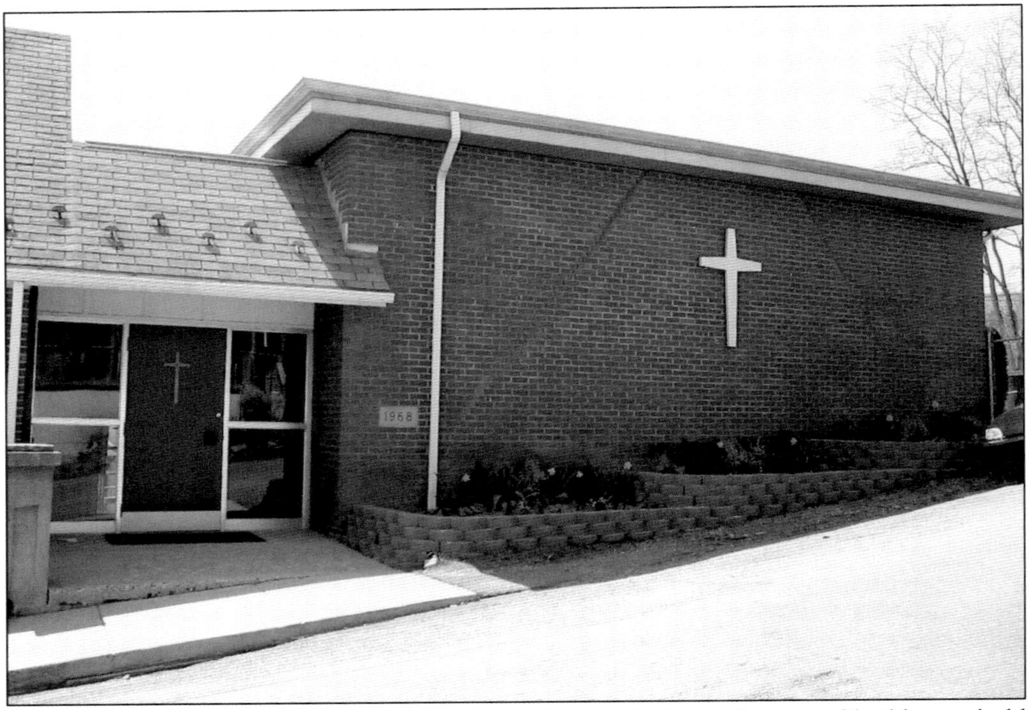

THE SUNDAY SCHOOL BUILDING. In 1968 the parishioners built an educational building to hold their Sunday school classes. Before this building the classes were held in a house that had to be torn down.

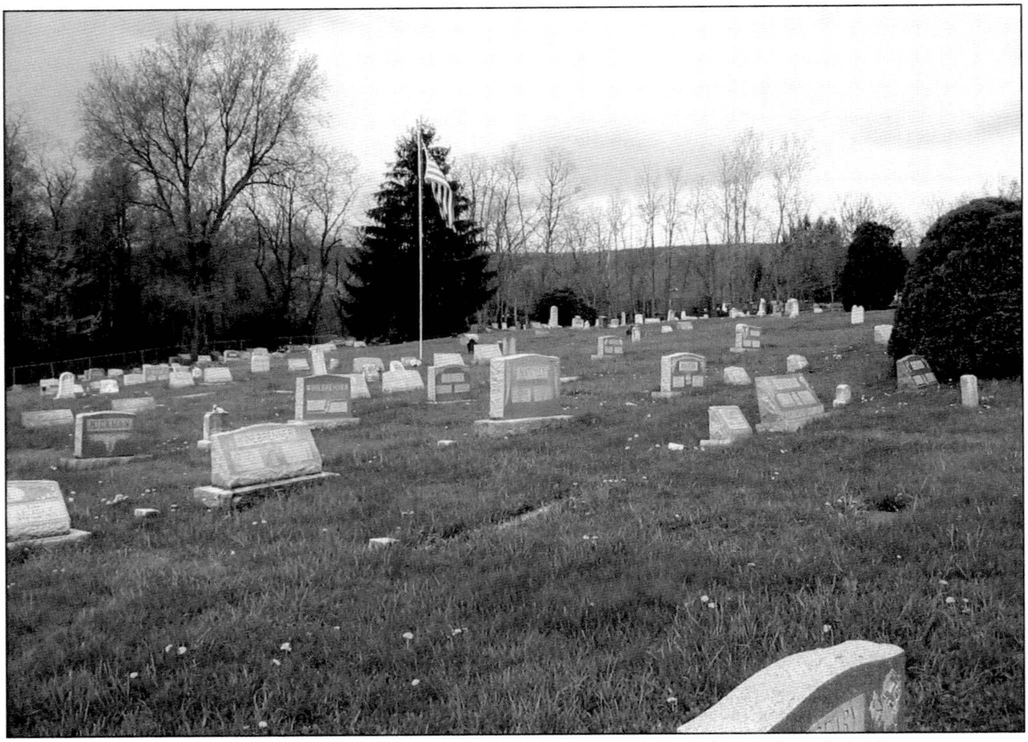

THE UNITED METHODIST CEMETERY. This cemetery is also located on Church Hill.

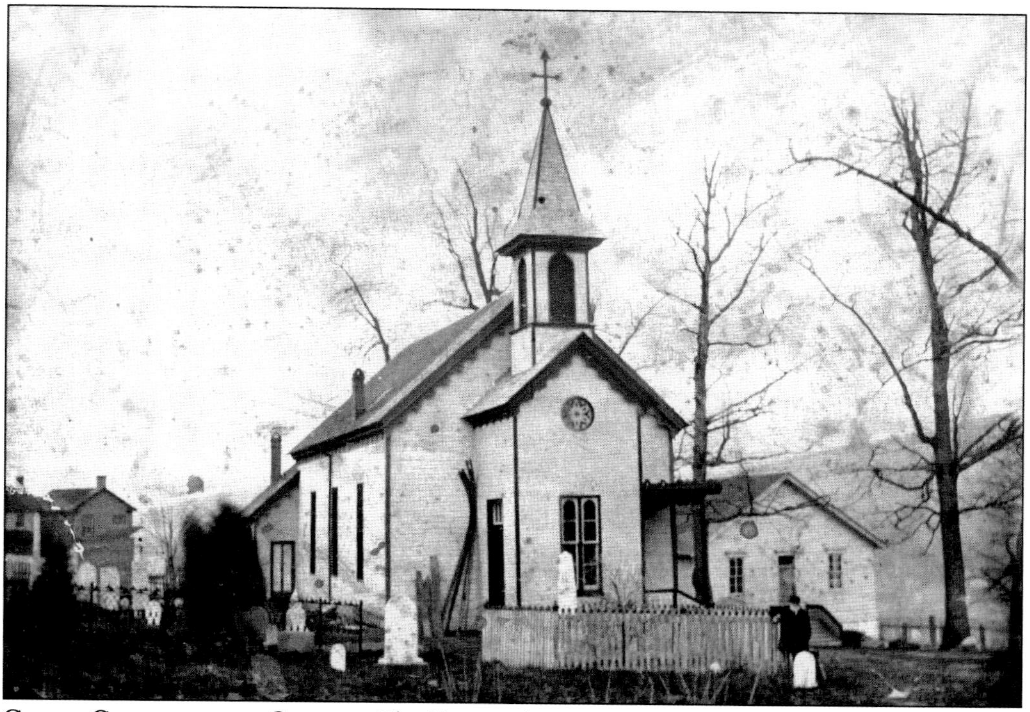

Christ Congregation Church. The Episcopal congregation started to meet in 1841 in one of the C & P shops. The first Episcopal church was actually named the Christ Congregation Church. This church was built in 1844, off of Church Hill on Zig-Zag Street. In 1877 the church was enlarged as the membership grew. (Courtesy of St. George's Episcopal Church.)

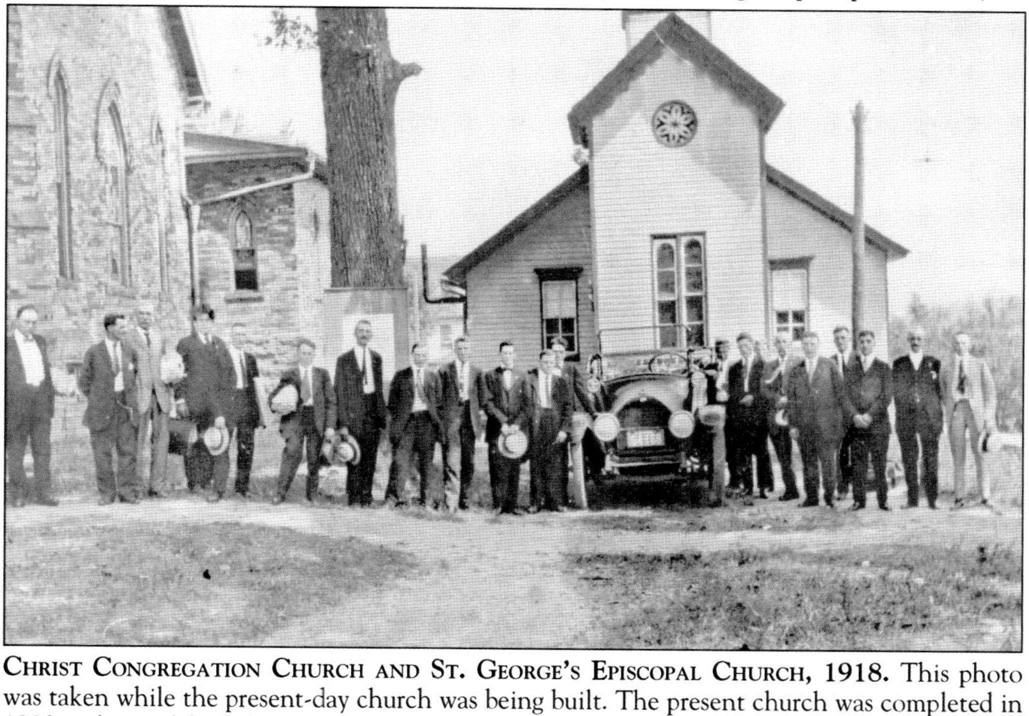

Christ Congregation Church and St. George's Episcopal Church, 1918. This photo was taken while the present-day church was being built. The present church was completed in 1903 with an edifice of stone and native brick. (Courtesy of St. George's Episcopal Church.)

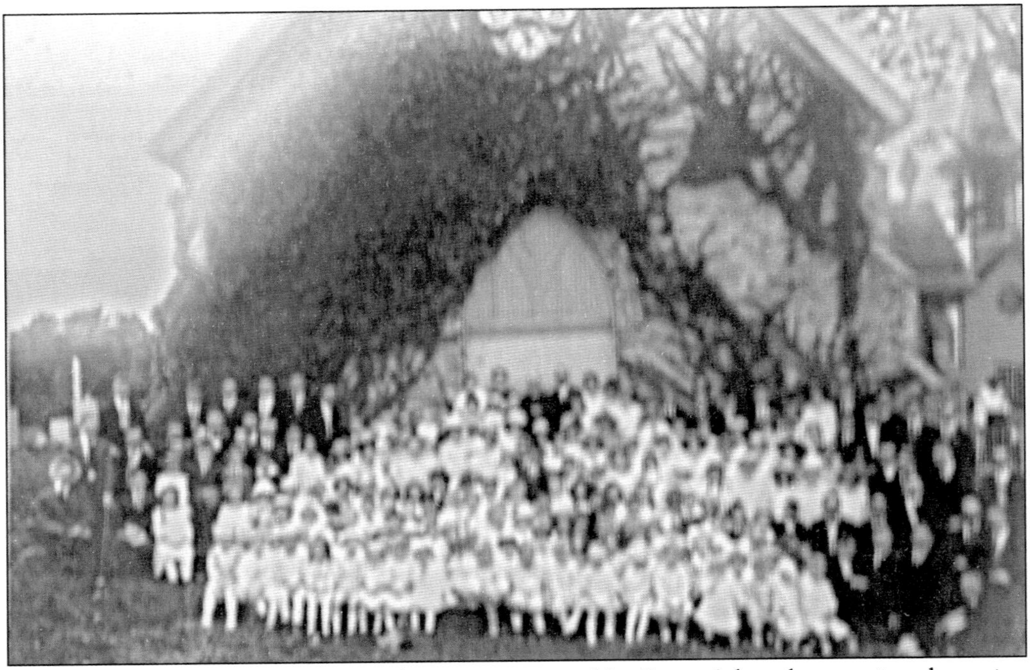

St. George's Episcopal Church. The congregation of St. George's has always enjoyed meeting to celebrate their church. (Courtesy of St. George's Episcopal Church.)

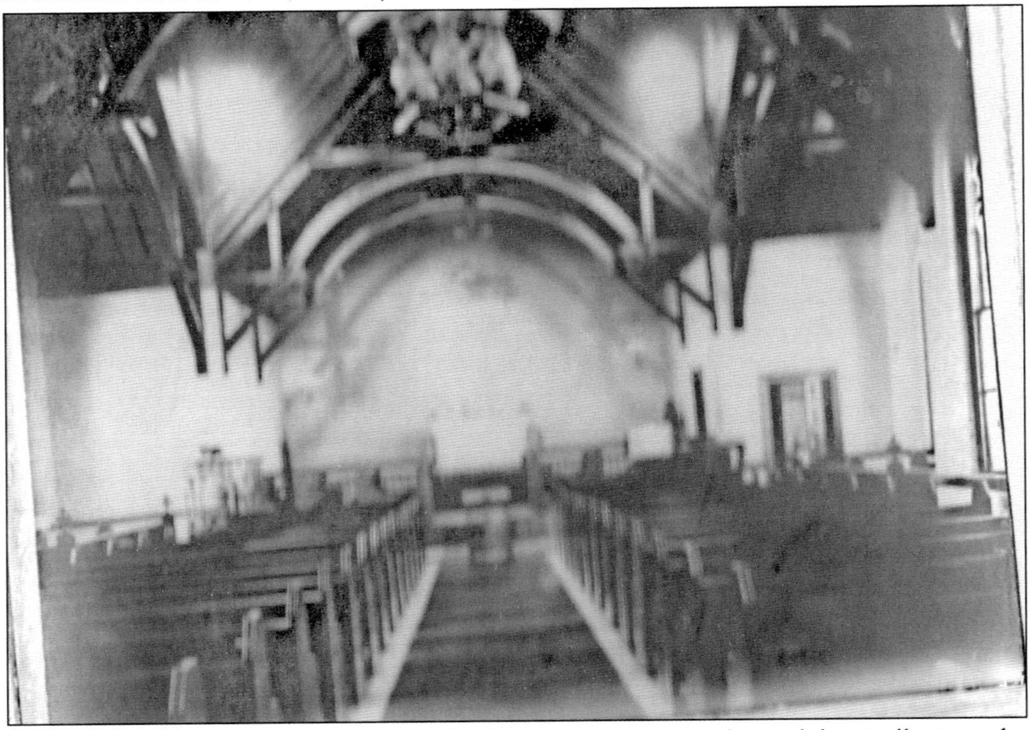

Inside St. George's Church. The inside of the church has not changed drastically since the structure was built in 1903. In the 1960s the church did undergo some renovations that replaced the gas/electric-powered chandeliers; some other minor changes were also done to the altar. (Courtesy of St. George's Episcopal Church.)

The Bell Tower. The stone bell tower at St. George's Episcopal Church was built in 1952. The tower was constructed with native sandstone except for 48 stones that were placed at the top of the tower. Every state of the nation at the time shipped a stone to represent their state in the tower. (Courtesy of Carol Barry.)

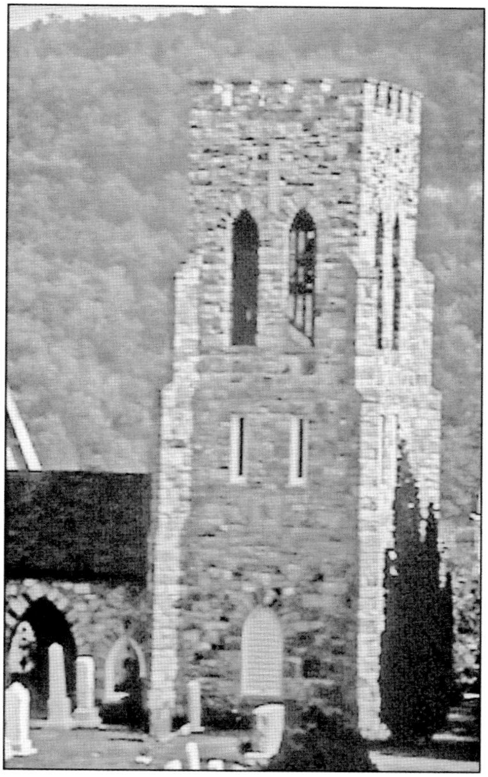

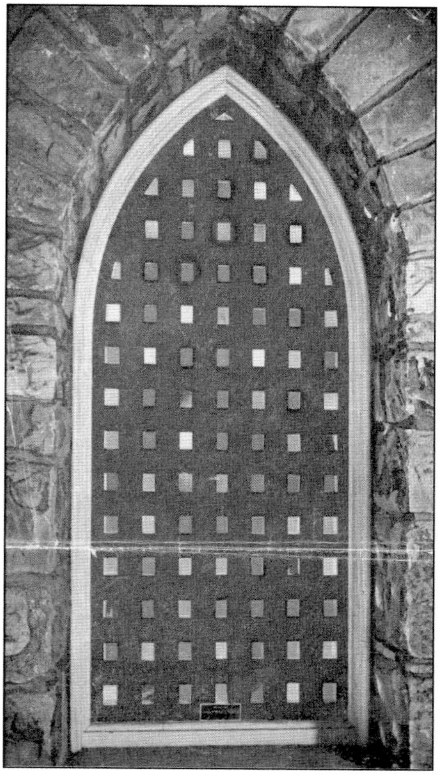

Stained Glass Window. This window was featured in *Life Magazine* in the April 1955 issue. It is a beautiful array of blue, red, and orange. (Courtesy of Mount Savage School.)

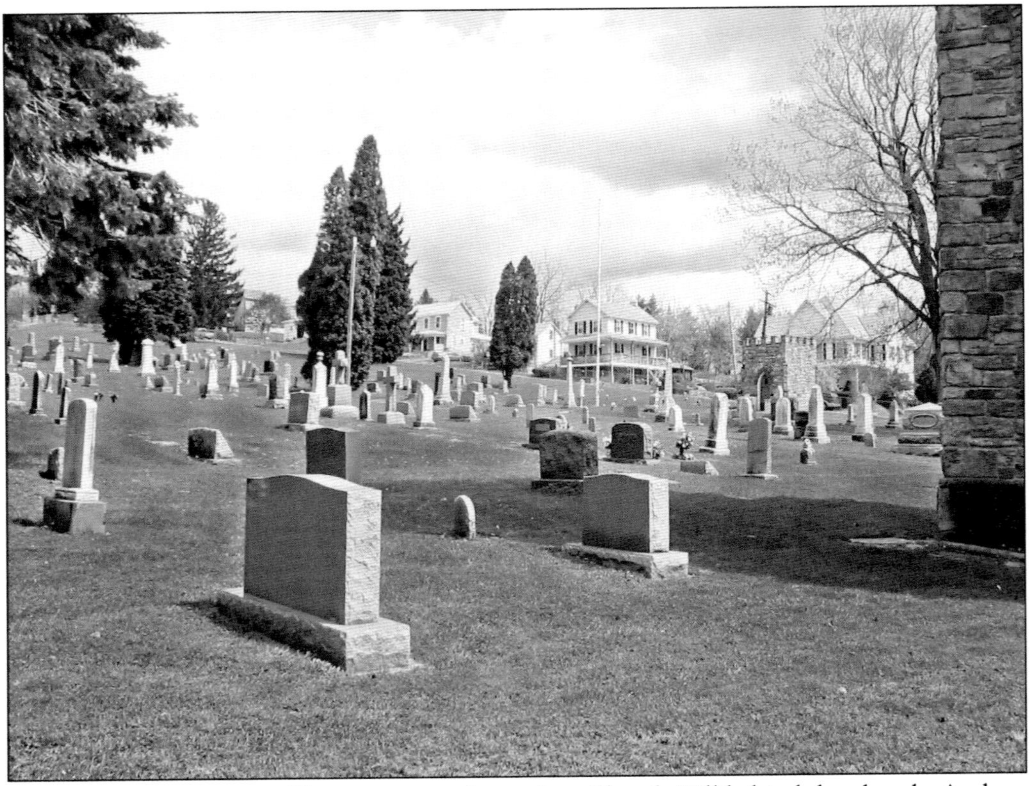

St. George's Cemetery. The cemetery is located on Church Hill behind the church. Andrew Ramsey, the famous brick maker, is buried here.

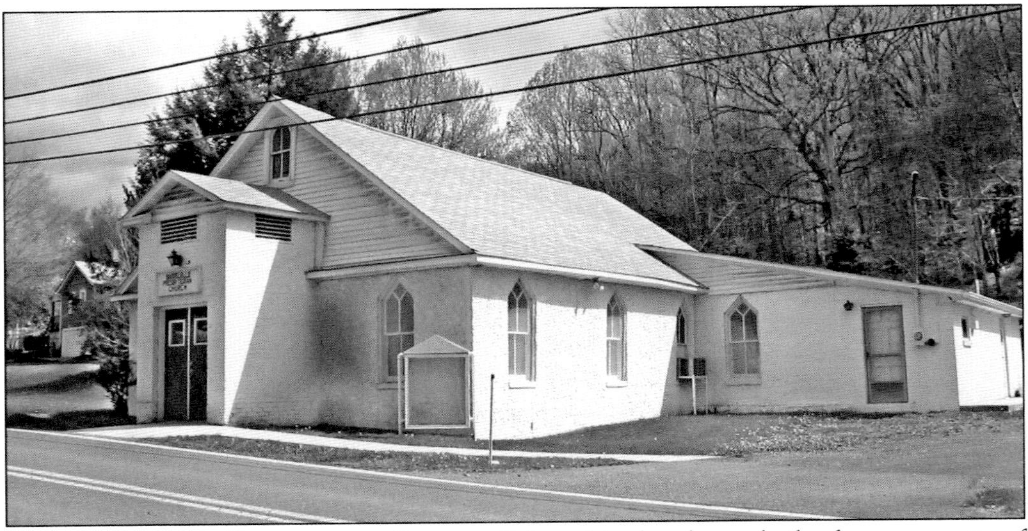

Barrelville First Presbyterian Church. Before this church was built, the community of miners attended church on the second floor of the company store. This small church was built in this little mining town for the miners in 1920s.

Six

SCHOOL SPIRIT
The Spirit of the Town

Education has always been important to the citizens of Mount Savage. Most of the original founders from Arnold's Settlement valued the education of their children and their children's children. They were taught the three R's—reading, writing, and arithmetic—by their parents. But not all emigrants to the area were as lucky as the members of Arnold's Settlement.

Most of the new emigrants who came to Mount Savage in the mid-1800s were of Irish descent and were not well educated, if educated at all. But they had the American dream to give their children the things that they did not have in the old country. Because of this great desire to better their children's lives, the company towns came to the realization that the workers' children deserved to learn to read and write.

The company town donated land for schools to be built and purchased classroom wares for the schools. In and around Mount Savage were several small schools. Children who lived near Mount Savage, Barrleville, Dutch Hollow, and Zihlman had a chance to attend school and learn. St. Patricks Church founded St. Patricks School, in addition to the public schools that were available.

Because of the desire for the education of the community, the schools became foundations of the town. They became meeting places and centralized social areas where townspeople would get acquainted.

The school as the center of the community really emerged when the Allegany County Board of Education decided to build a school that would accommodate school children in grades 1 through 12. The small schools in the other communities were consolidated, and the hill overlooking the industrial town became an educational base for children of Mount Savage.

Mount Savage School opened in the fall of 1952. In the beginning it served children in 1st through 12th grades. Kindergarten was later added in the 1960s when the school systems began to follow Germany's lead of including a pre-first grade. The largest class to graduate from Mount Savage was the class of 1965. These were the baby boomers of the area. The last class to graduate from Mount Savage School as a K–12 school was the class of 2000. Today the school is newly remodeled and caterers to kindergarten through 8th grade.

Even though the school has gone through some changes, it is still clear that the school is what holds the town together. The education system is the one constant that has stayed and evolved even after the boom time of industry disappeared. The spirit of the Mount Savage Indians, the school mascot, stays alive in the town with the children and their parents. The spirit of the town is indeed education, and alumni are proud to have been a part of the town's history.

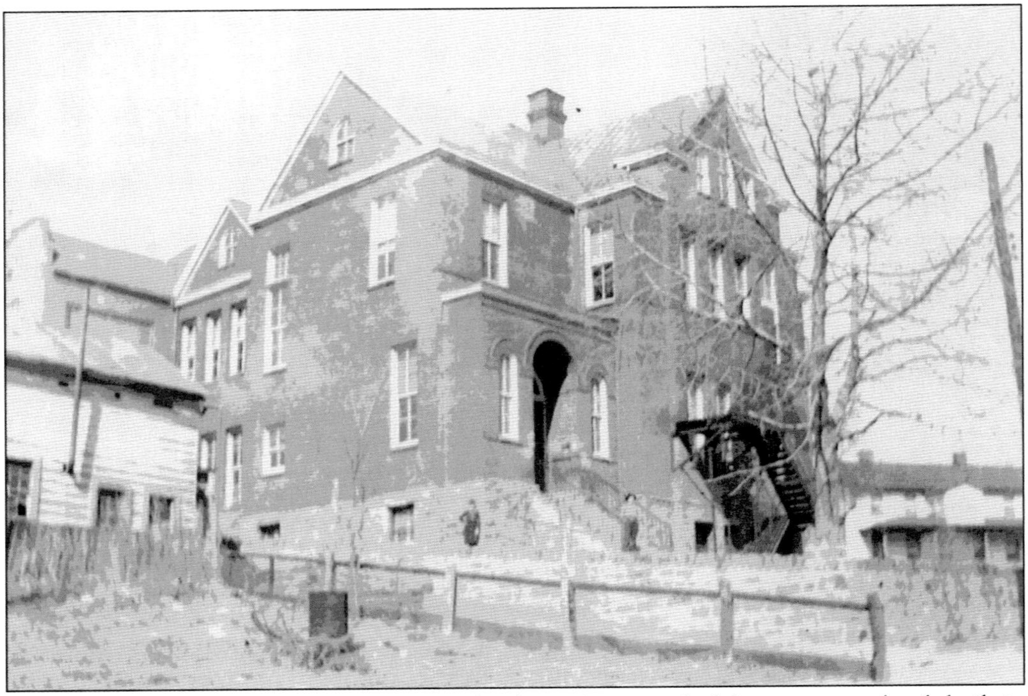

Mount Savage School. Mount Savage School was the second of the two new schools built in the Mount Savage area at the turn of the 20th century. (Courtesy of Cora Carter.)

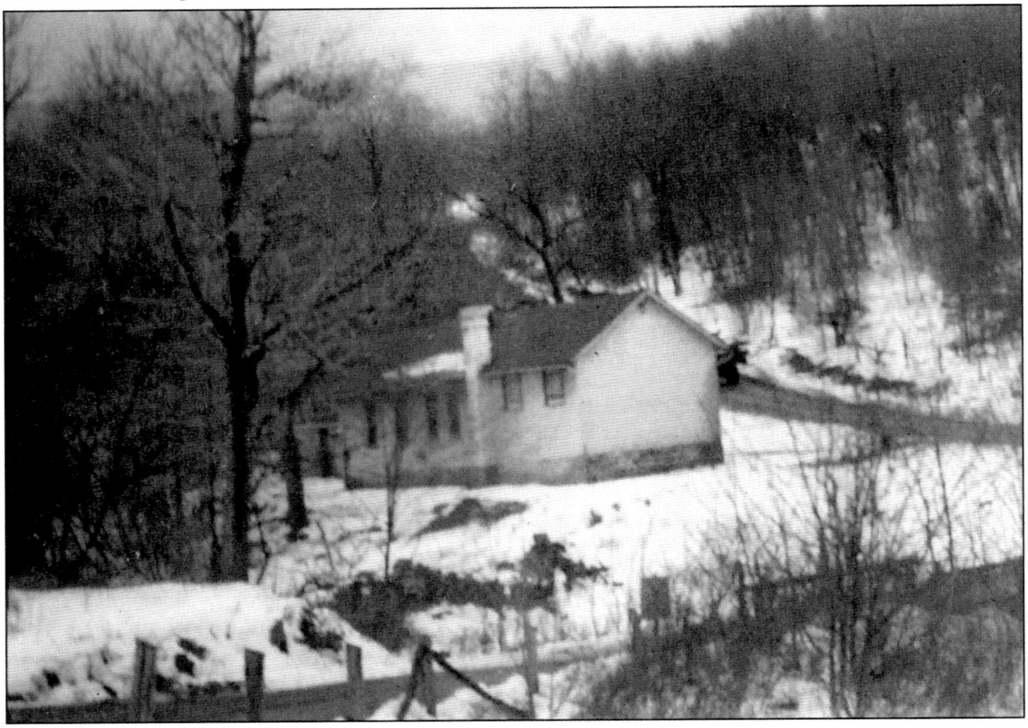

Dutch Hollow. This school was in use until the fall of 1952. After the new Mount Savage School was built, the first and second schools were consolidated into the new school. (Courtesy of Paula Fuller.)

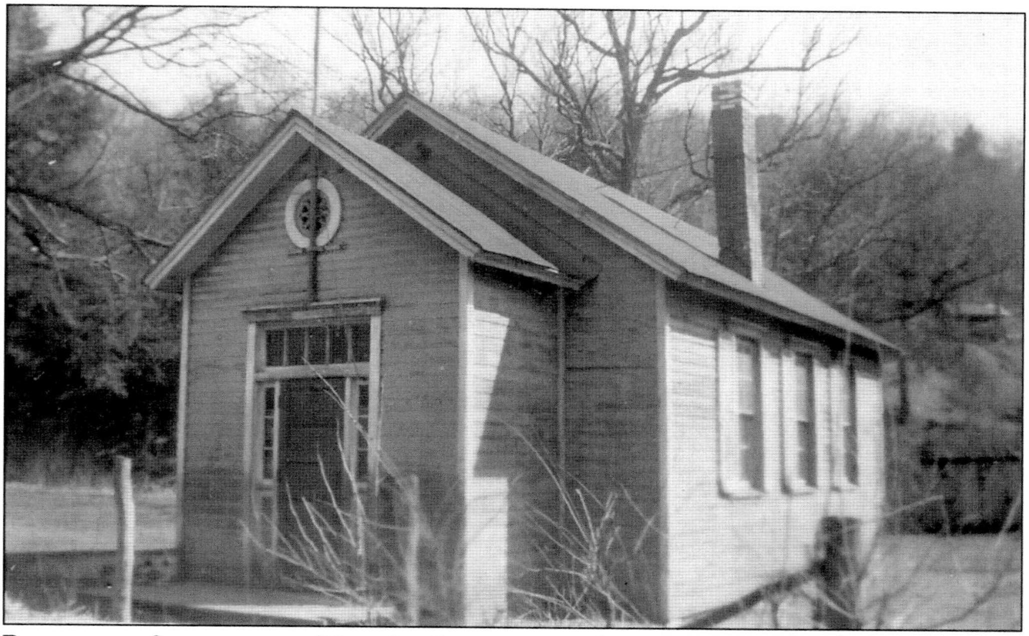

Barrelville Schoolhouse. The schoolhouse is one of two one-room schoolhouses that were located in Barrelville. This building housed grades one through three.

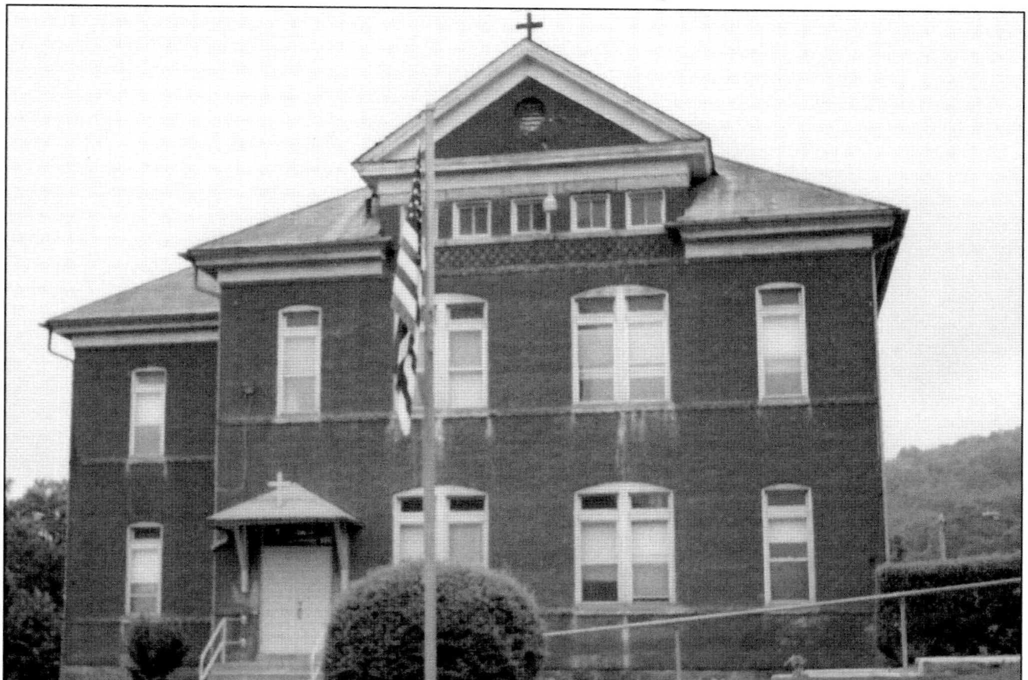

St. Patricks Parochial School. In 1896 Reverend Father Williams, who was in charge of the Ursuline Sisters, established St. Patricks school. In 1899 the Ursuline Sisters were recalled to Kentucky and placed the school in charge of the Sisters of Notre Dame. An actual school building was not constructed until 1900. A Catholic-based education was offered to students for $1 a month. (Courtesy of Bill Pratt.)

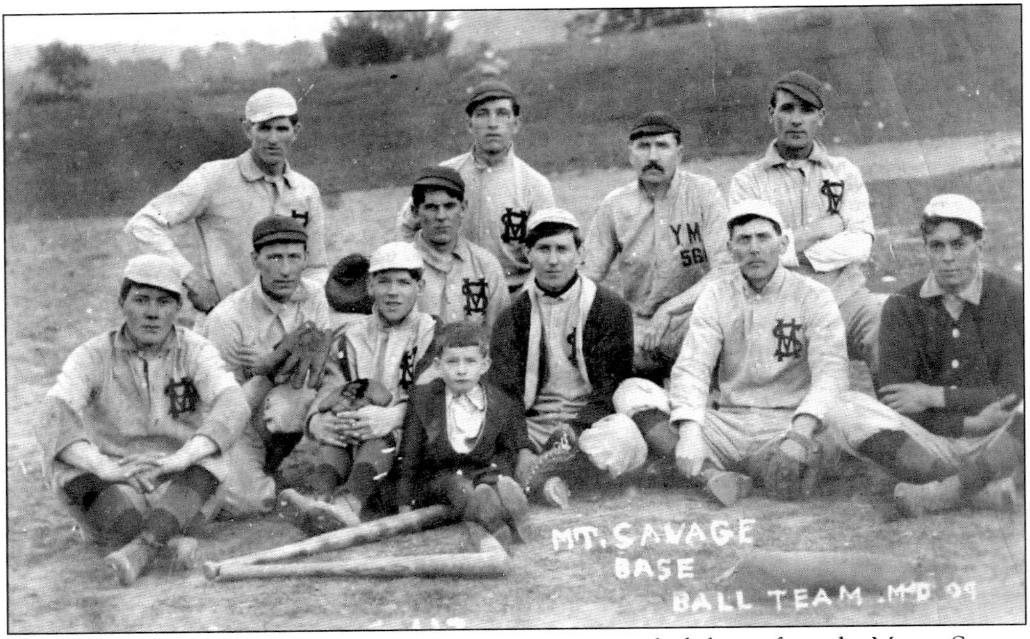

MOUNT SAVAGE BASEBALL TEAM, 1909. This team consisted of players from the Mount Savage area, not just from the town itself. The home field was located where the current Mount Savage School stands today. (Courtesy of Mount Savage Historical Society.)

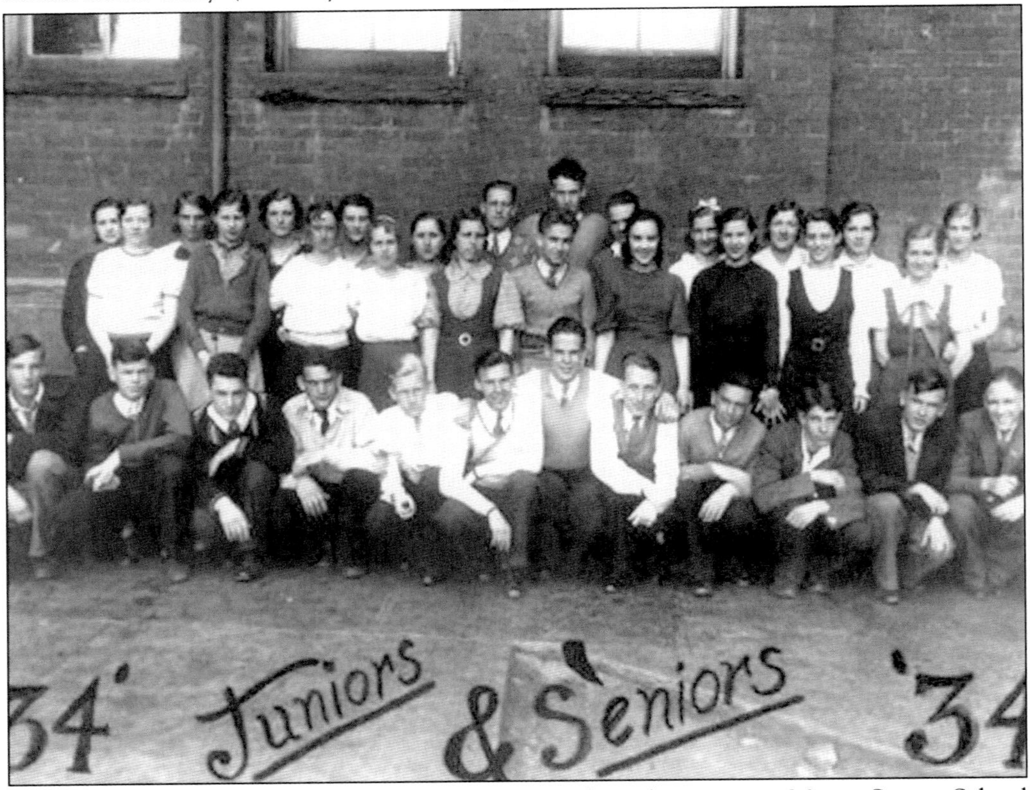

CLASS OF 1934. This is one of the graduating classes from the two-story Mount Savage School that was located across from St. Patricks Church. (Courtesy of Wilbert Paul.)

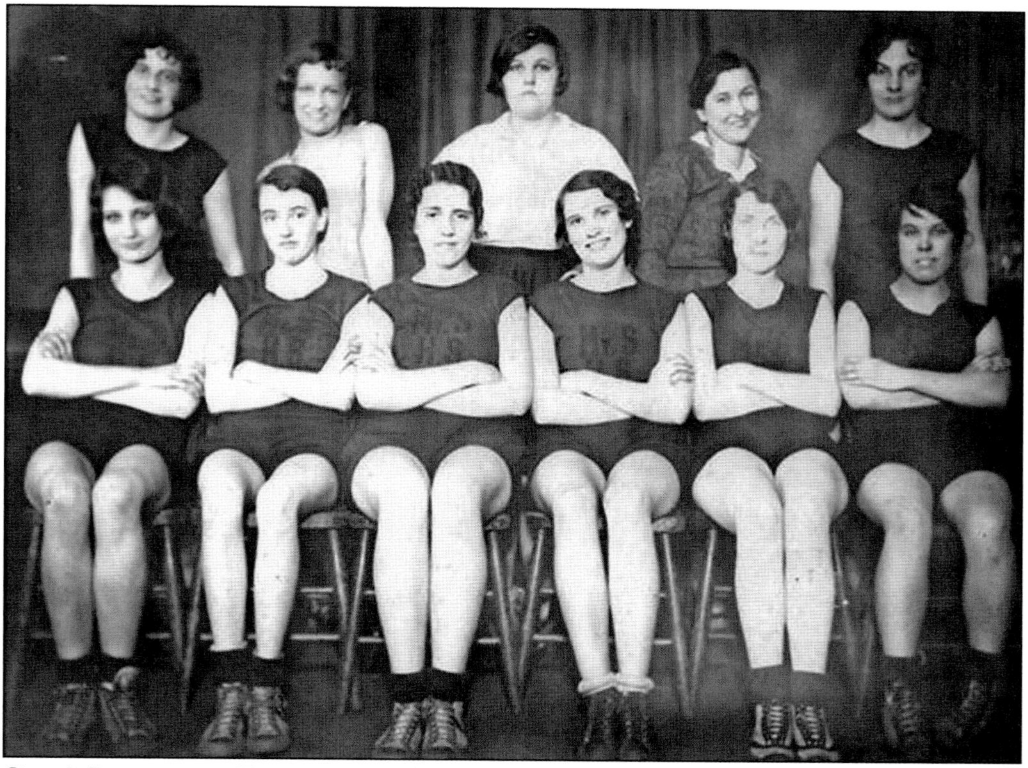

Girls' Basketball Team, 1932. Sports have always been important to the schools in and around Mount Savage. This is a photo of an early girls' basketball team. (Courtesy of Wilbert Paul.)

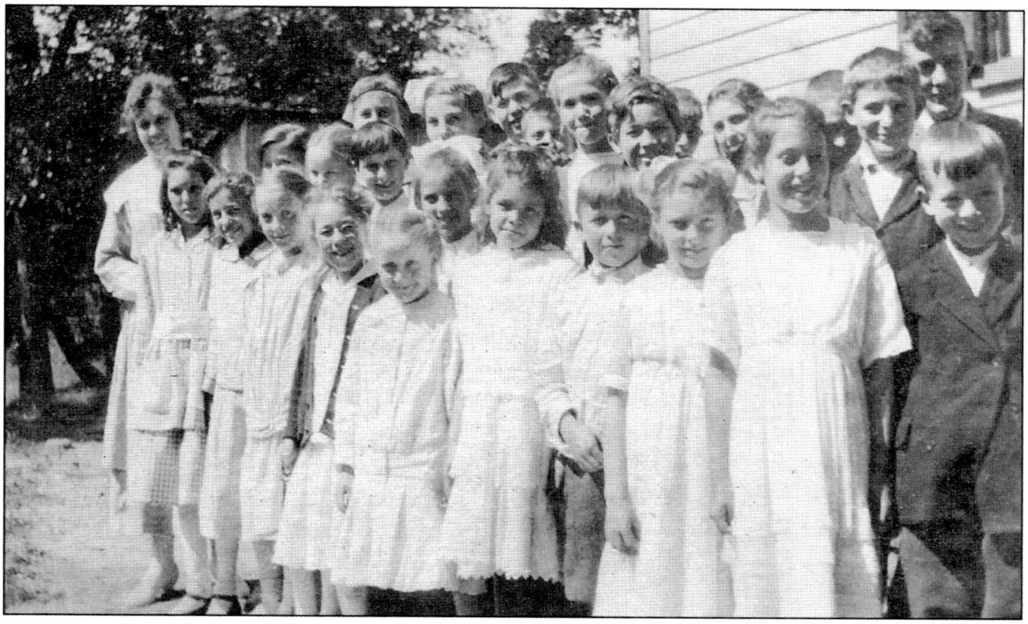

Dutch Hollow School Students, 1930s. This school only had two rooms and two teachers. One room was for the first through third grades and the other room was for the fourth through eighth grades. (Courtesy of Cora Carter.)

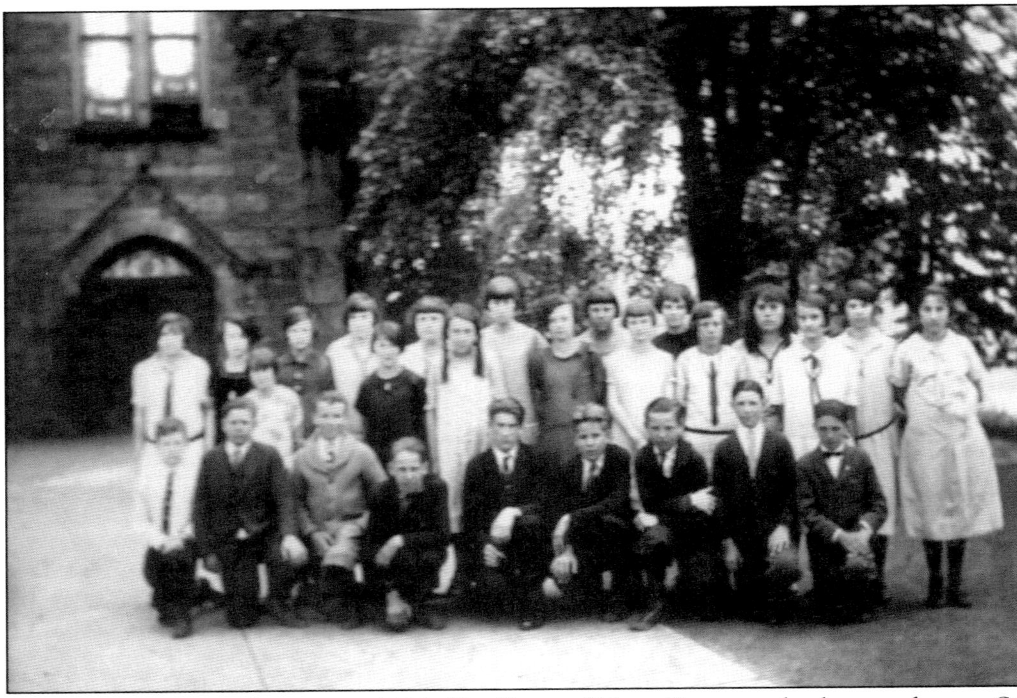

St. Patricks School Students, 1920. The Sisters of Notre Dame taught these students at St. Patricks. (Courtesy of Cora Carter.)

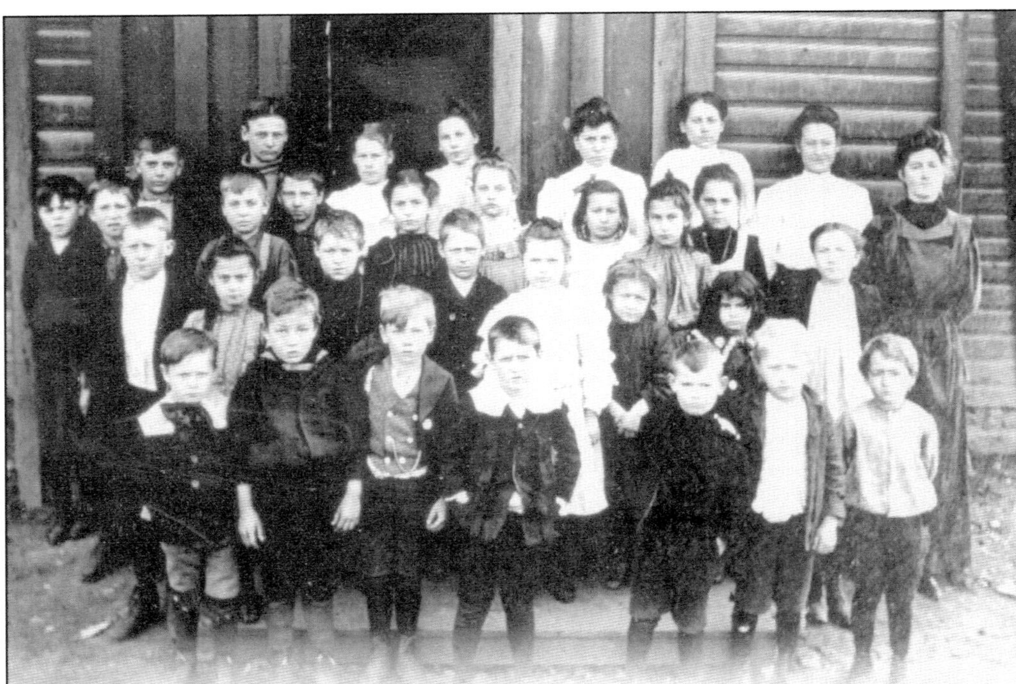

Students in Front of Barrelville School, 1905. Here is a group of students ranging from first to eighth grades. This school was also taken out of use after the fall of 1952. (Courtesy of Phyllis Reed.)

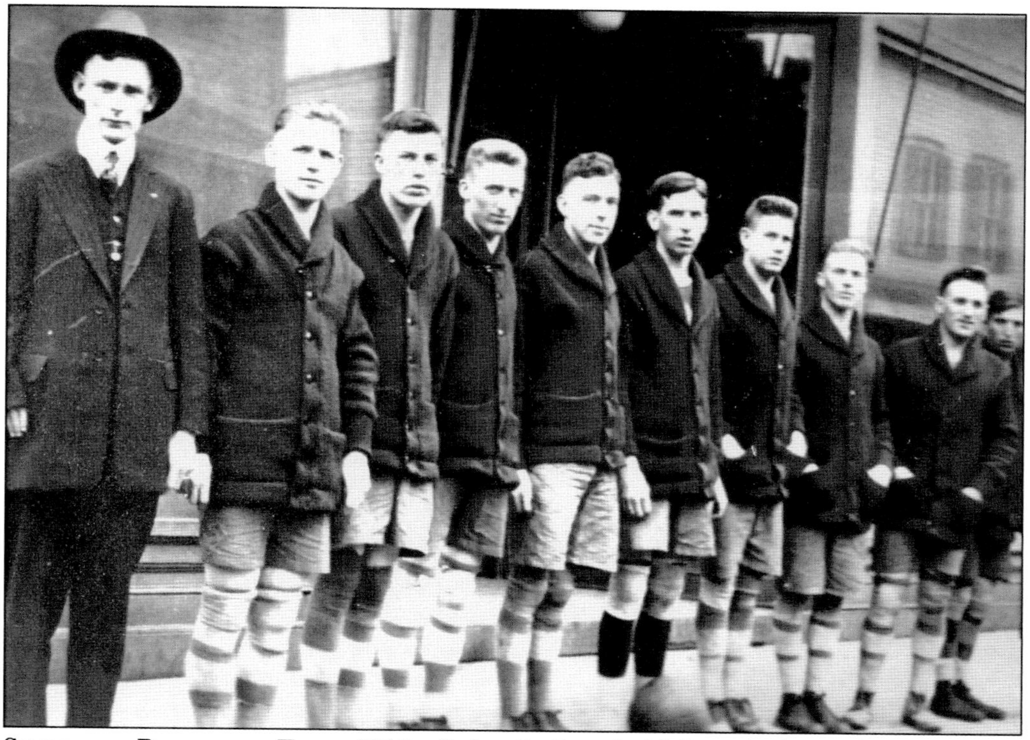

SHAMROCKS BASKETBALL TEAM, 1910S. Before St. Patricks Hall was built on Church Hill, the St. Patricks Shamrocks played on the second floor of the Mullaney Building. Team members were, from left to right, as follows: James Brannon, George Kootnz, Ralph Lashley, Ed Snyder, Tom Moran, James Graham, Chuck Lancaster, Joe Carter, James Shaffer, and Oscar Kootnz. (Courtesy of Naomi Hummelwright.)

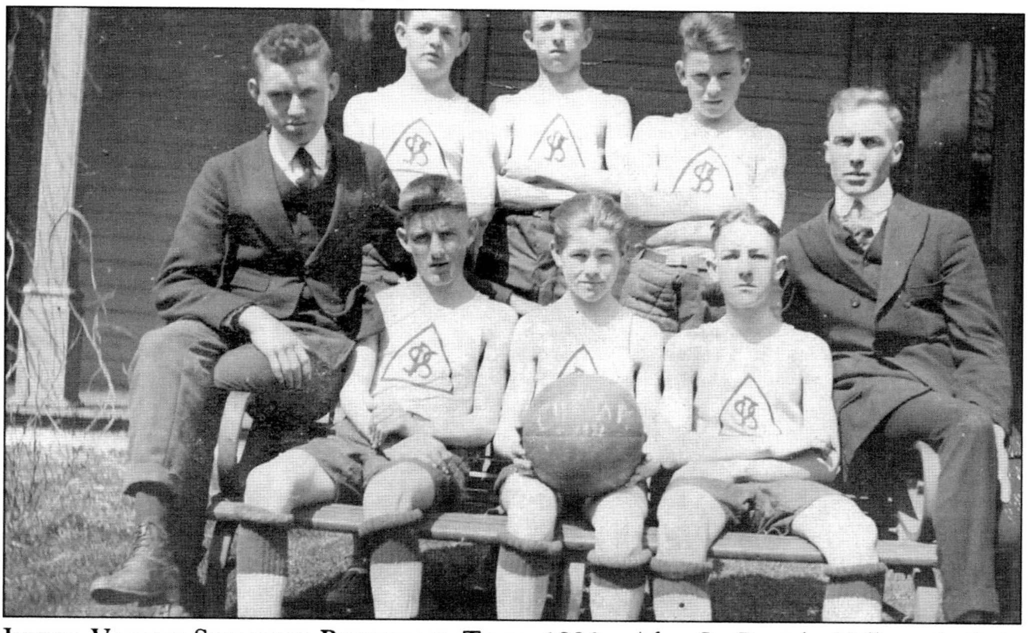

JUNIOR VARSITY SHAMROCK BASKETBALL TEAM, 1920S. After St. Patricks Hall was built in 1921, the Shamrocks played on the second floor of the hall. (Courtesy of Gary Delaney.)

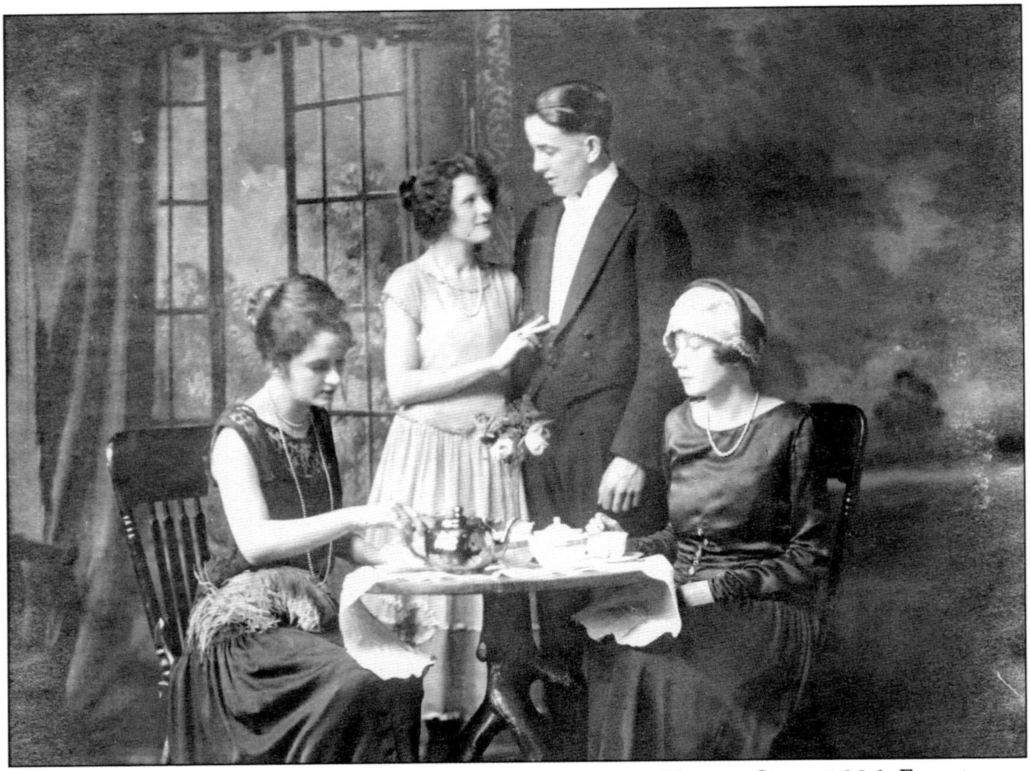

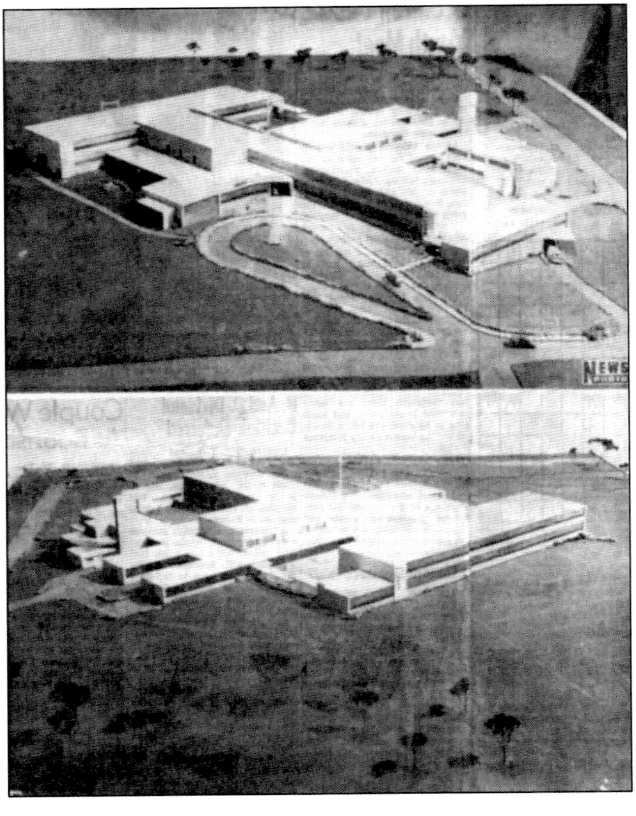

DRAMA CLUB, 1926. Even in the small two-story school, the students were interested in the stage. This was the first year that the school included grades 1 through 12. The class entered a drama competition for Allegany County and won for their performance of *Betty's Butler*. The actors, from left to right, are Christina Porter (sitting), Dorothy Rinard (standing), Lester B. Reed (standing), and Zella Soustnine (sitting) (Courtesy of Phyllis Reed.)

MODEL DEMOS OF MOUNT SAVAGE SCHOOL. In the early 1950s the Allegany County Board of Education started to consolidate small community schools into large elementary and high schools. Here is an architectural model of the planned Mount Savage School. (Courtesy of Mount Savage School.)

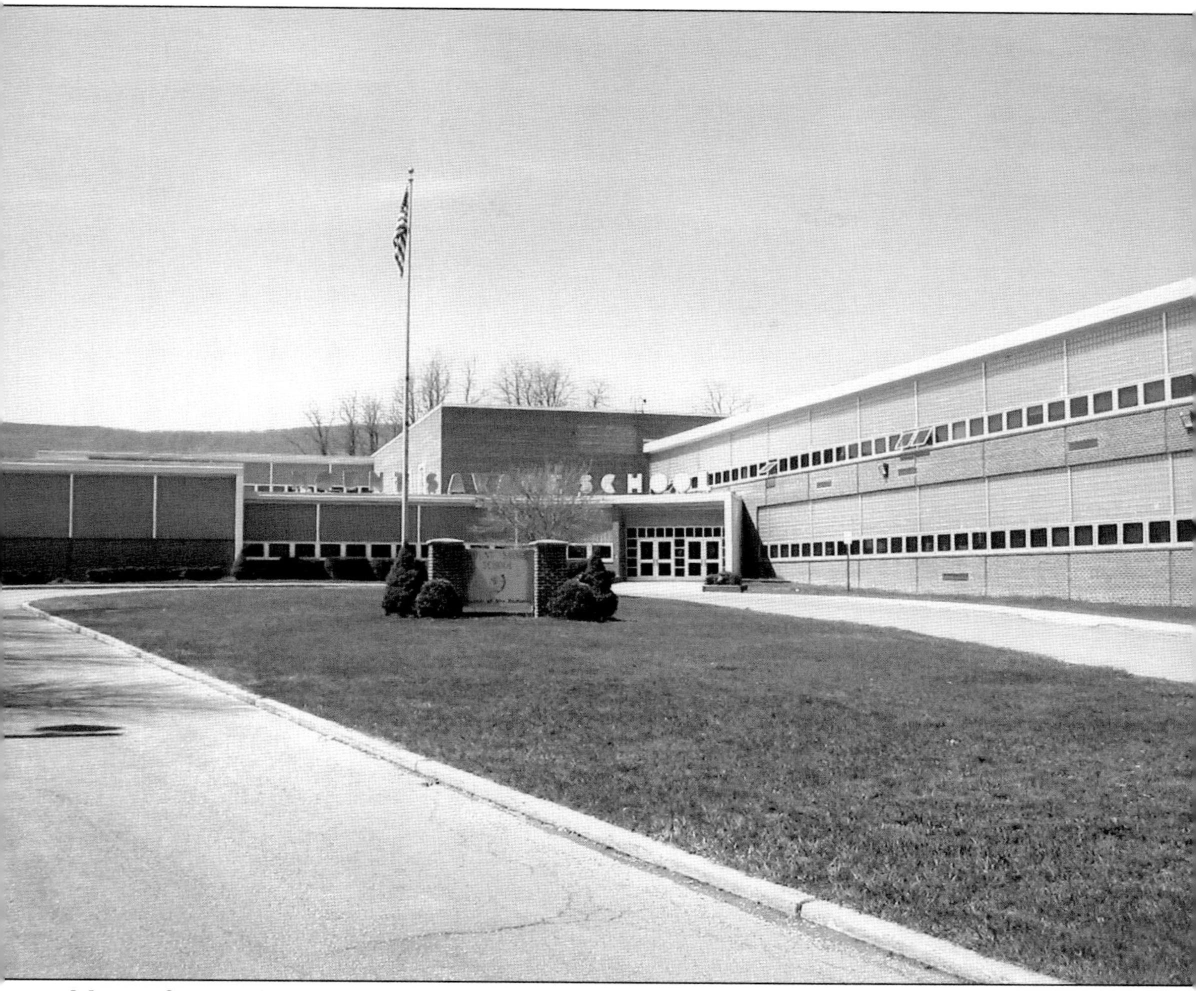

MOUNT SAVAGE SCHOOL. The current school was opened in the fall of 1952. It was built at a cost of 65¢ a square foot. The indian was chosen as the school's mascot, because the school was built near the site where Shawnee Indians once dwelled. The school colors are green and gold.

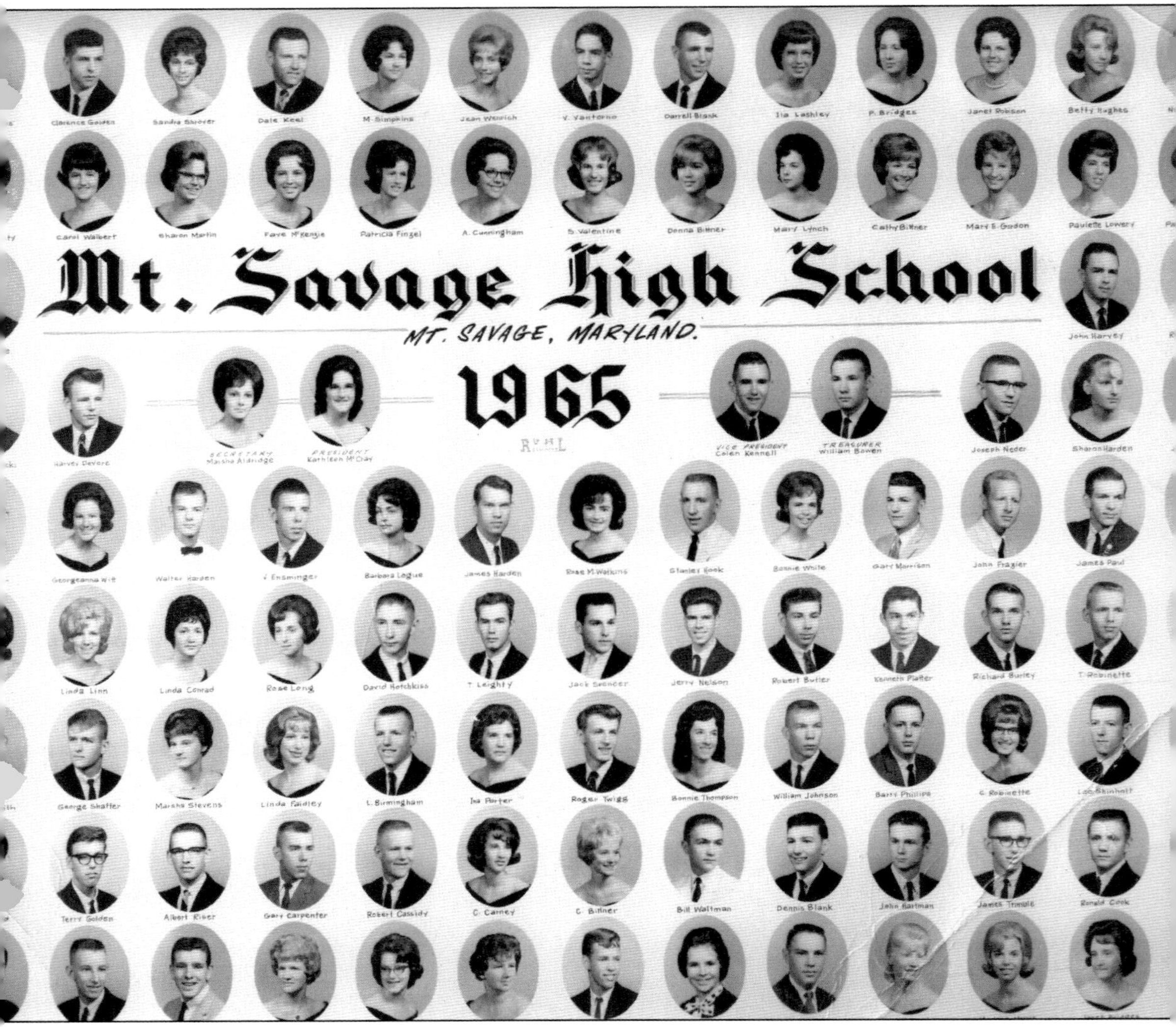

CLASS OF 1965. The class of 1965 was the first class to attend the school from 1st through 12th grade. This class was also the largest graduating class from Mount Savage School.

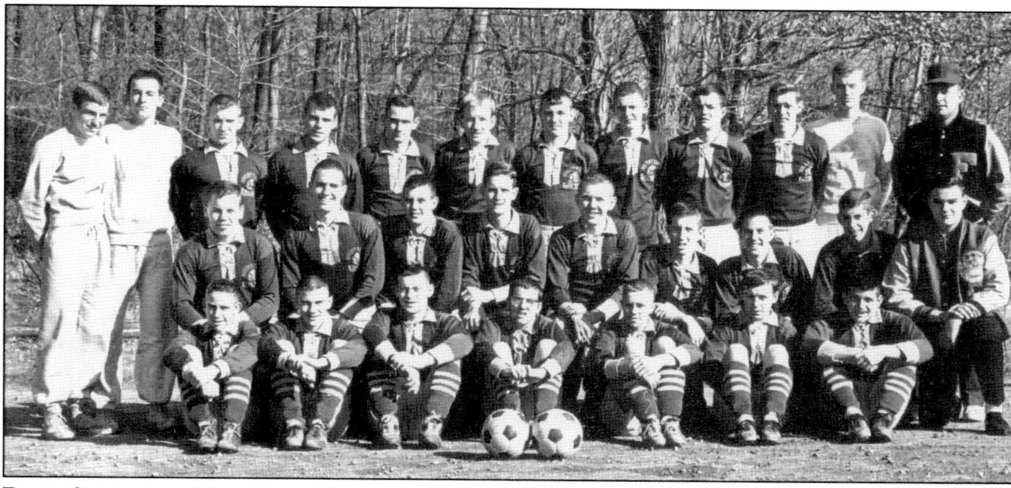

Boys Soccer, 1966. From the opening day of the new school, soccer was Mount Savage School's sport because the school was not large enough to accommodate football. Later, in the 1980s through 1990s, Mount Savage had the pleasure of having one of the area's greatest soccer coaches, George BiShields. He led the team to more playoffs and championships than any other coach.

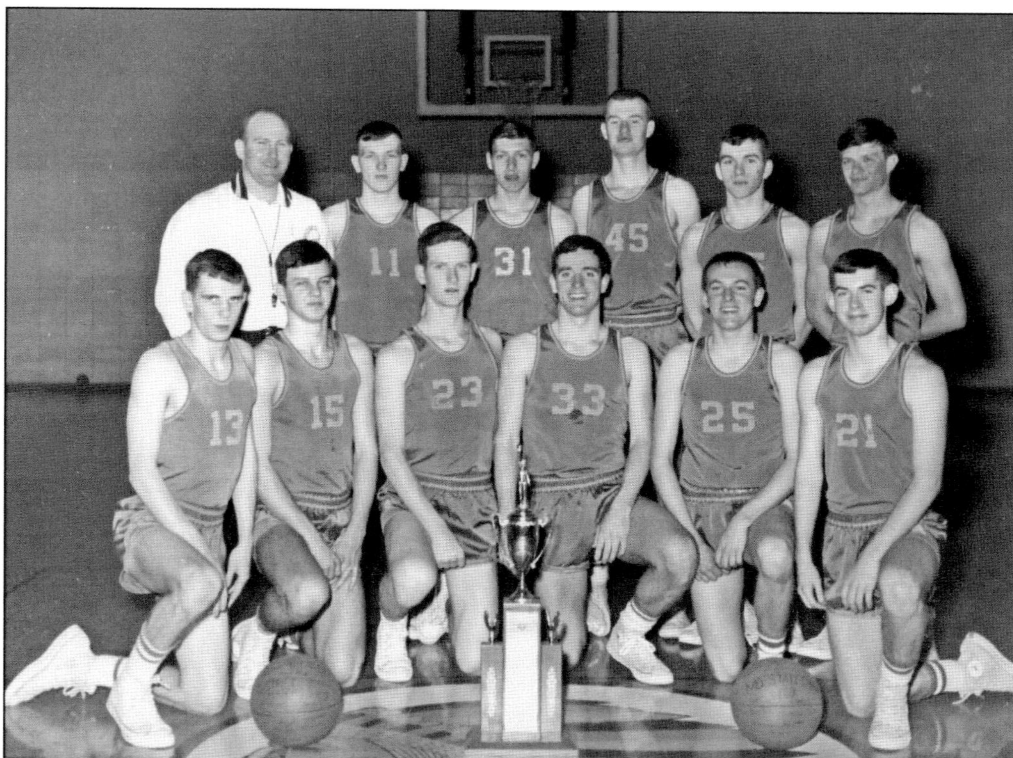

Boys Basketball, 1967. This Mount Savage School team was one of the winners of the Maryland State Basketball Championship. They won against Poolesville 56–54 in the class "C" crown. Coach Robert Kirk, who is now the head coach for Allegany College of Maryland's basketball team, led them.

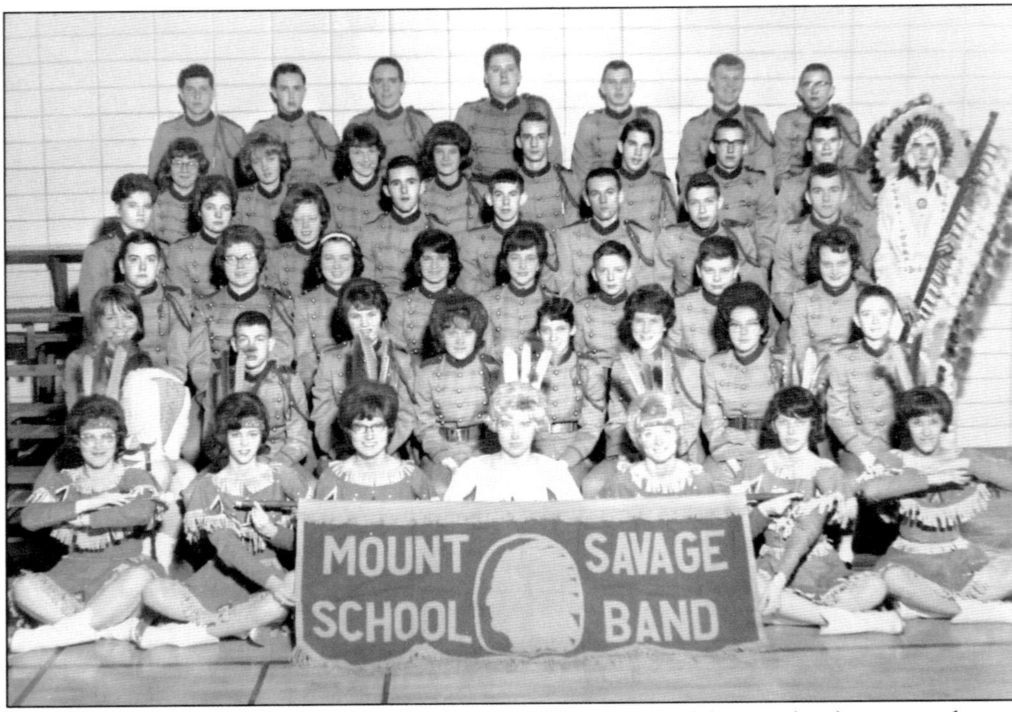

Mount Savage Marching Band, 1964. How can a school have school spirit without a marching band?

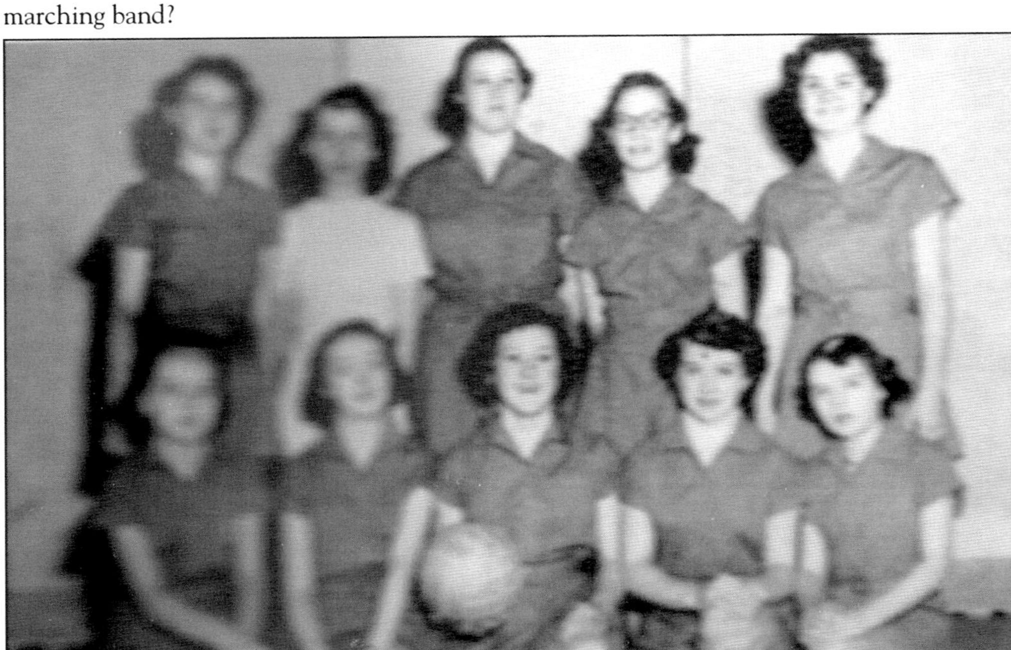

Girls' Volleyball Team, 1953. The girls' volleyball team has always been a popular sport for Mount Savage School. They had many wins over the several years they played for the high school, especially under the coaching of Joanne Nickel. The team is identified from left to right as (front row) J. Holt, R. House, J. Logsdon, P. Dorman, and N. Cook; (back row) N. Deffenbaugh, C. Lucky, C. Geary, R. Lashley, and C. Reagan.

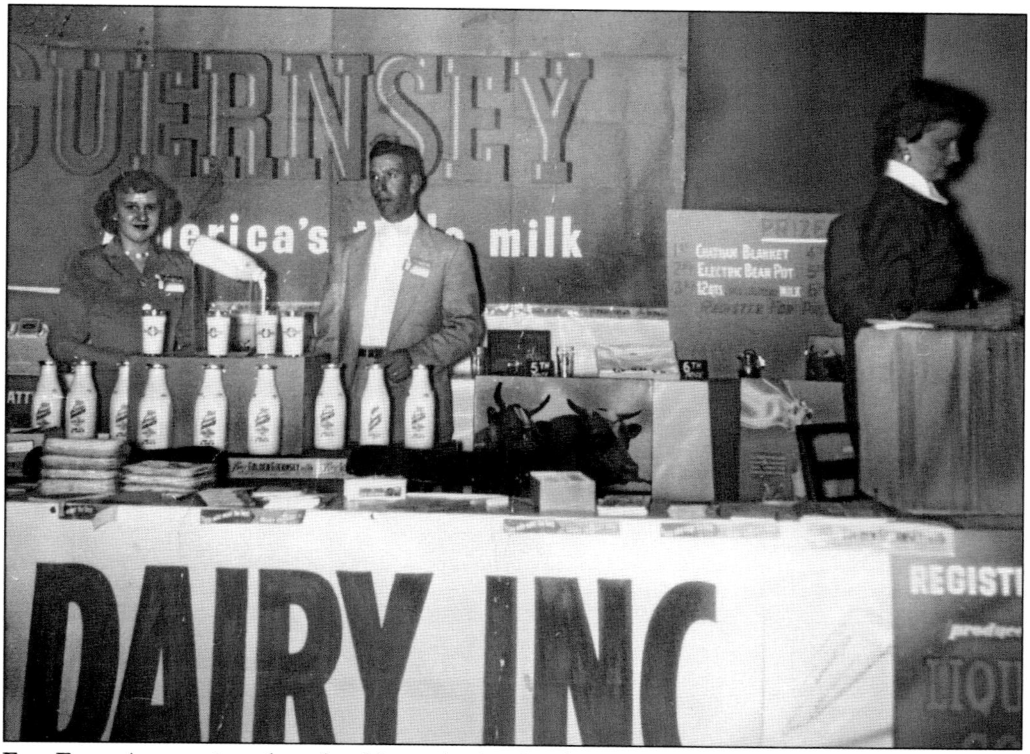

Fun Fair. At one time the school hosted a fun fair for its students to educate them about their surroundings. Here, the Glen Savage Dairy booth is displaying the process of bottling milk. (Courtesy of the James Robison family.)

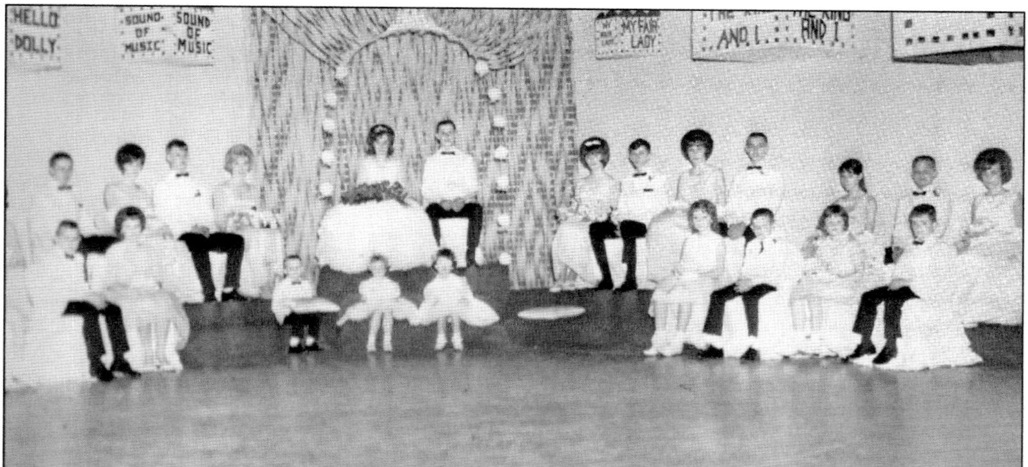

May Day 1965, "Broadway Musicals." Mount Savage School was the last school in Allegany County to celebrate the talent show tradition of May Day. This school-wide show always took place on the first Thursday of May. The last May Day celebration took place in 2000.

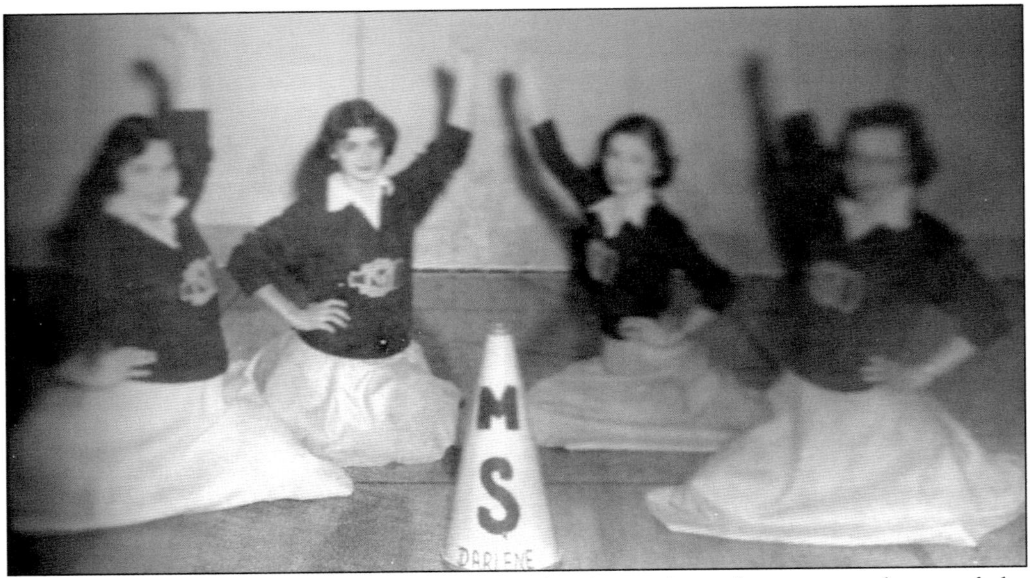

CHEERLEADERS, 1954. Mount Savage cheerleaders have always been a proud part of the school's history. They attended many competitions in the mid- to late 1990s. The cheerleaders shown here, from left to right, are Alphie Watkins, Rosalie Femi, Laura Jean House, and Jane Rizer.

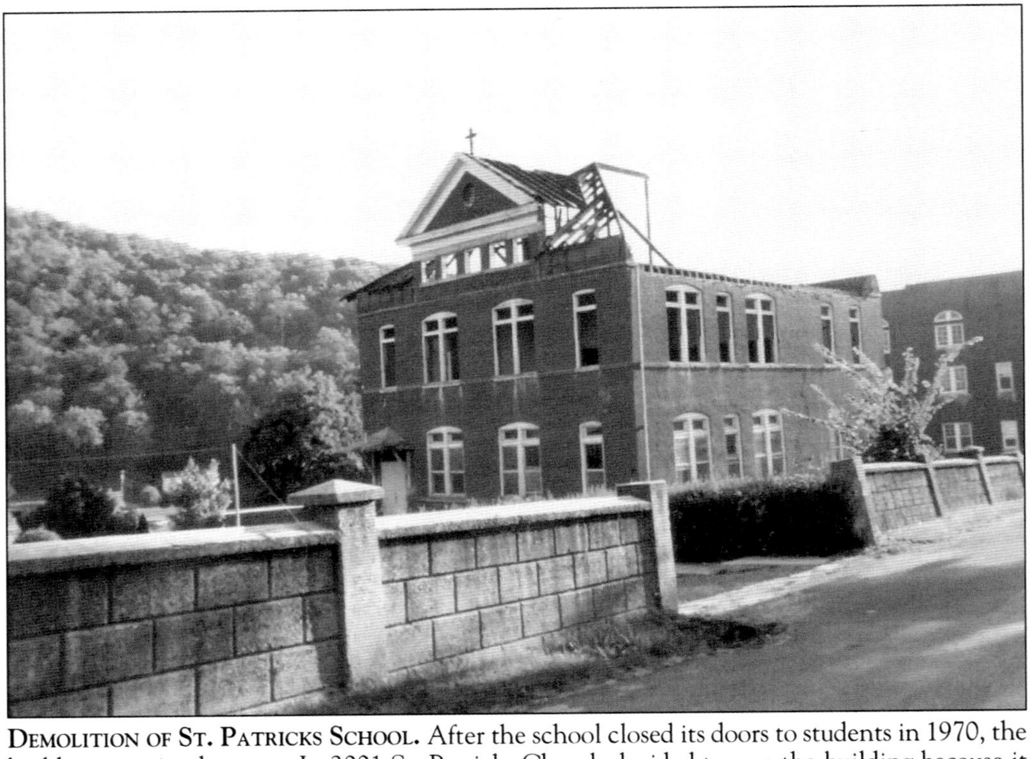

DEMOLITION OF ST. PATRICKS SCHOOL. After the school closed its doors to students in 1970, the building remained vacant. In 2001 St. Patricks Church decided to raze the building because it had become unsafe. (Courtesy of Margaret Winner.)

Seven

VOLUNTEERING
A Town Tradition

It is amazing how many volunteer organizations the small town of Mount Savage has had in its history. Of course, there have always been the church and school auxiliaries that were and still are popular. There were many men's and women's volunteer groups in the town.

One of the most important and most popular volunteer groups is the Mount Savage Volunteer Fire Department. It was started by a group of men who worked for the C & P Railroad. They saw the need for a firemen corps to protect the community from the imminent danger of fire.

Other volunteer groups were not as prevalent in the community as the fire department, but they also helped the community in their own ways. Many of these groups were union-based or religious-based groups such as the Odd Fellows, the Rebeccas, the Knights of Columbus, and the Masons. Many of these groups are still active today.

The Veterans of Foreign Wars has become a large part of the community. They have a large meeting building on Main Street. Through the years the town has honored the veterans of foreign wars in various monuments and memorials. American pride has been a major part of Mount Savage.

Many groups have disbanded, such as the Odd Fellows, but over the years new organizations have developed or organized in Mount Savage, like the school alumni group and the historical society. Lions Club International also has a local chapter that meets twice a month in town.

All of these organizations have one thing in common: the desire to make Mount Savage a safe, beautiful, and great place to live. These groups are made up of local citizens who take pride in the place that they live. Without the volunteer groups working behind the scenes, the town of Mount Savage would fall into despair. The churches, fire department, and other civil organizations are the blood that flows through the heart of the town.

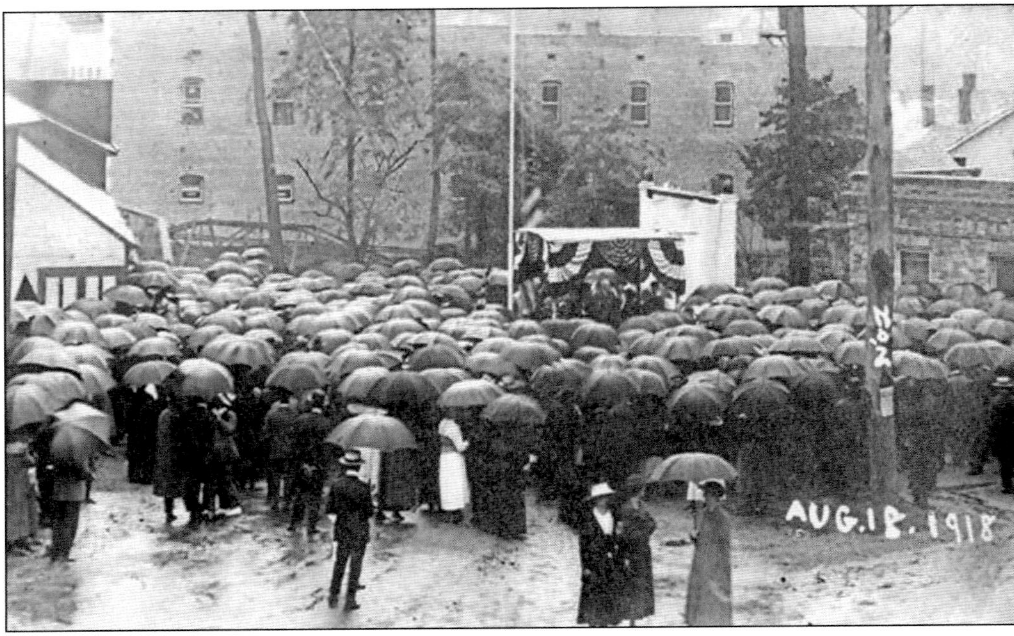

Unveiling of the World War I Honor, 1918. The citizens of Mount Savage came out in the rain to dedicate this memorial. (Courtesy of Wilbert Paul.)

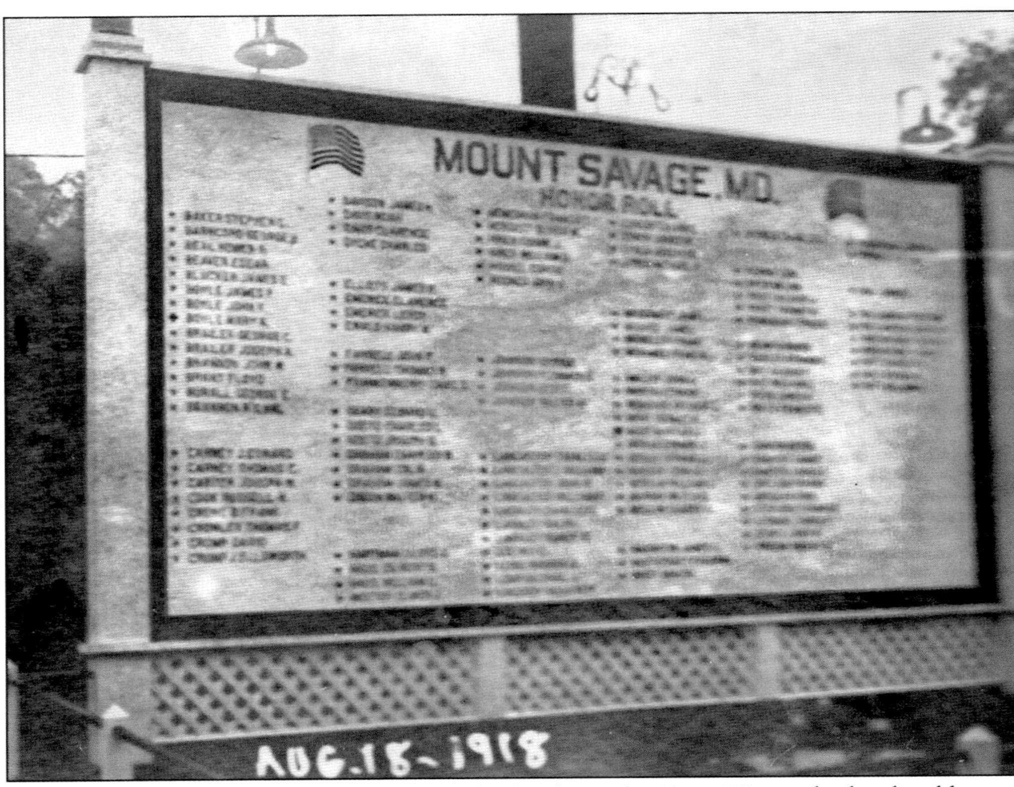

Honor Roll. This list included the men who fought in the Great War and other local heroes. (Courtesy of Wilbert Paul.)

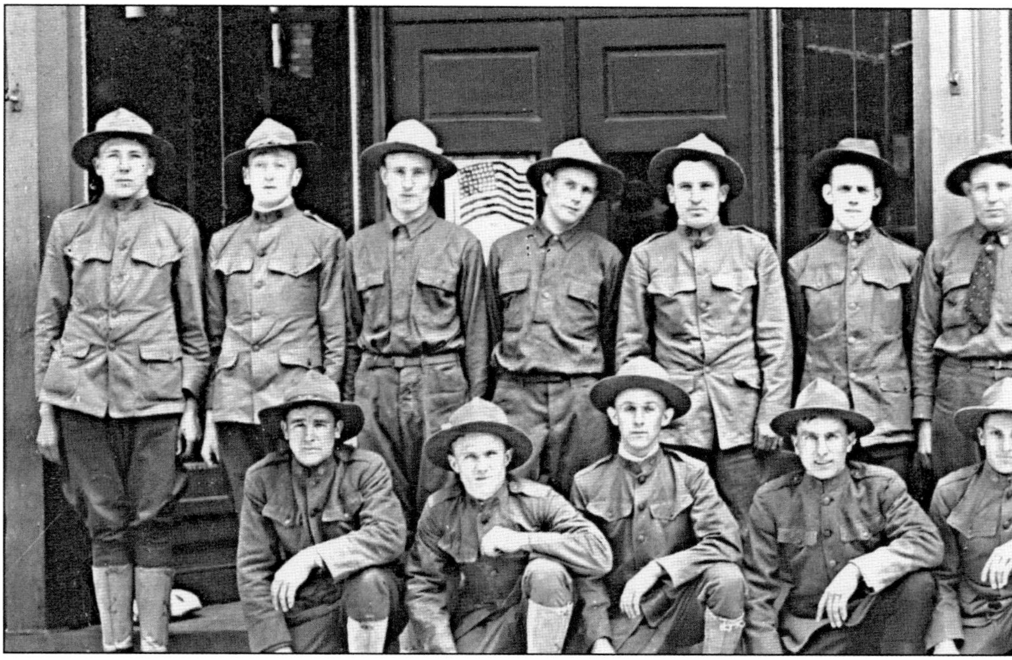

Dough Boys of Mount Savage. Young men pose for a photo in front of Mullaney Brothers Store before leaving for Europe to fight in the Great War. Almost all males of military age volunteered for the service. (Courtesy of Gary Delaney.)

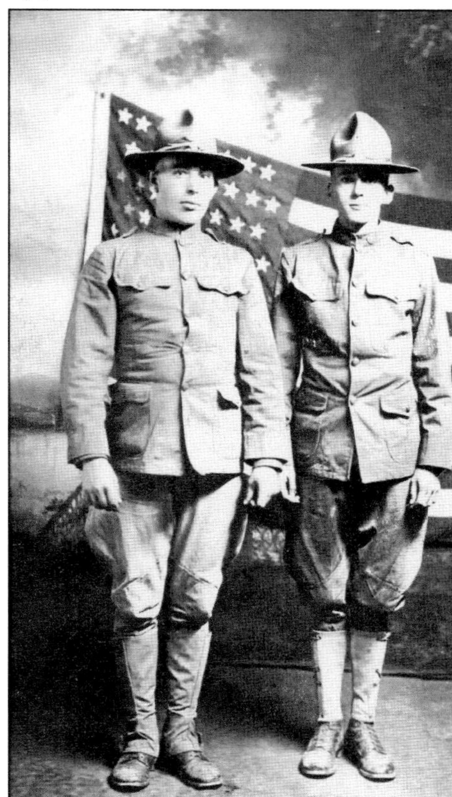

World War I Volunteers. These are two more men who volunteered to fight the Germans in World War I. Not only did the healthy young men of the town help with the war effort, but the town was the first to go "over the top" in the Fourth Liberty Loan Drive and was one of the few towns in the county to have two stars in its Honor Flag. (Courtesy of St. George's Episcopal Church.)

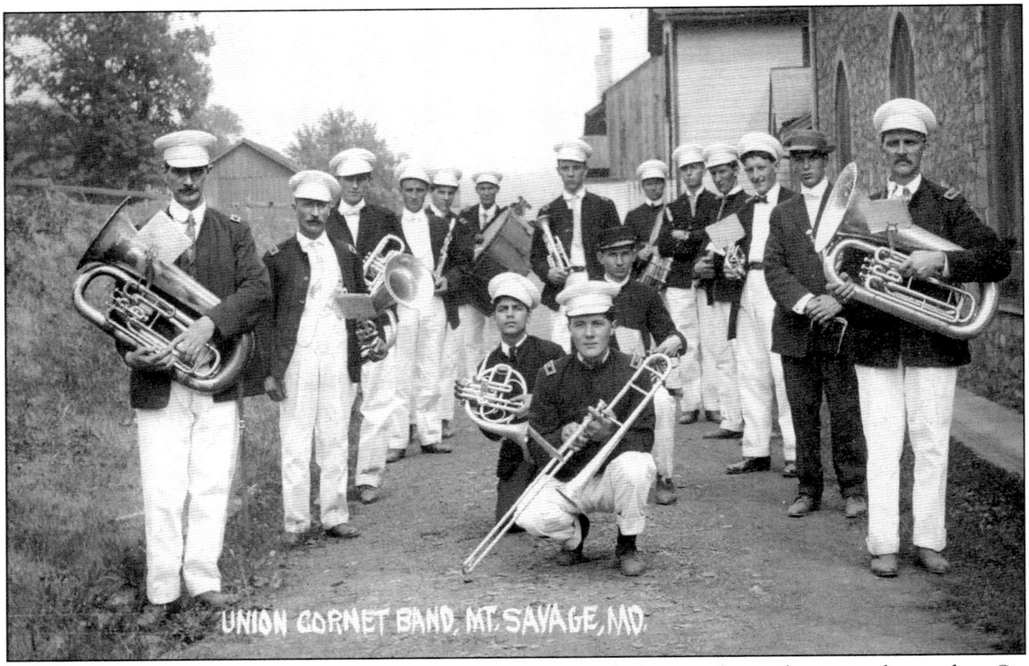

UNION CORNET BAND. Everyone loved the cornet band that performed in parades and at St. George's Episcopal Church. (Courtesy of Gary Delaney.)

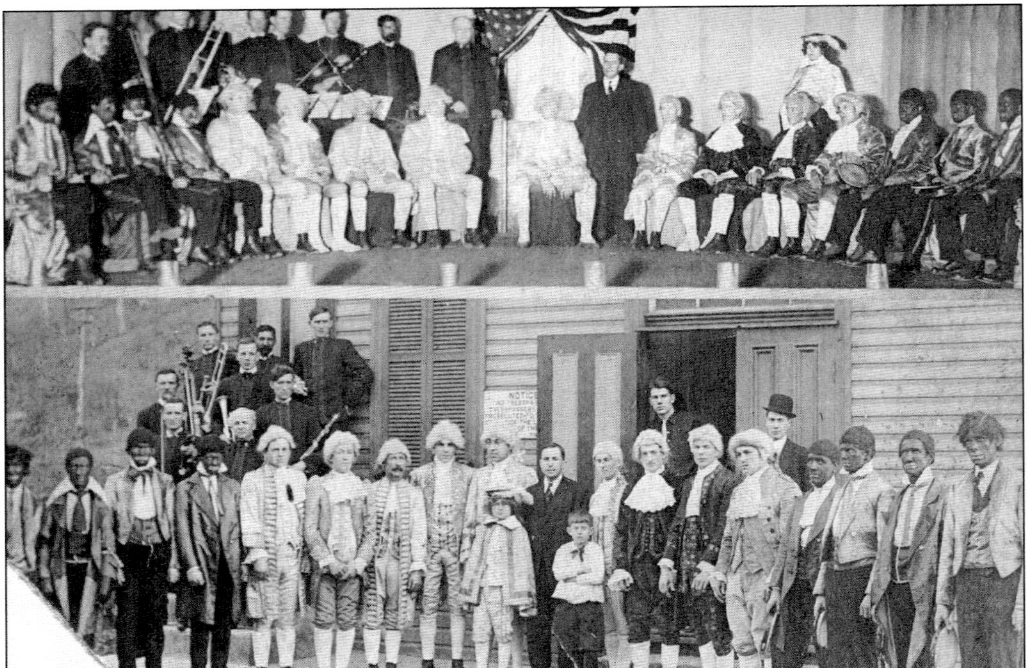

UNION CORNET BAND FOLLIES. Follies were performed at the Christ Congregation Church (St. George's Church) at the turn of the 20th century by the Union Cornet Band. Crowds would pack the church activity hall to see these comedy-filled shows. (Courtesy of Gary Delaney.)

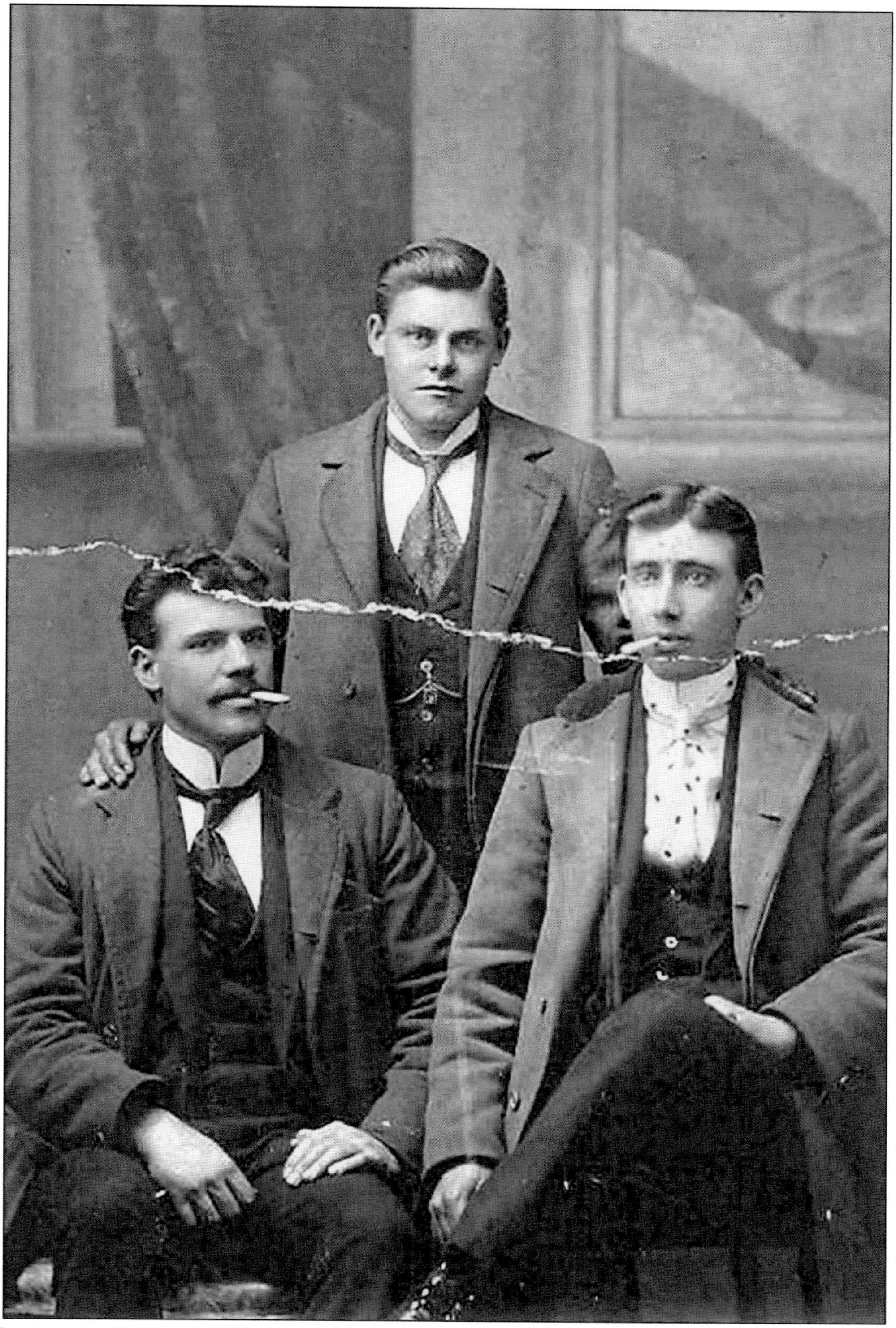

Knights of Columbus. Here are three members of the Mount Savage Knights of Columbus Council #1058. The council first organized in 1905. The Knights have met for years on the second floor of Pat Fannon's store (now Bill's Market). (Courtesy of Theresa Swanson.)

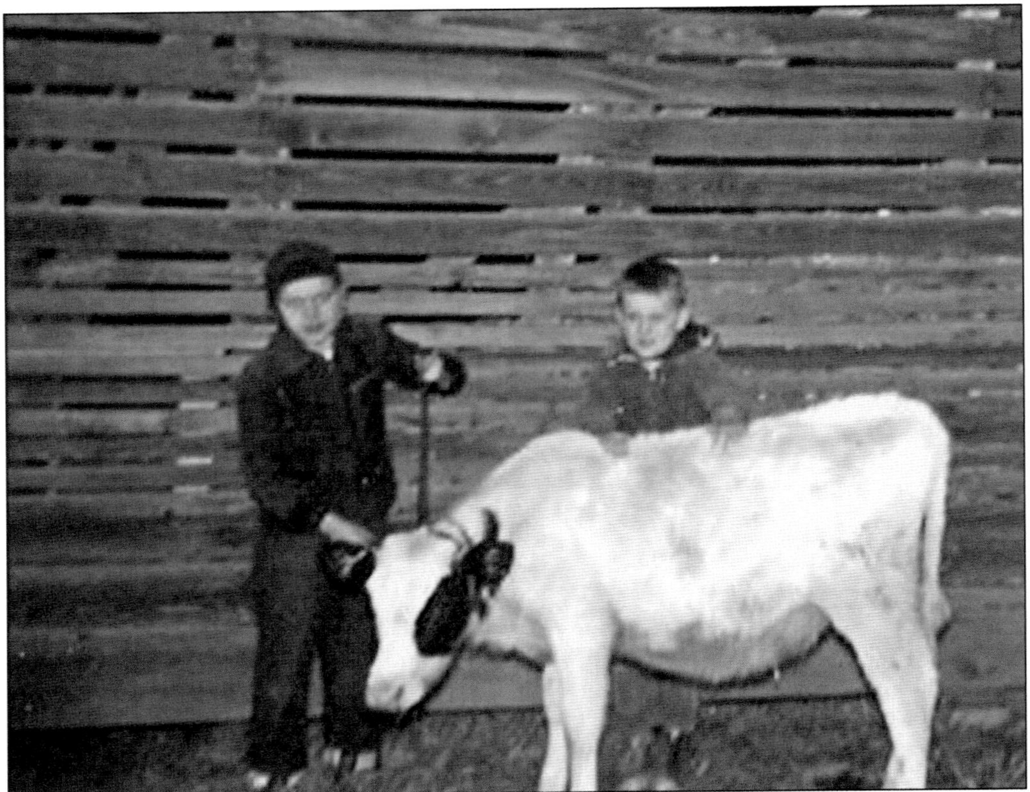

Future Farmers of America. The FFA, along with other organizations like the Soil Conservation, was a big part of the farming community. In 1955 these boys from the FFA joined with the Methodist church in the Heifer Project, a project to help Puerto Rico begin dairy farms. Slitz the calf was sent to Puerto Rico for the project. On the left is Jim Paul, and on the right is Gene Paul.

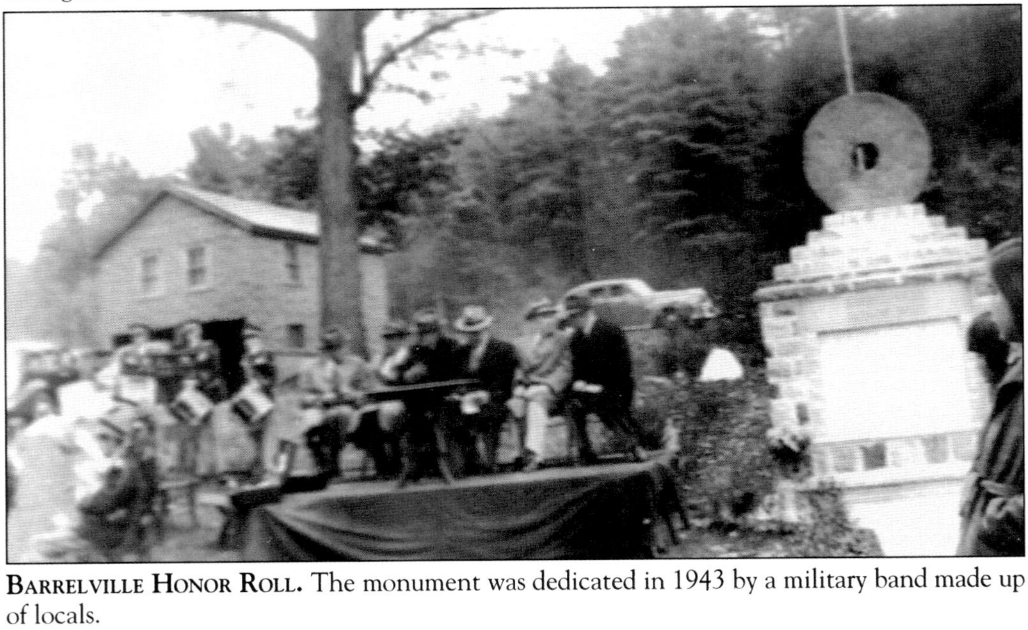

Barrelville Honor Roll. The monument was dedicated in 1943 by a military band made up of locals.

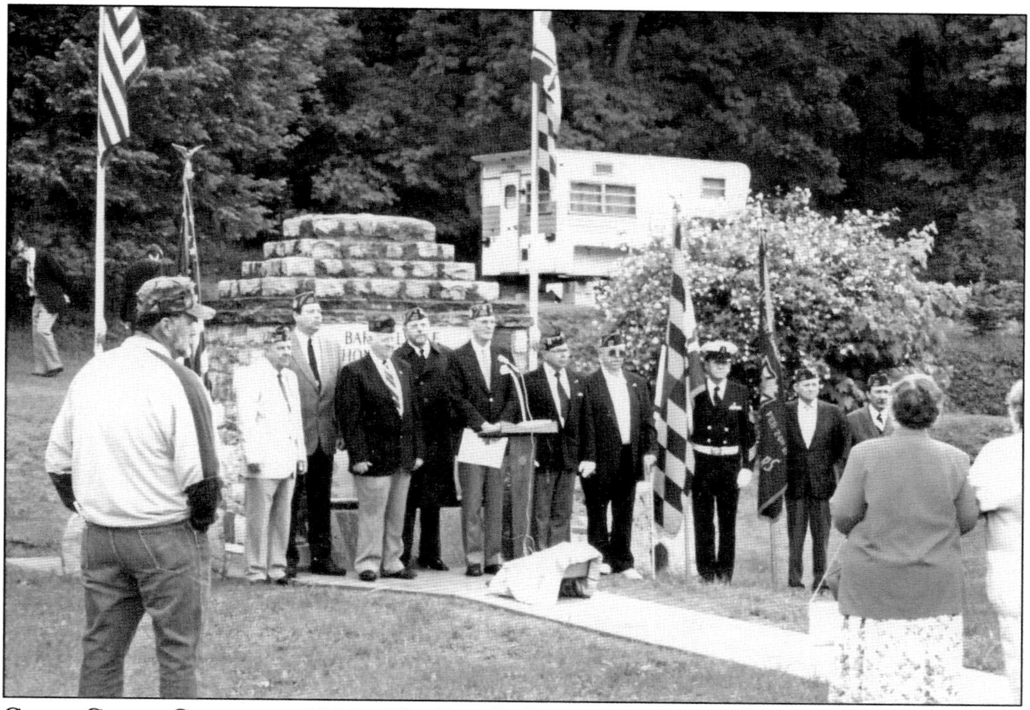

COLOR GUARD CEREMONY, 1990s. The Barrelville Honor Roll monument was enlarged in the 1960s with the help of the Barrelville Outdoor Club's donations. Here, the Color Guard from the Old Iron Rail Post #6025 honor people newly nominated to the roll.

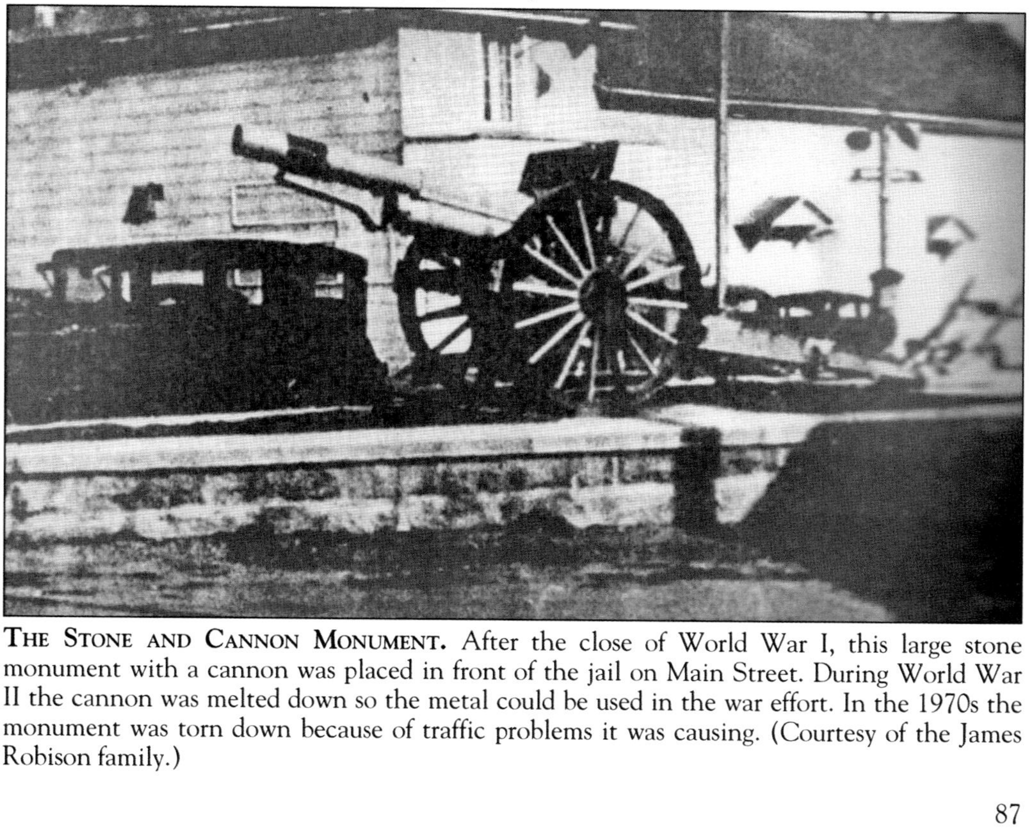

THE STONE AND CANNON MONUMENT. After the close of World War I, this large stone monument with a cannon was placed in front of the jail on Main Street. During World War II the cannon was melted down so the metal could be used in the war effort. In the 1970s the monument was torn down because of traffic problems it was causing. (Courtesy of the James Robison family.)

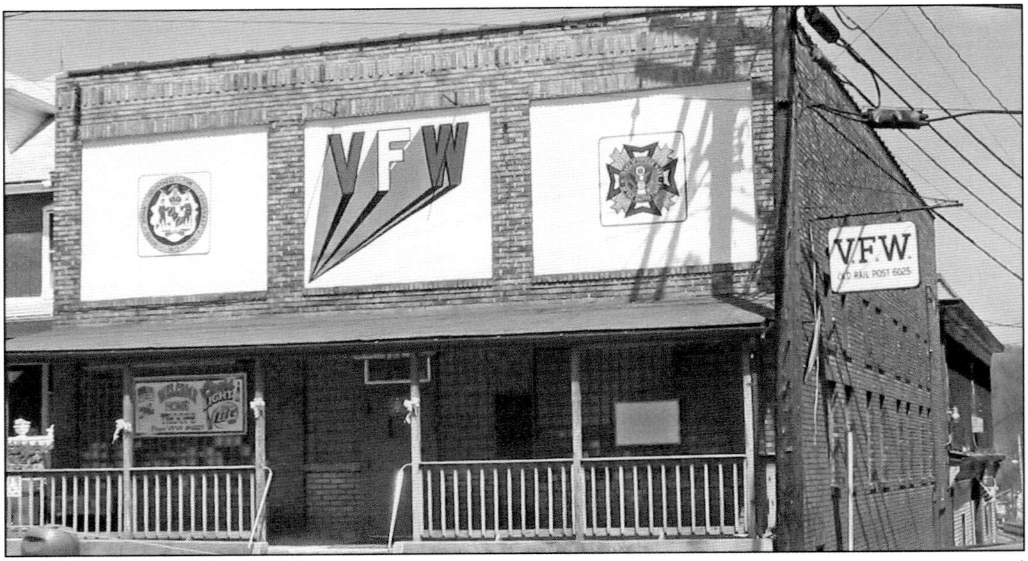

VETERANS OF FOREIGN WARS. The Veterans of Foreign Wars Old Rail Post #6025 was chartered in 1946. They purchased this half of the hotel building around the same time.

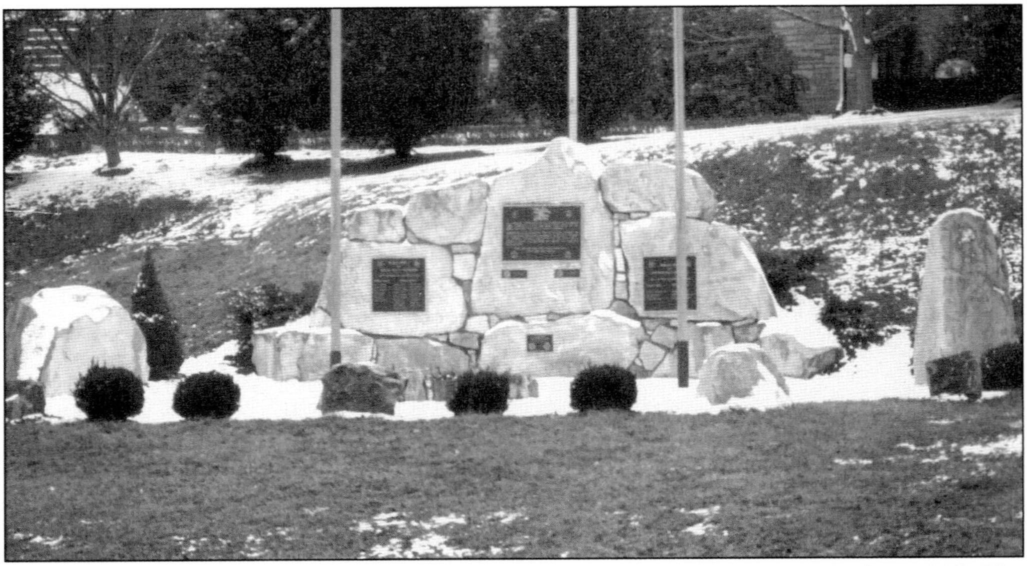

WAR MONUMENT AT THE PARK. The memorial was placed in Mount Savage Park in 1995. The monument immortalizes the Mount Savage men who lost their lives in World War I, World War II, the Korean War, and Vietnam. (Courtesy of Cora Carter.)

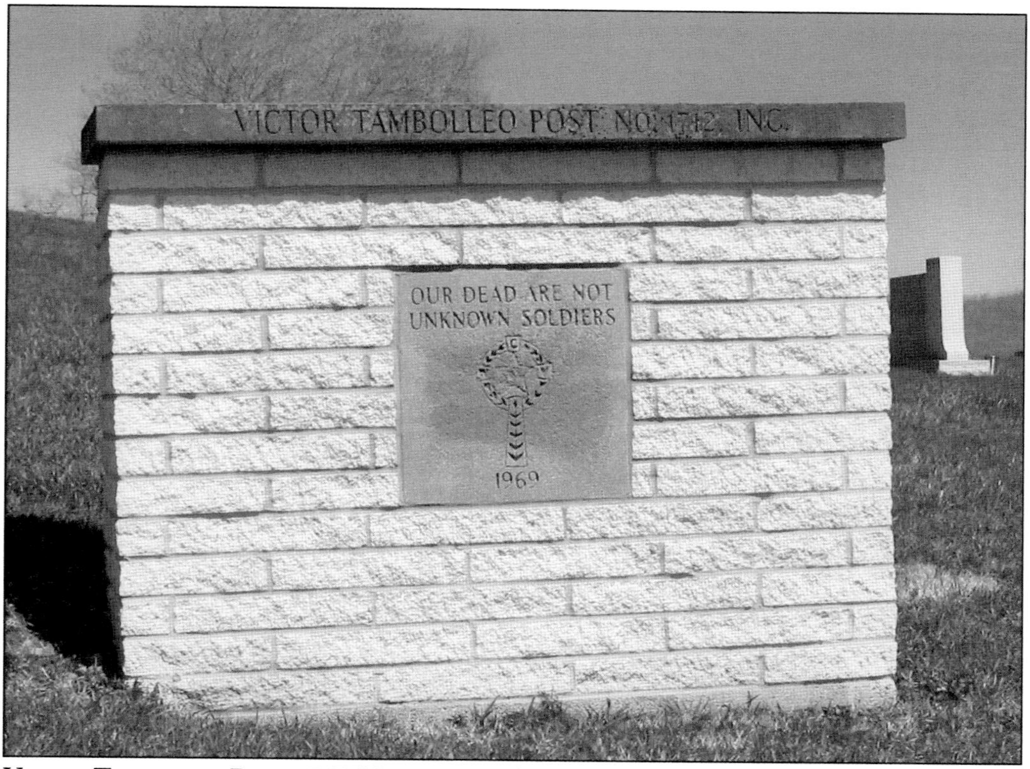

VICTOR TAMBELLEO, POST 1742 MONUMENT. This monument was placed in St. Patricks Cemetery in 1969 to remember the men who volunteered their lives for our nation.

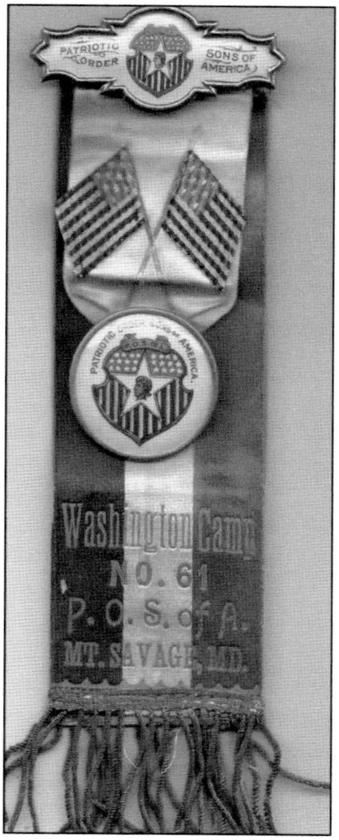

PATRIOTIC ORDER SONS OF AMERICA. Here is a wonderful look at one of the lapel sashes from a fraternal group that was in town. The sash is reversible; the side showing is red, white, and blue and was worn to meetings and parades. The reverse side is black and silver and was worn to funerals and wakes. (Courtesy of Earl Pope.)

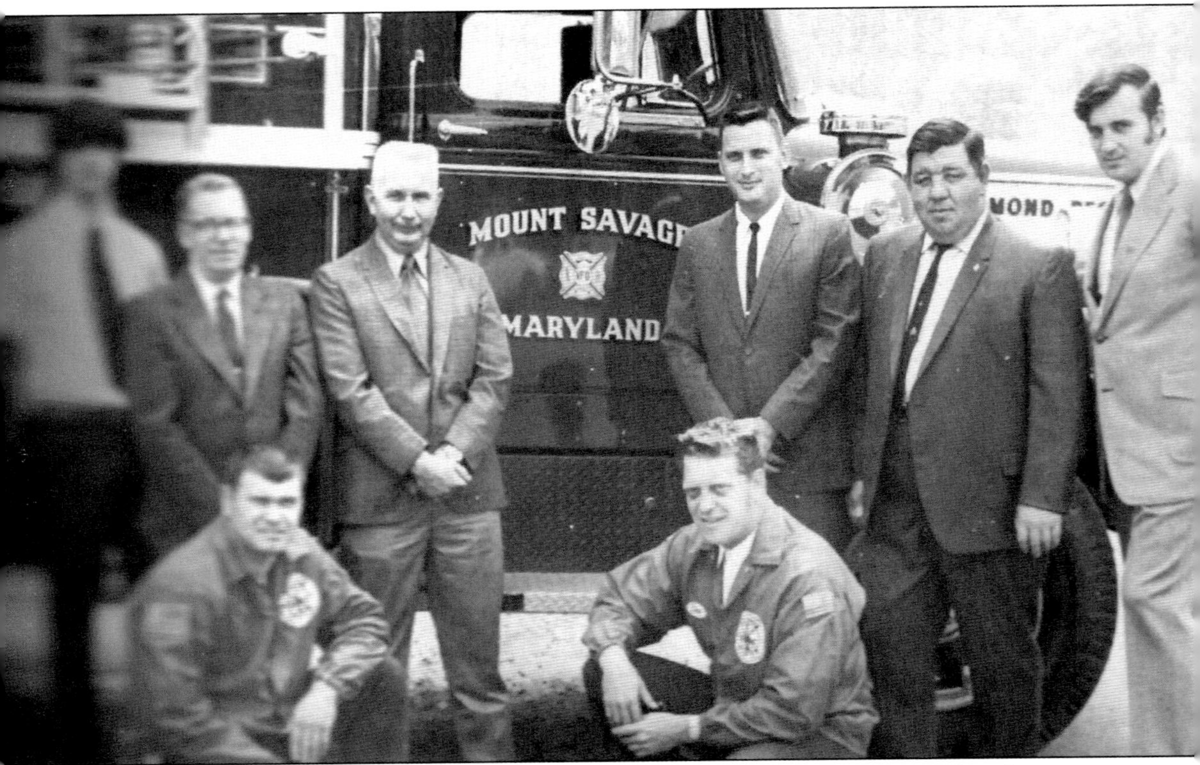

Members of the Fire Department and Truck. The members of the town's fire department have always been proud of the equipment they have purchased over the years. The community has always supported them in donations and fund-raisers.

Eight

MAIN STREET
Yield to Oncoming Traffic

The Main Street in Mount Savage is not like most Main Streets in the country. When most people think of a Main Street, they picture a wide street with two-way traffic, lined with storefronts. The picture also includes parallel parking on both sides.

Mount Savage's Main Street appears to be a one-way street with parking on one side. The street does allow two-way traffic flow, but when driving through Main Street one must yield to oncoming traffic. The street is so narrow between the buildings and the parked cars on the southbound lane that traffic must allow the first vehicle that came to the street to pass before continuing. In addition to the narrow streets, it is common knowledge that you may park with or against the flow of traffic. In most towns or cities the parked cars would be ticketed for parking against traffic; in Mount Savage, they are not.

The narrow Main Street has been this way since the development of the storefronts in the mid-1800s. Many of the stores may be vacant now, but at one time Main Street had 15 taverns and 6 grocery and/or dry good stores. It is amazing that Main Street is only three blocks long, yet it housed so many businesses. It was said that at one time men would often be found lying in the streets, beastly drunk. Because of the problem with public drunkenness, a jail was built on Main Street to punish those accused of drunken disorder.

Entertainment could be found at locations other than the taverns that lined the street. Two "picture show" theatres went into business to entertain the masses. Plus, many of the stores used their second and third floors for bowling alleys and basketball courts. There was plenty to see and do in this three-block radius.

Other businesses existed along Main Street besides stores and taverns. Once the automobile came into use, two service stations were built, one at each end of the street. A bus station opened to accommodate the working commuters who took jobs outside the railroad and brick refractory industries.

Today, Main Street looks rather dreary with only one local grocery and three taverns, but it still is alive with the spirits of the past.

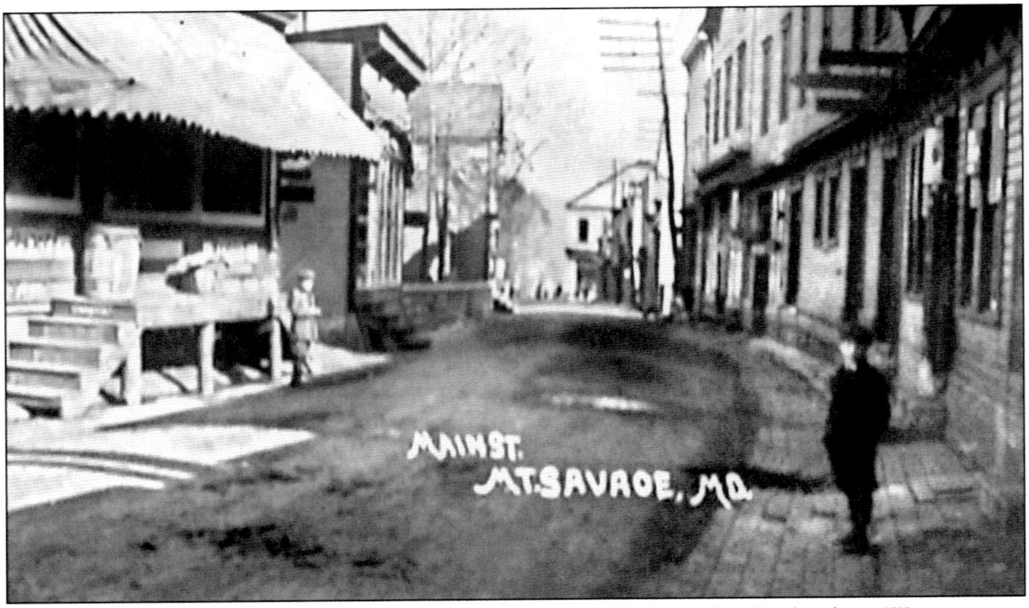

MAIN STREET, 1890s. Since Route 36 was constructed from Cumberland to Westernport, Mount Savage has been the mid-point of the route. (Courtesy of Carol Barry.)

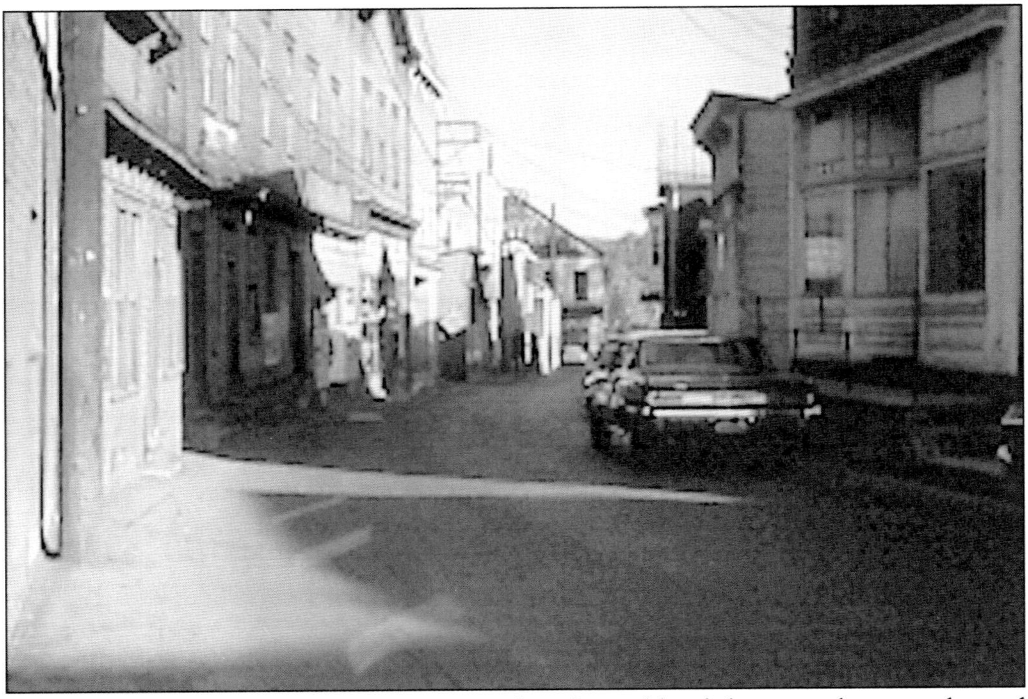

MAIN STREET, 1970s. It is amazing to see that the width of the street has not changed throughout the years. Drivers must always remember to yield to oncoming traffic. (Courtesy of Carol Barry.)

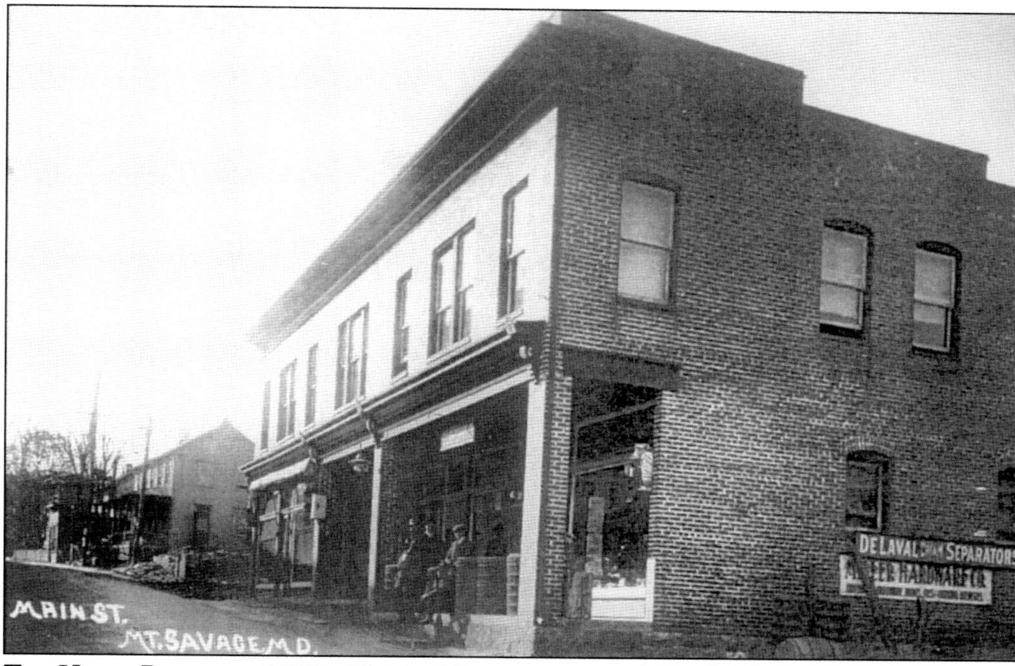

The Hotel Building, 1900s. This building at one time housed a doctor's office, a dentist's office, a couple of apartments, a store, and a movie theater, the Maryland. Today, the VFW occupies one side of the building and the other side of the building was the Varsity Pub (now Shaf's). (Courtesy of Cora Carter.)

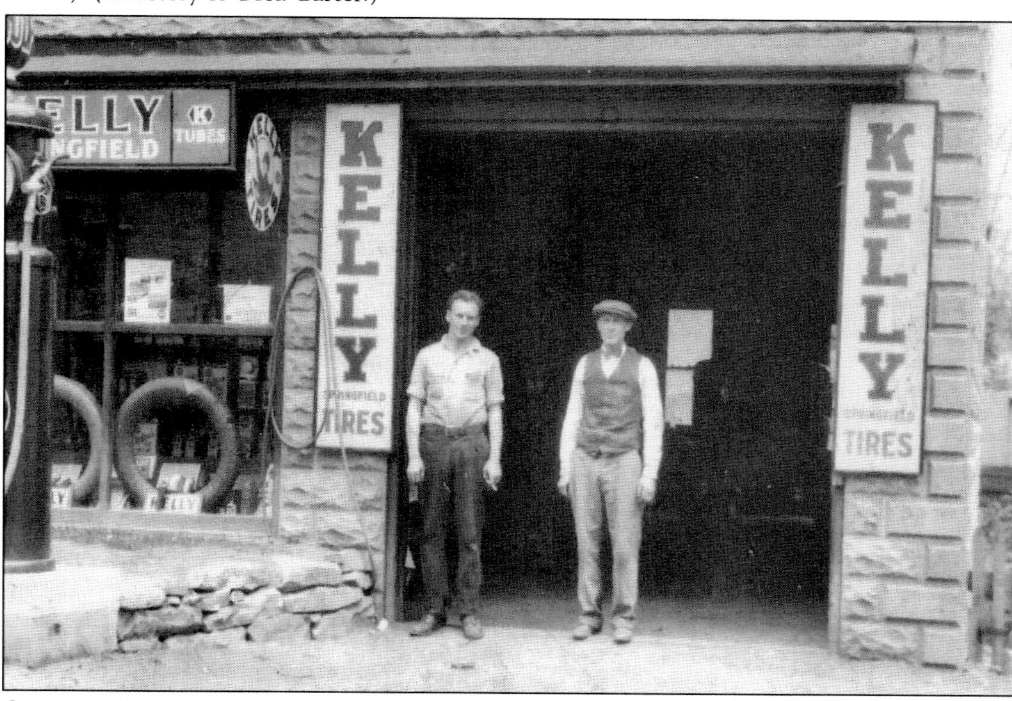

Carter's Service Station. This station was located at the corner of Columbia Street (Cobblestone Road) and Main Street. The Carter brothers operated a full-service station with Gulf Gasoline and a service station that sold Kelly Springfield Tires. (Courtesy of Cora Carter.)

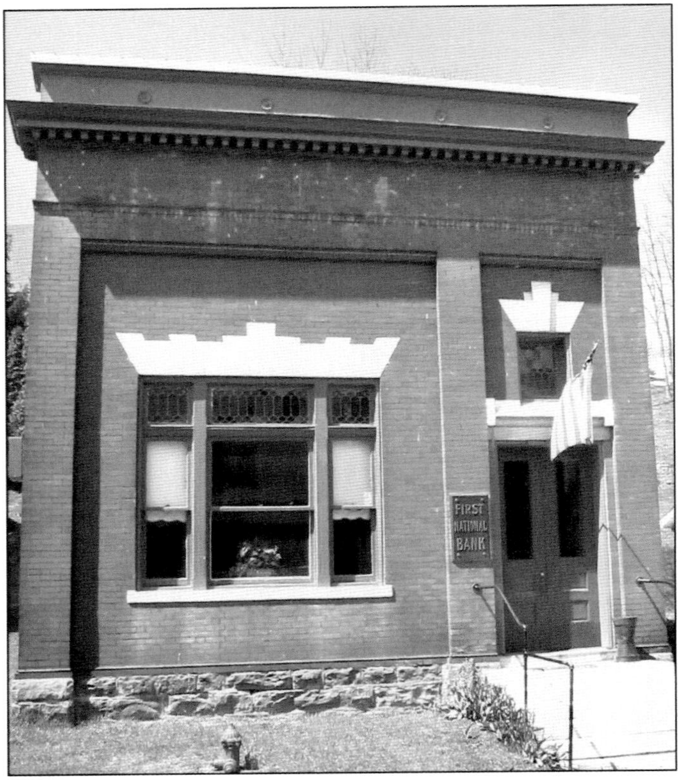

THE FIRST NATIONAL BANK. This bank opened its doors in 1902 and operated until 1984. Today it is owned and operated as a museum by the Mount Savage Historical Society.

GROCERY STORE. This is a great inside view of one of the grocery stores that operated on Main Street. It was one of many that lined the streets of Mount Savage. (Courtesy of Bill Pratt.)

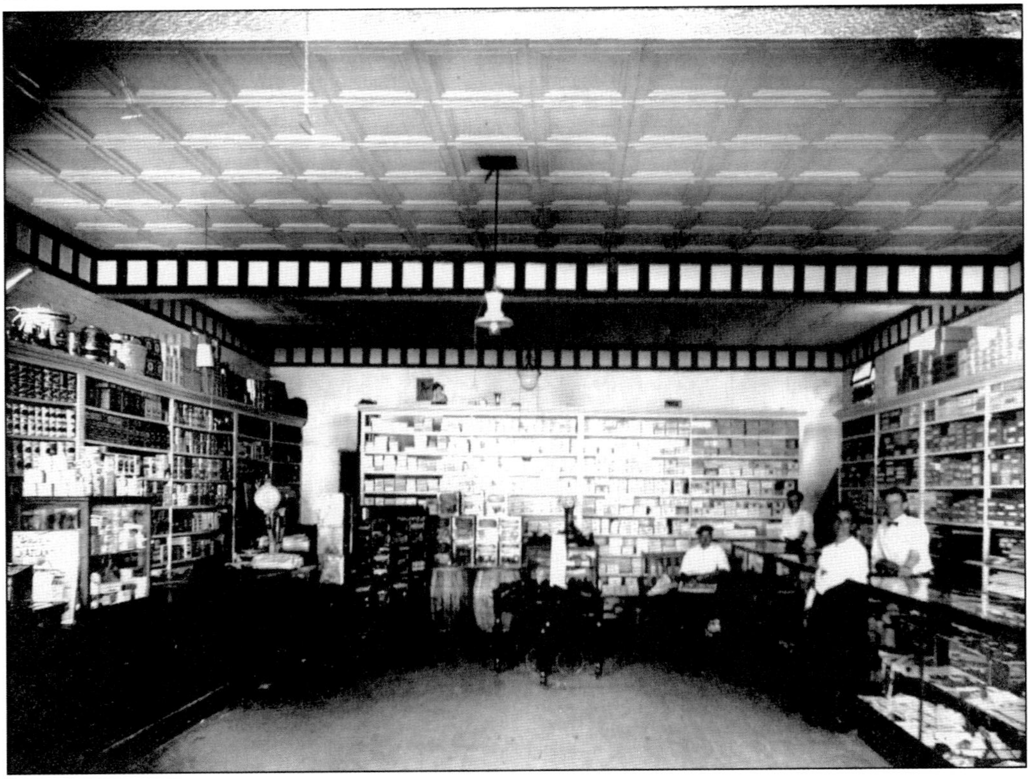

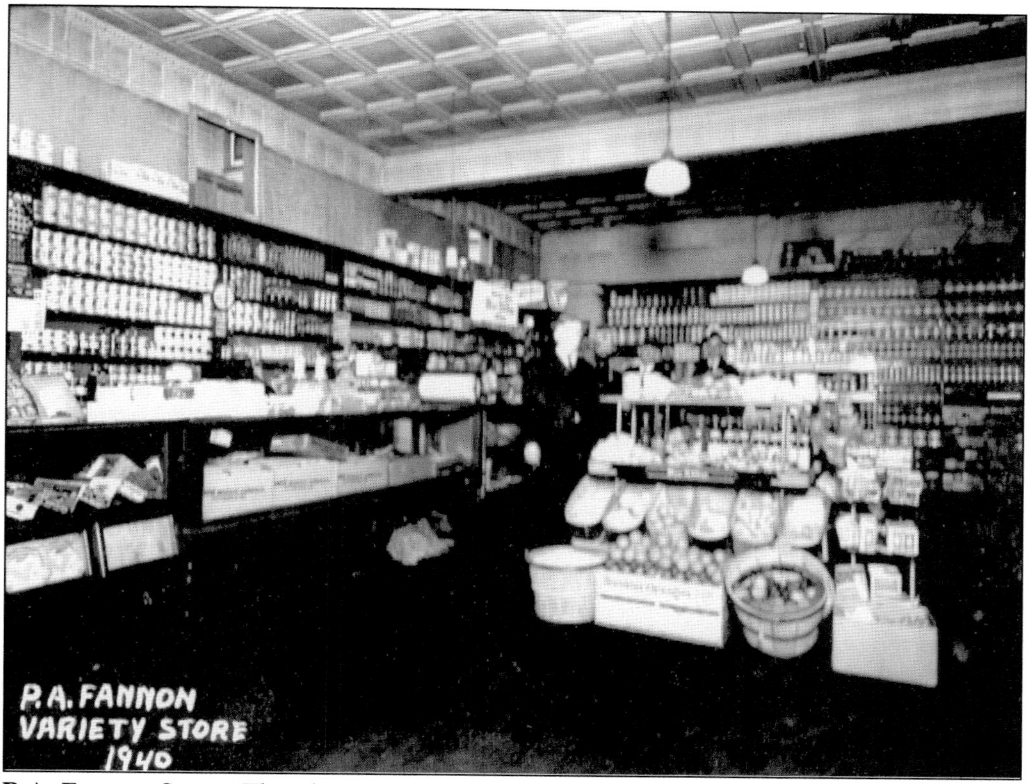

P.A. Fannon Store. This photo is an inside look at P.A. Fannon Store on Main Street. Later the store was sold to the Mulligan brothers. (Courtesy of Bill Pratt.)

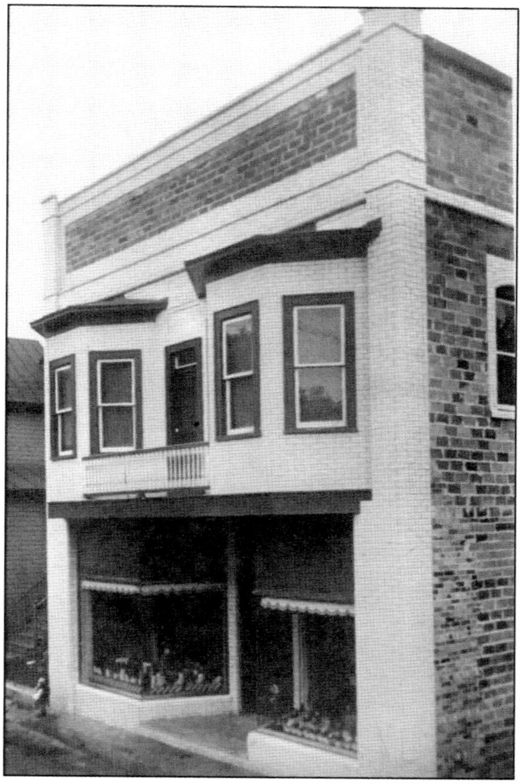

Bill's Market. Today the Mulligan brothers' store is owned by Bill Pratt. Bill's Market is still operating and offers delivery. (Courtesy of Bill Pratt.)

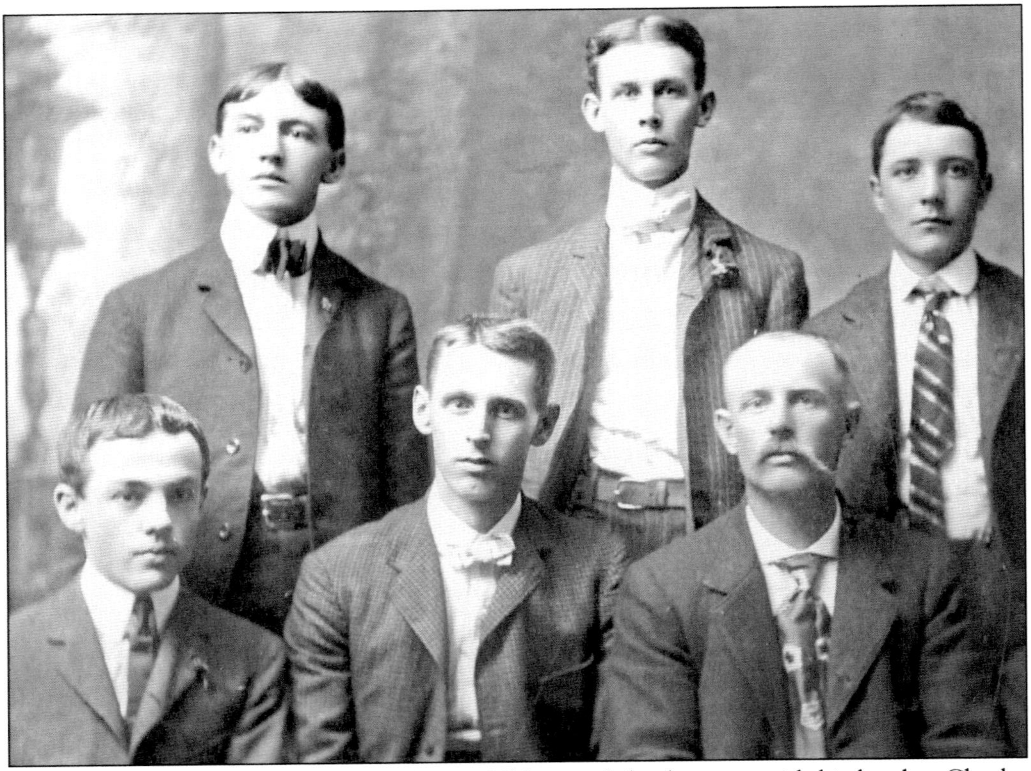

Uhl's Store Employees 1898. G. Clinton Uhl started this business with his brother Charles in 1897. Later Clinton was appointed to the Maryland State Roads Commission in 1916. This portrait is of the Uhl Store's employees. This store was another grocery that operated on Main Street. (Courtesy of St. George's Episcopal Church.)

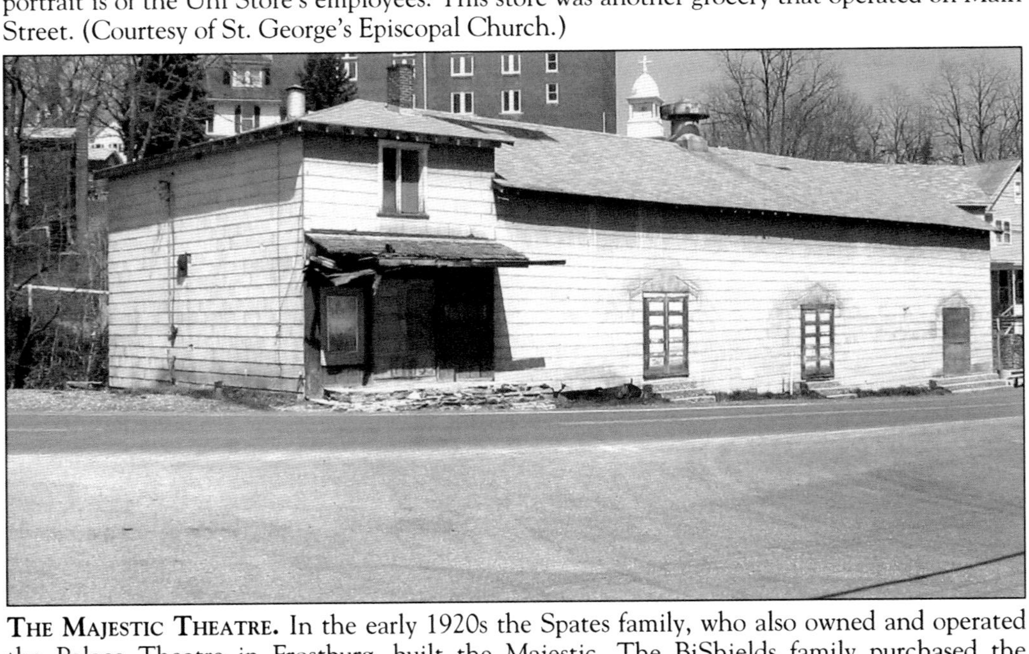

The Majestic Theatre. In the early 1920s the Spates family, who also owned and operated the Palace Theatre in Frostburg, built the Majestic. The BiShields family purchased the 1,200-square-foot parcel of land that included the theatre for $10 in 1926. The BiShields owned the theatre until 1965. It reopened for a short time in the 1980s.

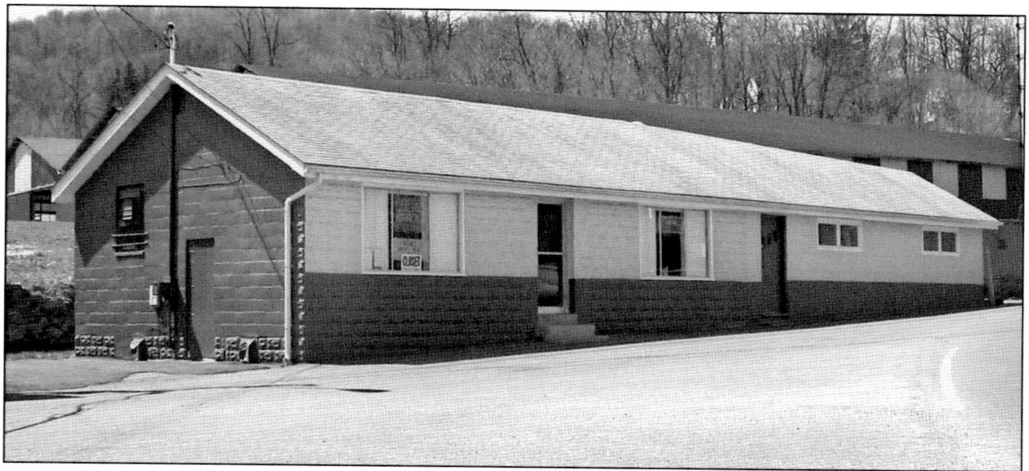

The Green Arrow Restaurant. This is the only restaurant in town. It was originally Shines, but the name was changed to the Green Arrow when the current owners purchased the restaurant in the 1970s. They named the restaurant to keep with the school mascot, the Mount Savage Indians, and the school colors, green and gold.

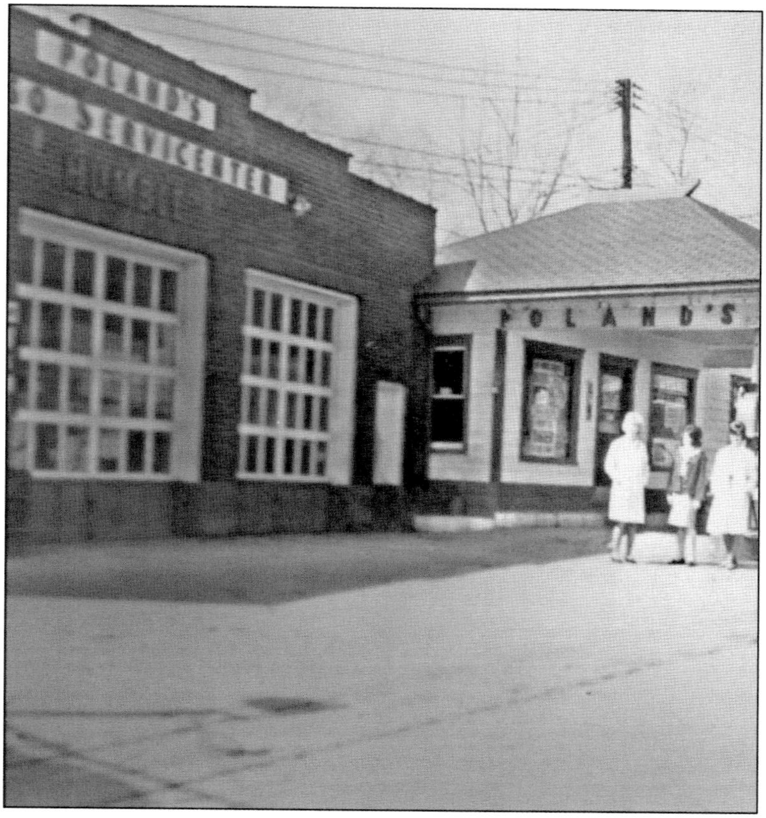

Poland's Service Center. This station was another full-service station on Main Street. At one time, its owners tried to attract customers with a choice of four different types of gasoline—Esso, Gulf, Sunoco, and Mobil.

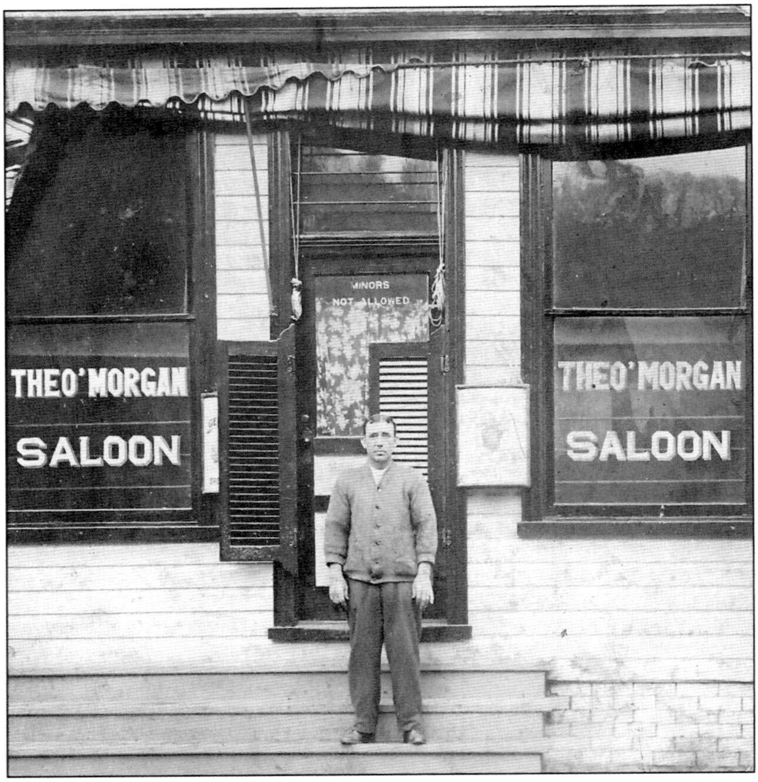

SALOON. This is a photo of just one of the 15 bars that lined the Main Street of Mount Savage. Pictured is the owner, Theopoluius (Theo) Morgan. (Courtesy of Theresa Swanton.)

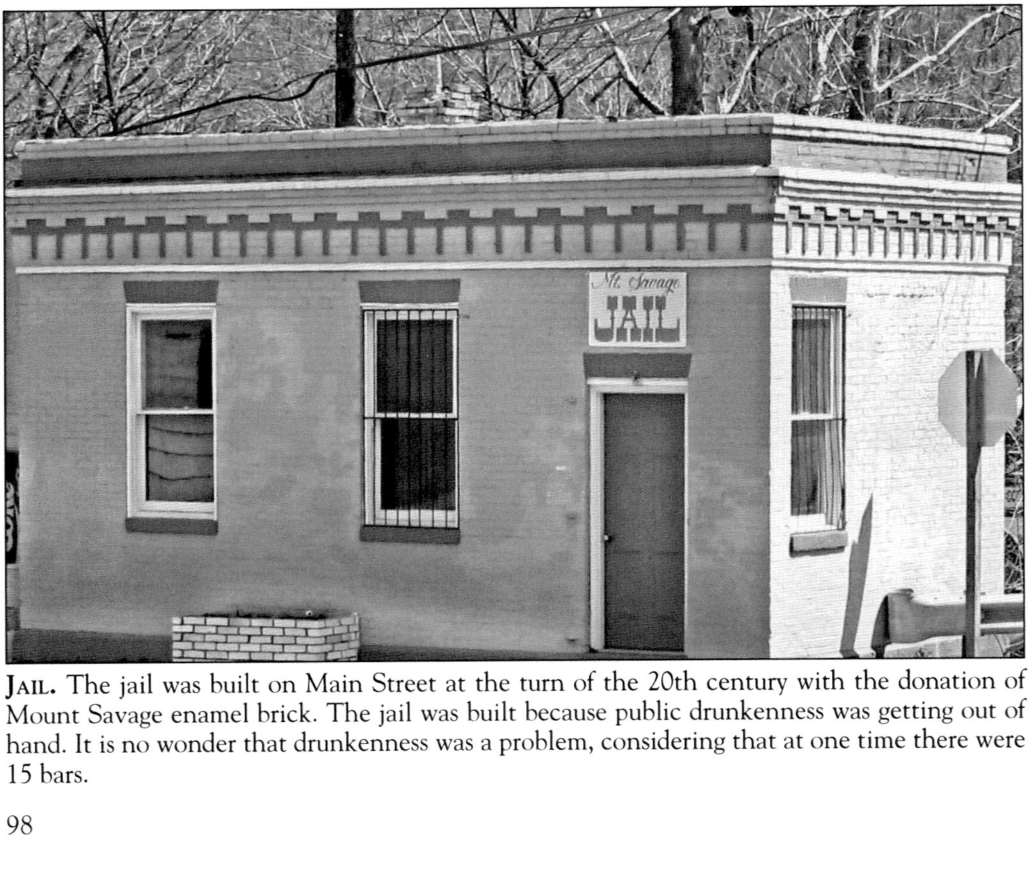

JAIL. The jail was built on Main Street at the turn of the 20th century with the donation of Mount Savage enamel brick. The jail was built because public drunkenness was getting out of hand. It is no wonder that drunkenness was a problem, considering that at one time there were 15 bars.

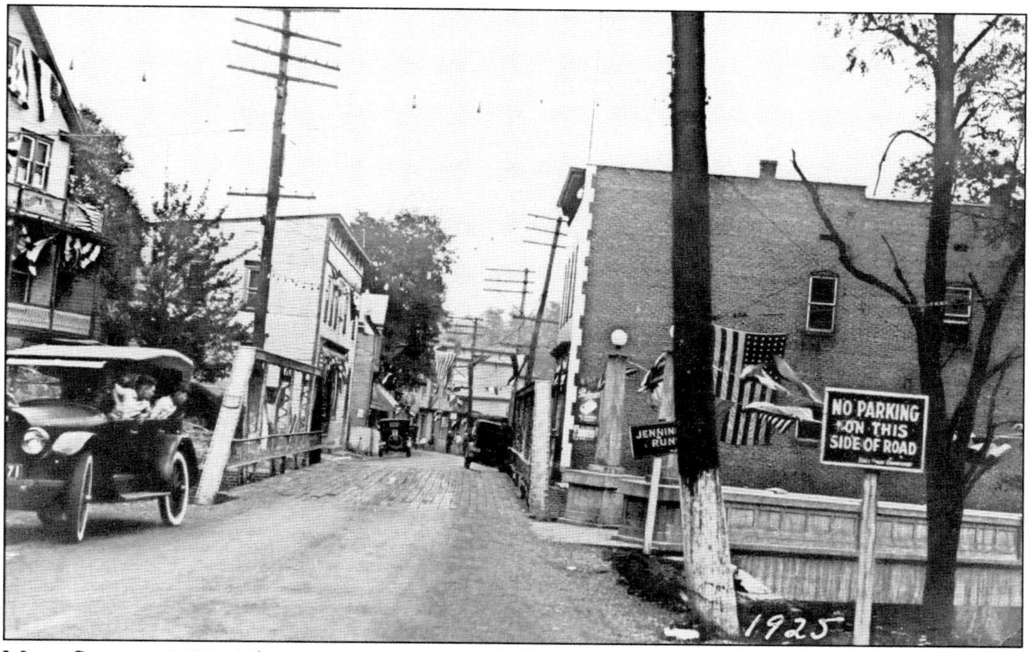

Main Street, 1925. The town is getting ready for a celebration. (Courtesy of Paula Fuller.)

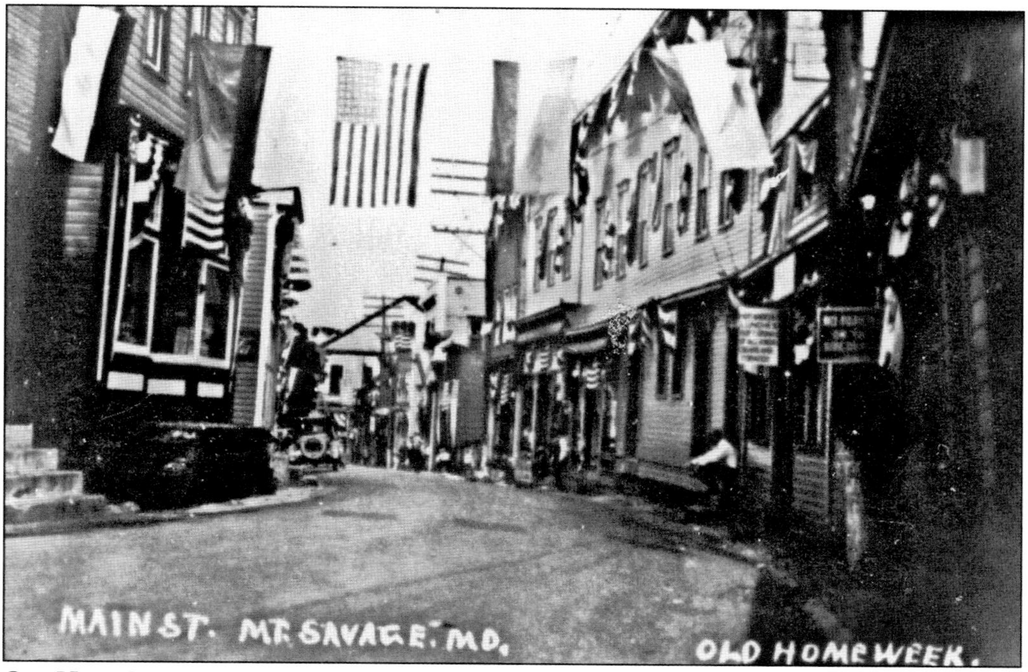

Old Home Week, 1925. This view of Main Street shows all the businesses that once lined the street. (Courtesy of Paula Fuller.)

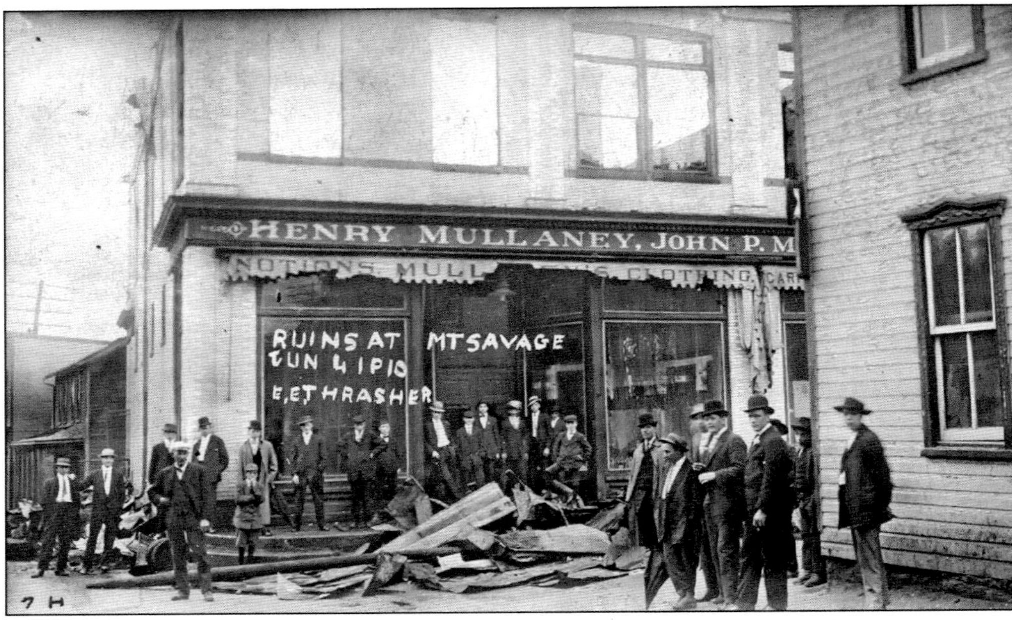

Henry Mullaney Building, 1910. This photo was taken at the corner of Main Street and Columbia Street. The onlookers are peering at the bad luck of others after a fire went through town. (Courtesy of Gary Delaney.)

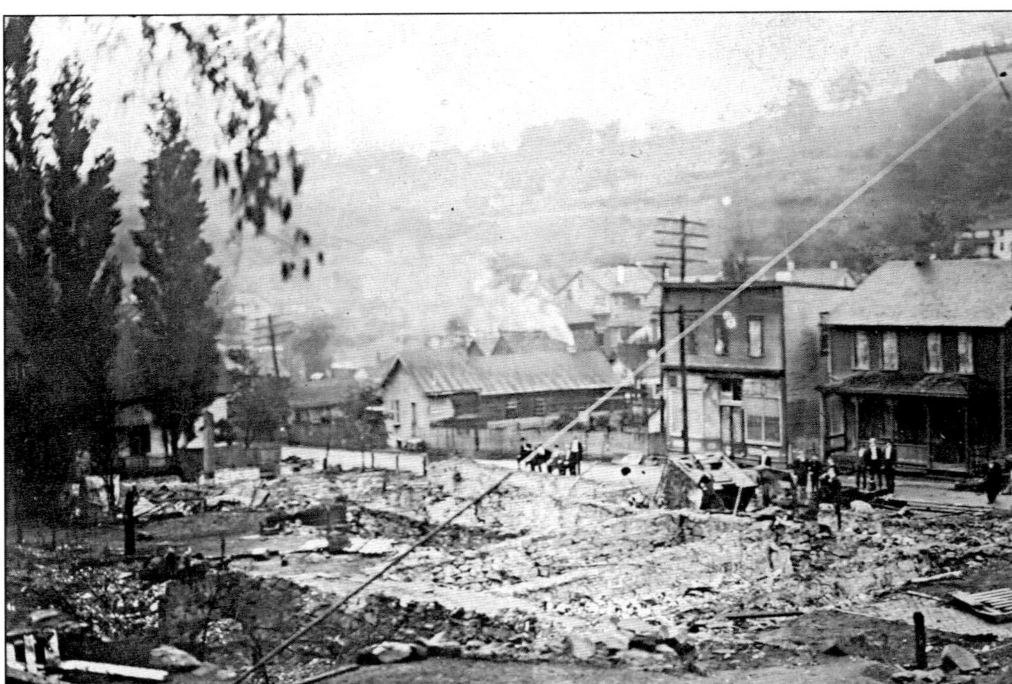

Mount Savage Fire, 1910. Houses were leveled to the ground after this fire swept through town in 1910. (Courtesy of Gary Delaney.)

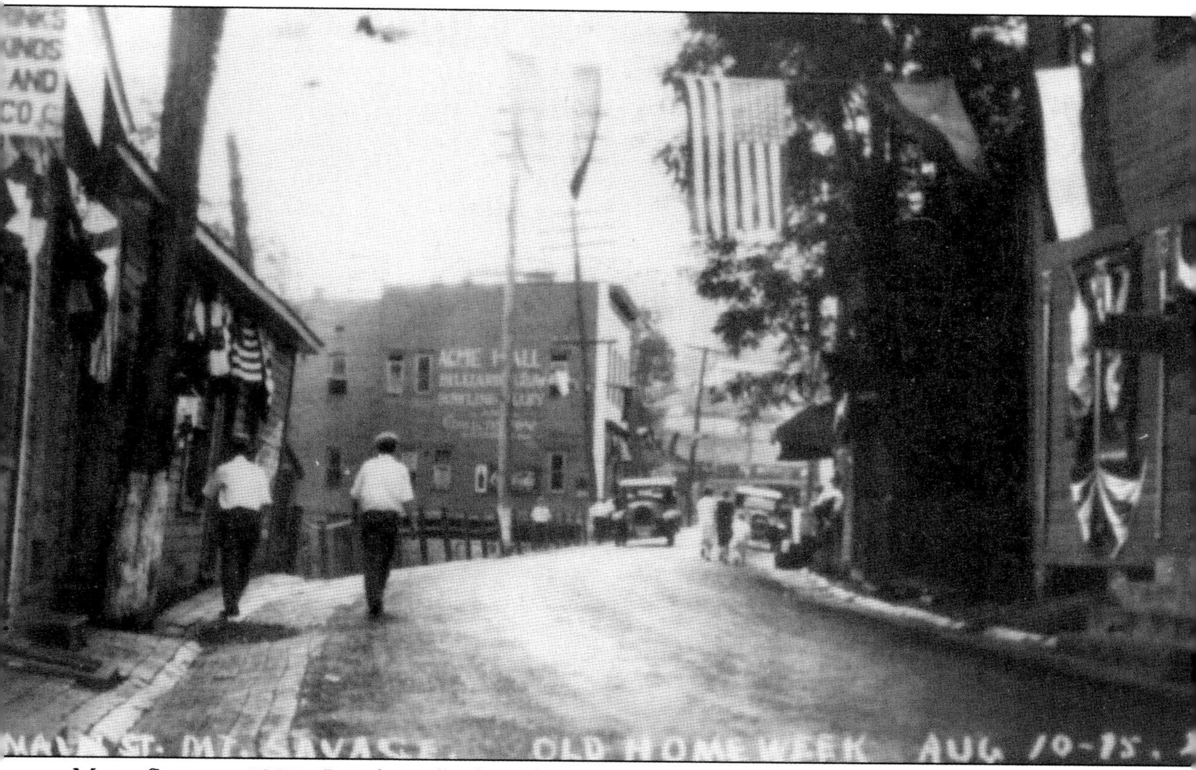

MAIN STREET, 1920. People walked in the streets during this time because there were no sidewalks. At one time Mount Savage was featured in *Ripley's Believe It or Not*. Ripley's articles stated that the people walked in the streets and drove on the sidewalks.

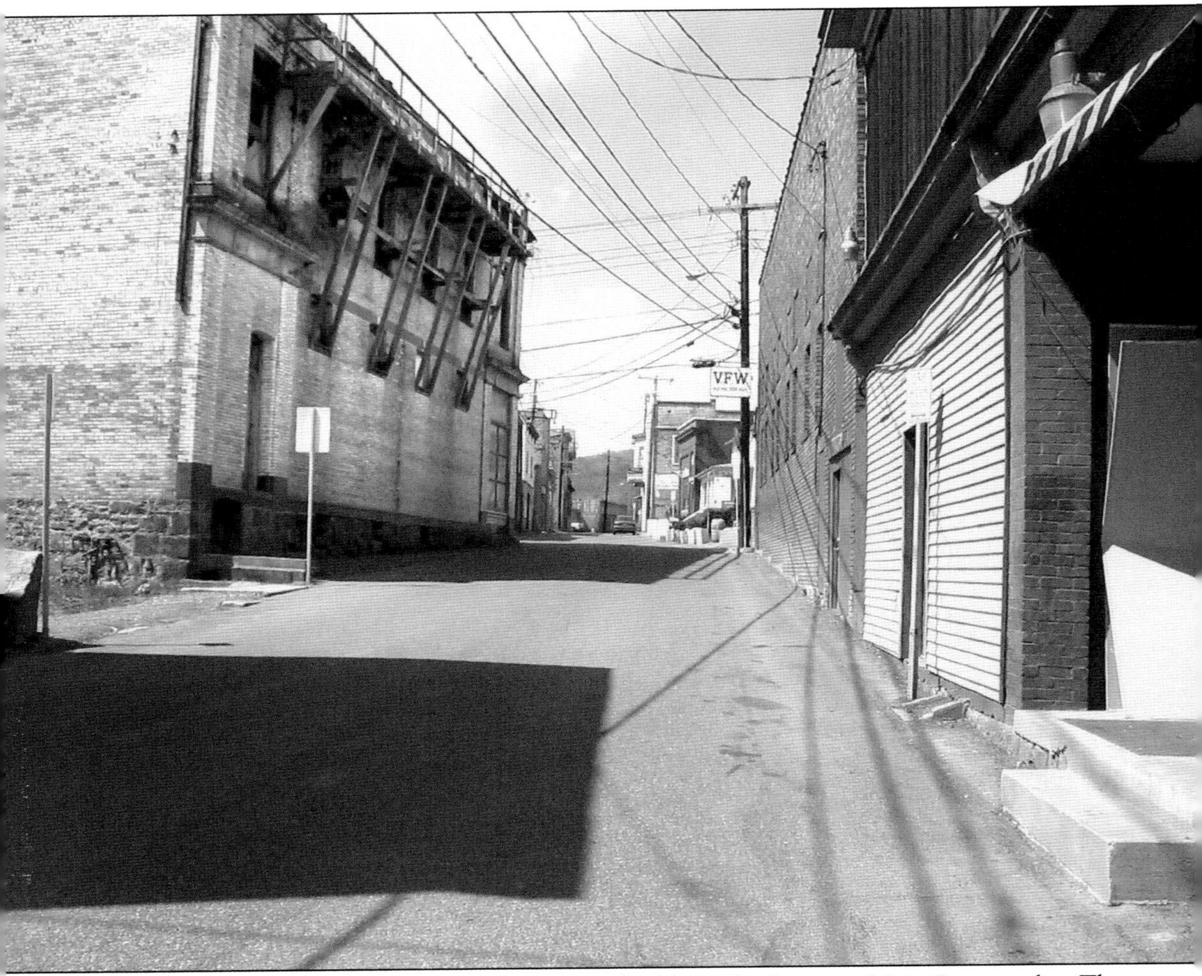

MAIN STREET, PRESENT DAY. Most of the same buildings shadow over Main Street today. The only major change to the street is that there are a few sidewalks.

Nine

THE COUNTRYSIDE

If you were to look at Mount Savage from an aerial view, you would see that the houses and buildings are built in close proximity to each other. They focus around Main Street and Route 36 and fan up the hills from the valley. But once outside of town there are beautiful farmlands that stretch across the mountains.

The mining companies built many large houses to attract doctors and foremen to move and work in the industrial town. The Bruce House and The Castle are two of these homes. When they were first built, they were a little removed from the town, but as time went on and the population grew, these homes were swallowed up by the town.

As the town grew beyond its small limits, areas like New Town were developed on Route 36. Woodcock Hollow and Sunnyside developed along the C & P Railroad line. The town of Barrelville also grew out of the expanding mining, the C & P Railroad line, and the Barrelville Brick Refractory.

Beautiful homes on the outskirts of town, like the Evergreen House and many of the original settlement houses from Arnold's Settlement, can be found in the rural areas of Mount Savage. These homes became the agricultural center of the town. At one time there was a dairy and bottling plant on Mile Lane. The local dairy farms would sell their milk to the Glen Savage Dairy. The dairy would then pasteurize and bottle the milk for sale.

In the 1940s the countryside of Mount Savage was full of dairy farms. There were eight dairies in a six-mile radius. These farms were small, family-operated businesses that depended on the land to raise their families. So it was typical for the farm children to want to go to town and get out of the country for leisure activities.

The countryside was not only a favorite place to build and develop land but also a place where Mount Savage's citizens could escape for picnic and family gatherings. In the summer and wintertime, families would have parties to celebrate various happenings, and the countryside was a favorite place to hold square dances, picnics, and sledding parties.

Churches loved to have outings in the country. It was a great experience to get away from the troubles of the industrial town for a day and enjoy the fresh air of the landscape. The church groups could see God's glory firsthand in the wilderness.

Today, the countryside of Mount Savage is still one of the most beautiful areas in Western Maryland. It has not been overdeveloped, and local families are still farming the majority of the land. It is just another unchanged wonder of Mount Savage.

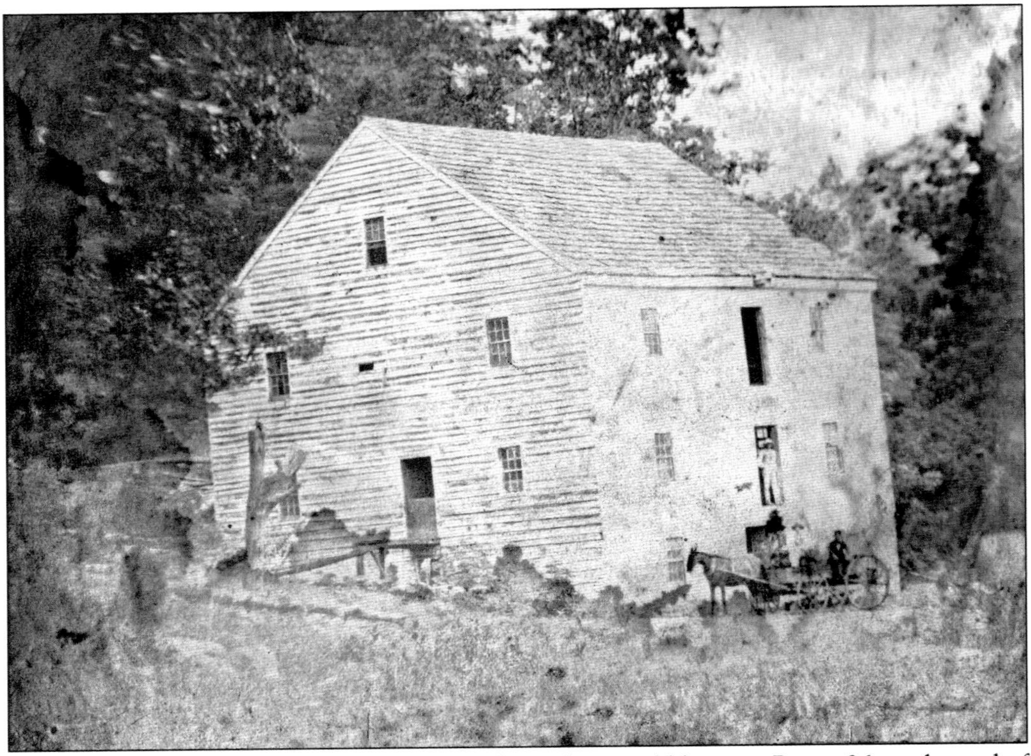

Arnold's Mill, 1860. This mill was located on what would become Route 36, at the end of Sunnyside Road (Woodcock Hollow Road). (Courtesy of Mount Savage Historical Society.)

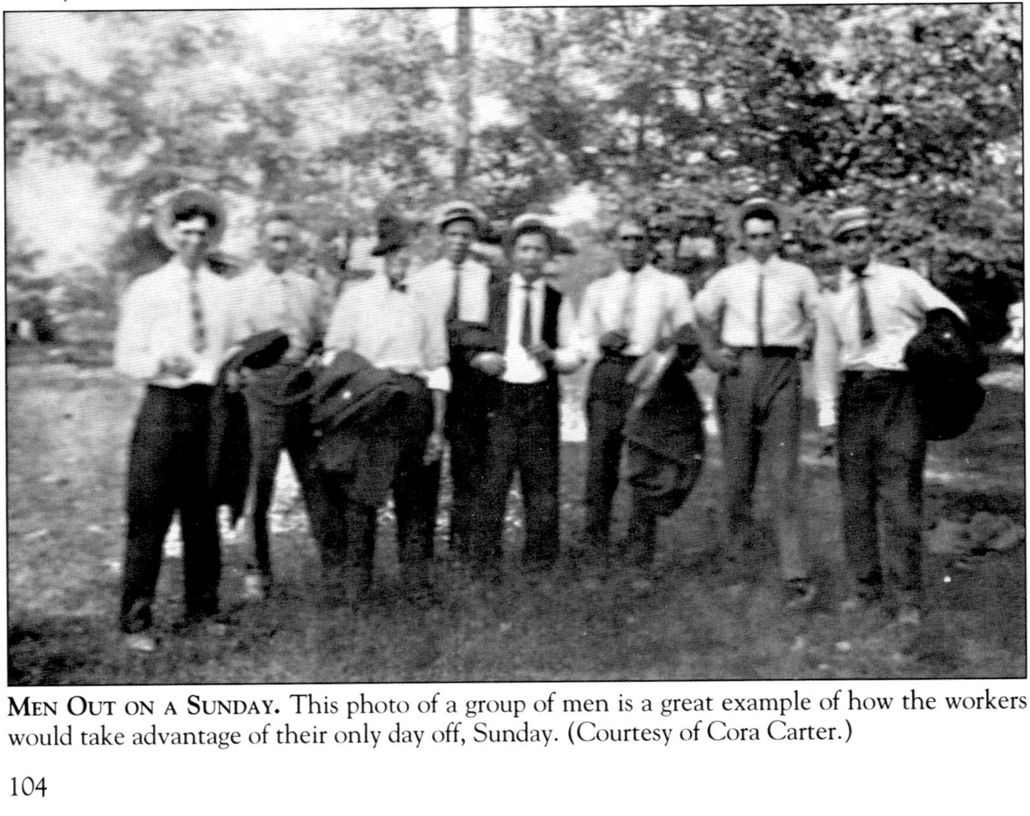

Men Out on a Sunday. This photo of a group of men is a great example of how the workers would take advantage of their only day off, Sunday. (Courtesy of Cora Carter.)

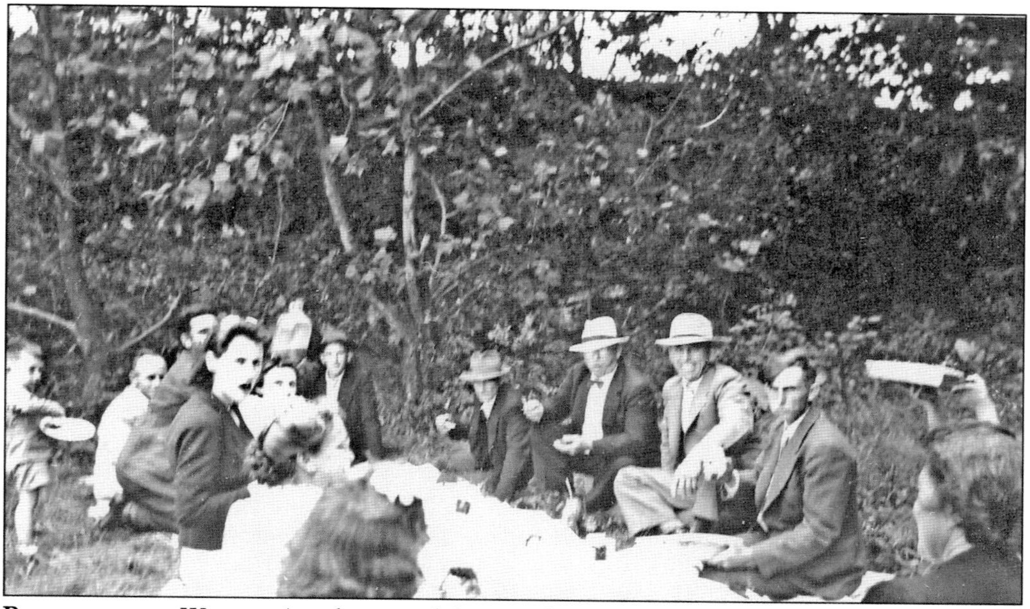

PICNICS IN THE WOODS. Another social favorite for people in the area was to get away from the industrial town and have a picnic in the woods. This is a photo of the Delbrook and Lepley families picnicking. (Courtesy of Wilma Delbrook, in memory of Stewart.)

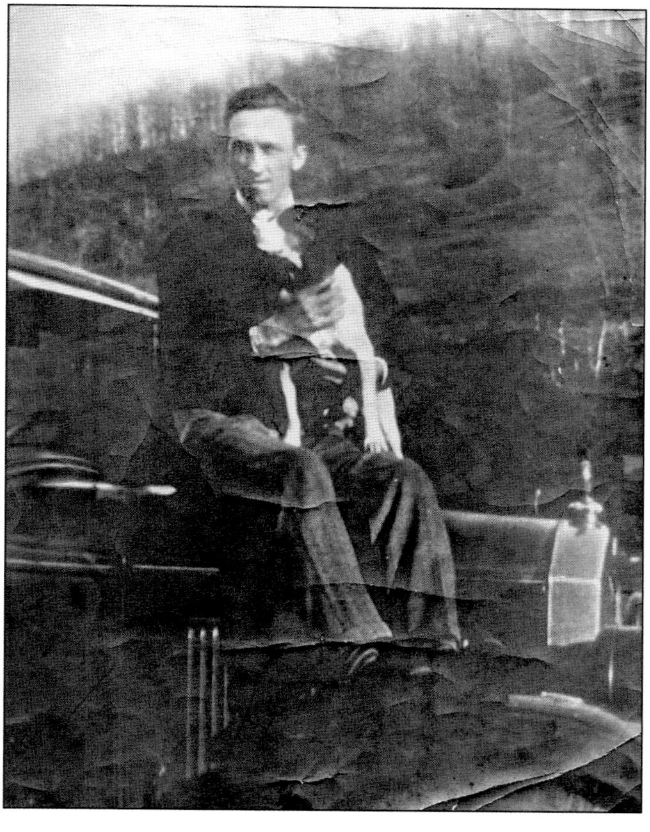

MAN AND HIS HOUND. Another favorite way to get away from the hectic life of the town was to go hunting. Gene Ruppert and his dog pose for a photo outside of town.

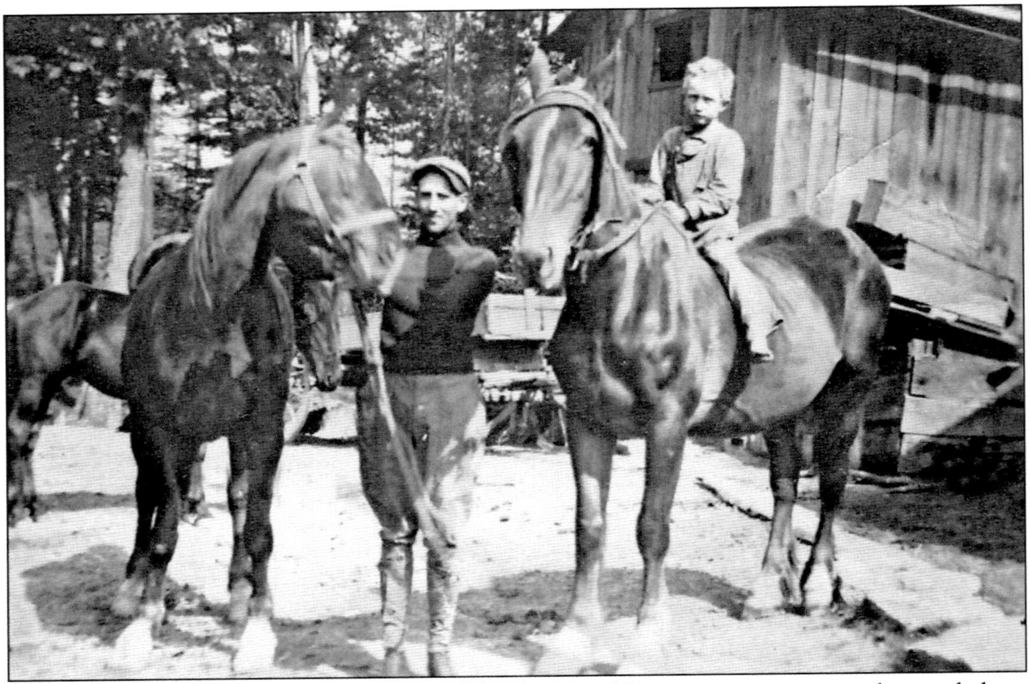

A GOOD-LOOKING PAIR OF MULES. Rural families would many times get together and show off their prize animals. Here, the Beal family members pose with their mules. (Courtesy of the Beal family.)

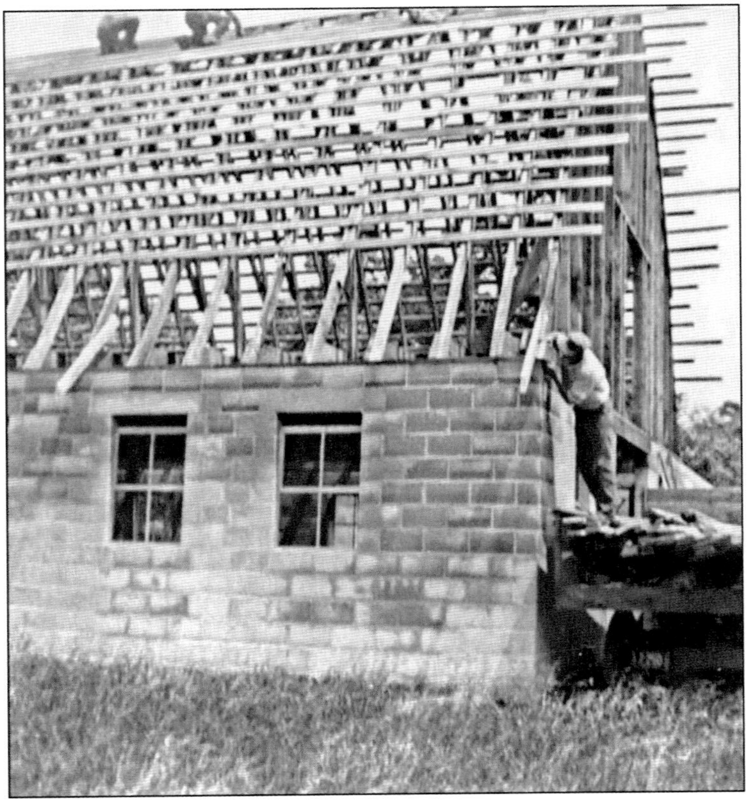

BARN RAISING, 1952. Building a barn was a community affair. The neighbors would come together and help the farmer build his barn. Many times people would stay overnight in the meadows under a tree so they could get an early start the next day.

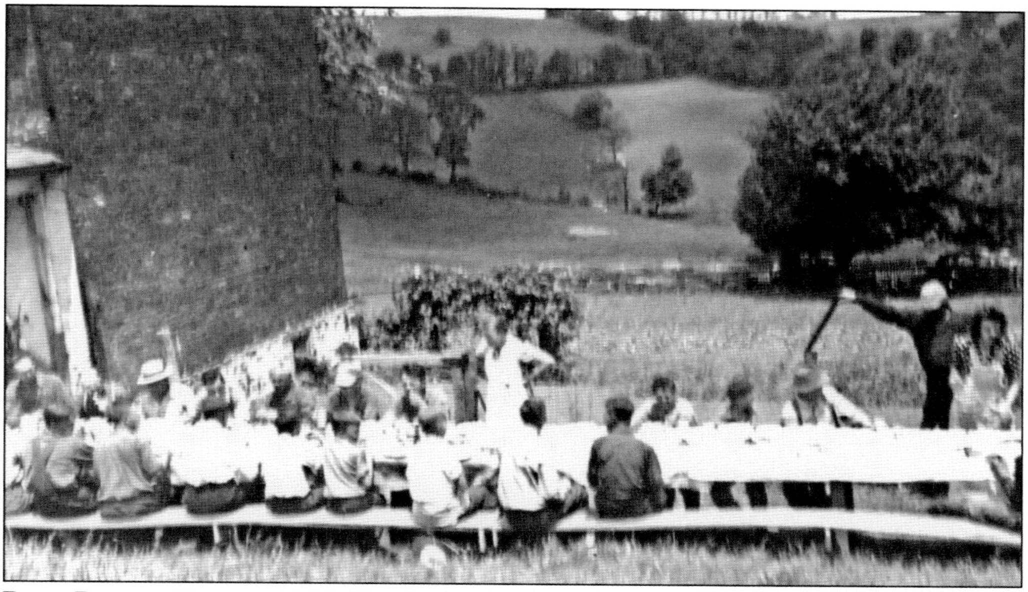

Barn Raising Dinner, 1943. The Lepley family had so many people coming to help them build their barn that they had two long tables full of people to feed at dinner and suppertime. (Courtesy of Wilma Delbrook, in memory of Stewart.)

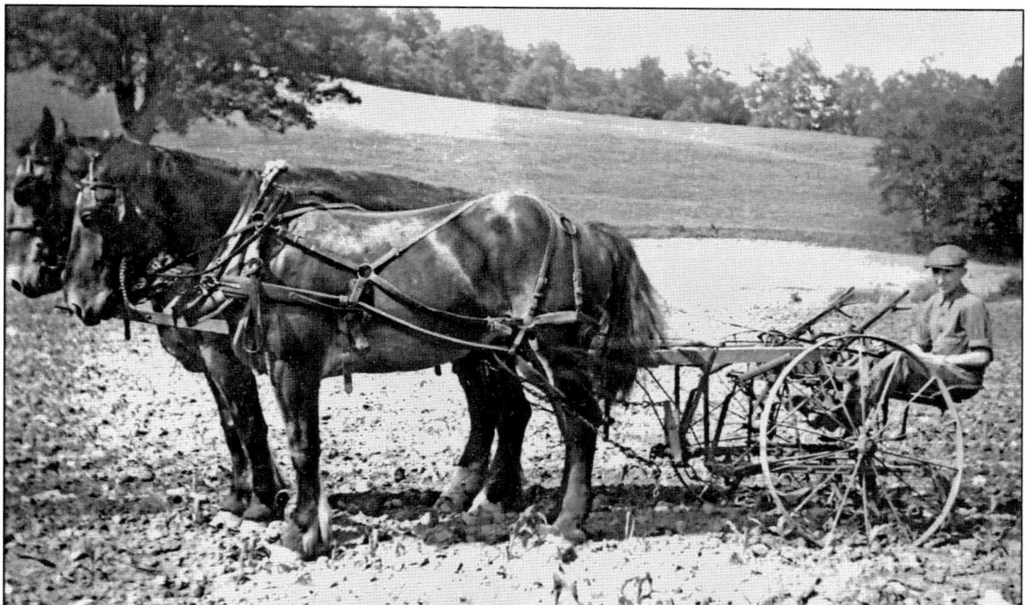

Cultivating Corn. Here Stewart Delbrook is cultivating corn with a two-horsepower machine. (Courtesy of Wilma Delbrook, in memory of Stewart.)

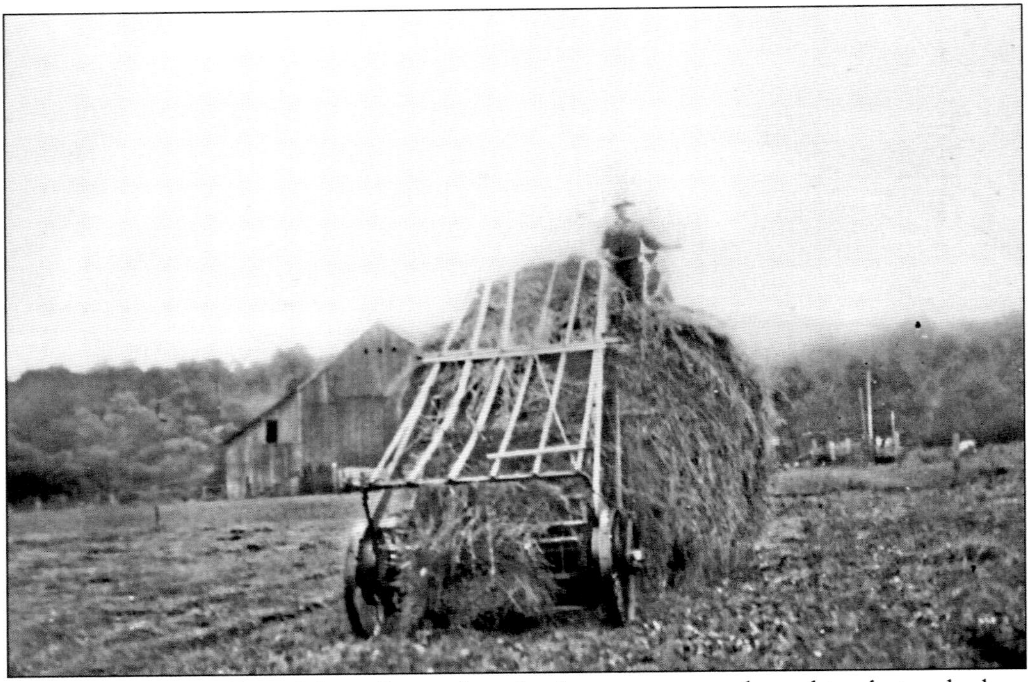

Hay-making Time. From July to September, the farmer seems to do nothing but make hay. Here is Lester Beal forming a haystack with a loader. (Courtesy of the Beal family.)

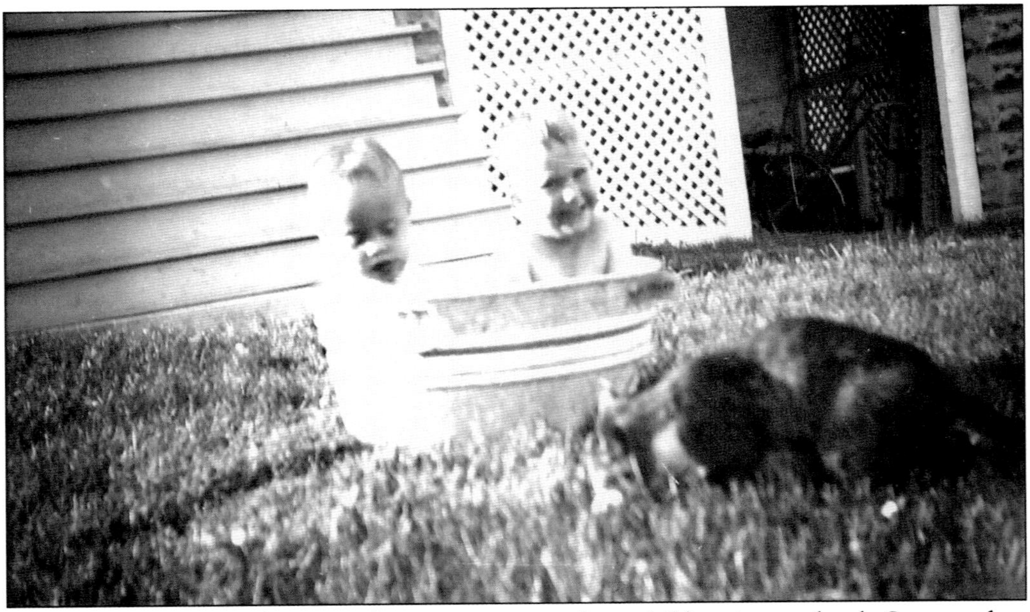

Rub A Dub. It is quite fun to see this country scene of two children in a wash tub. Summer days were great for taking a bath in the yard. (Courtesy of Wilma Delbrook, in memory of Stewart.)

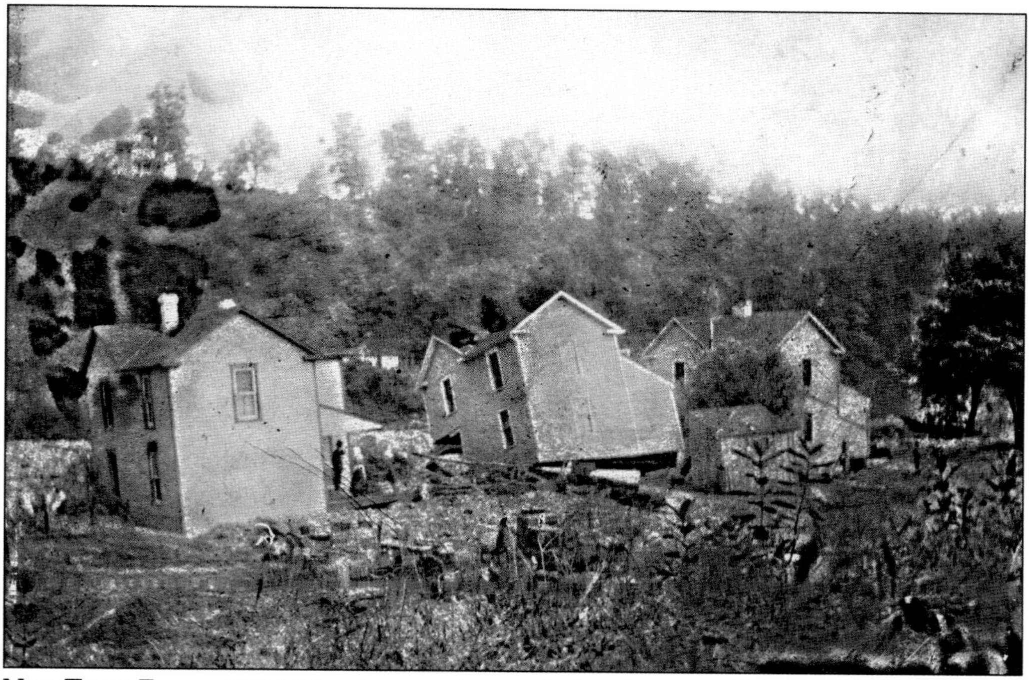

New Town Flood, 1906. Here is an unpleasant look at houses in New Town that have been knocked off their foundations after a flood on August 7, 1906. (Courtesy of Gary Delaney.)

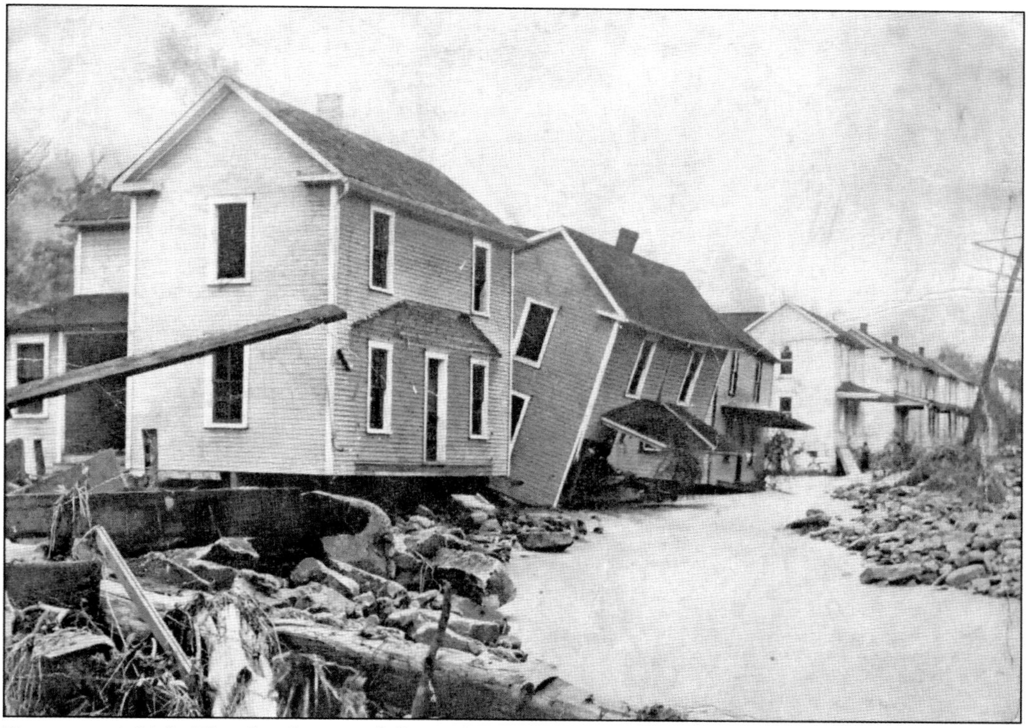

Flood of 1906. The flood water followed Route 36 and pushed houses off their foundations. After the flood the three most damaged houses were torn down. The plots were vacant until the Masonic Temple bought the land and built its lodge. (Courtesy of Phyllis Reed.)

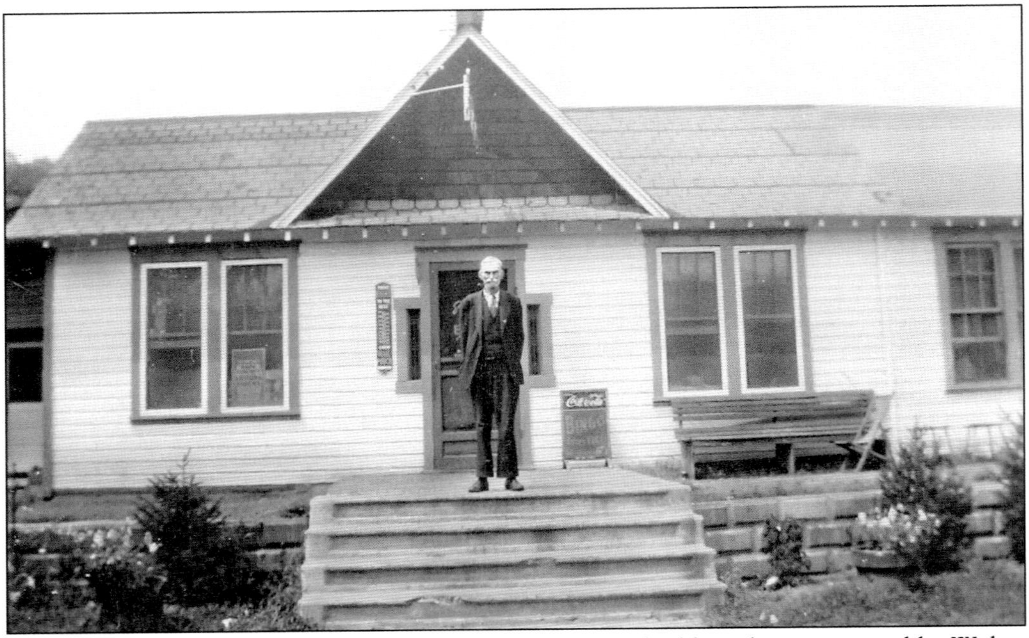

MELODY MANOR, 1940S. The Manor was a multi-purpose building that was owned by Walter Robertson for years. It was located near Barrelville on Route 36. It was a popular place to see a band play, play bingo, or just dance to the juke bar.

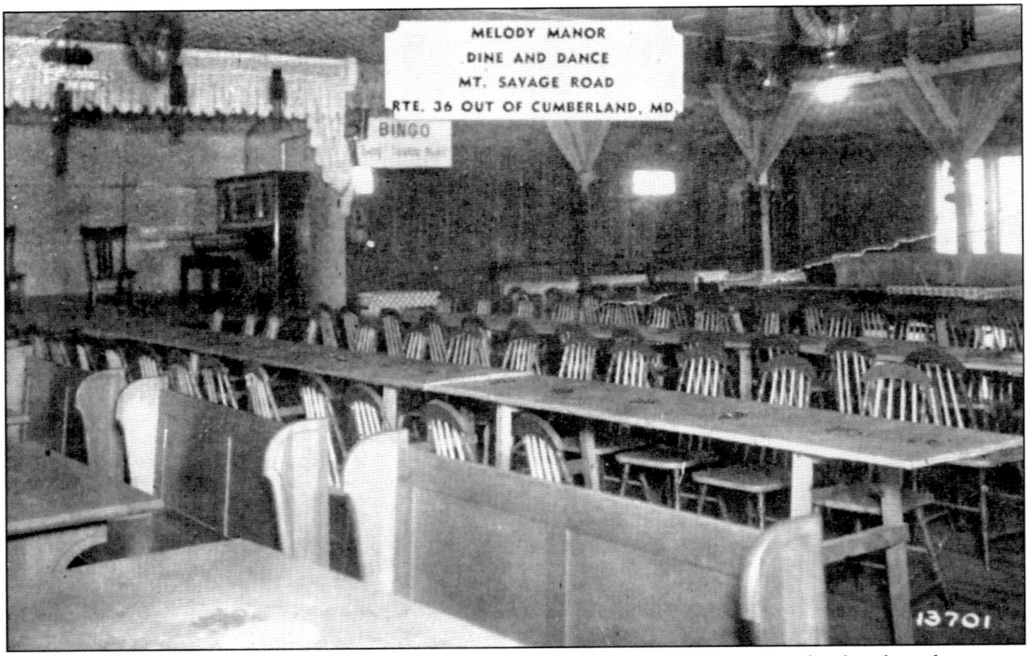

MELODY MANOR. This dance hall was so popular that buses ran from Cumberland to dances at the Manor. Here the dance hall is set up for a firemen's bingo. (Courtesy of Gary Delaney.)

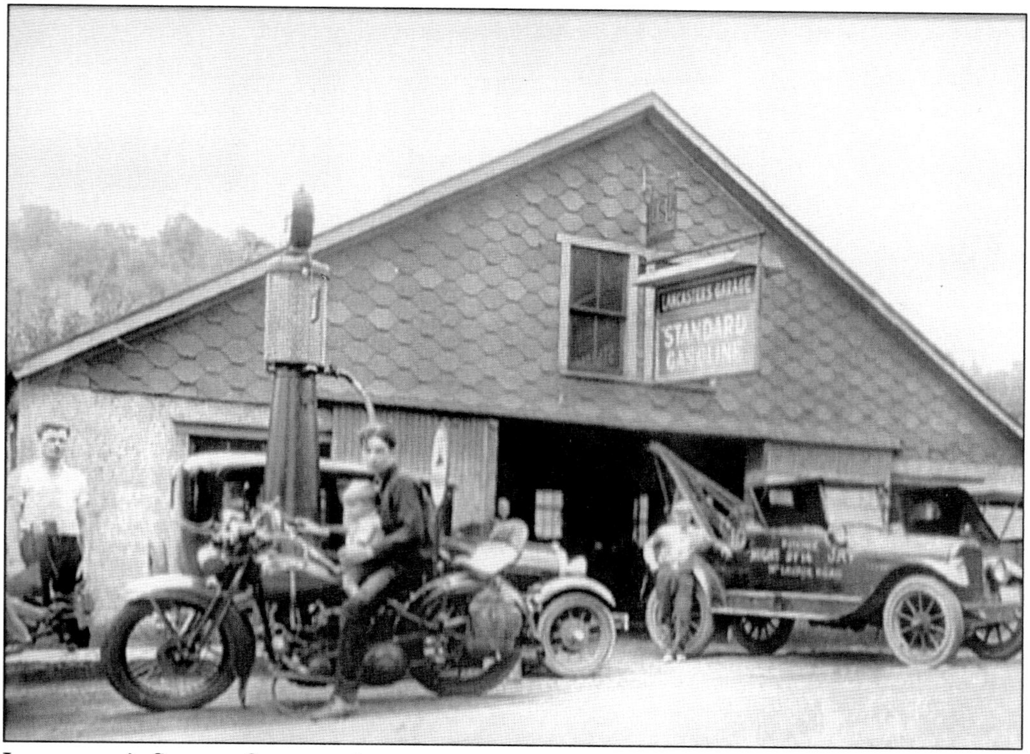

LANCASTER'S SERVICE STATION. Just down the street from the Manor were two gas stations, Wingard's and Lancaster's. Lancaster's sold Esso gasoline. Lancaster's went out of business in the 1950s, and Wingard's closed in 1990. (Courtesy of Earl Pope.)

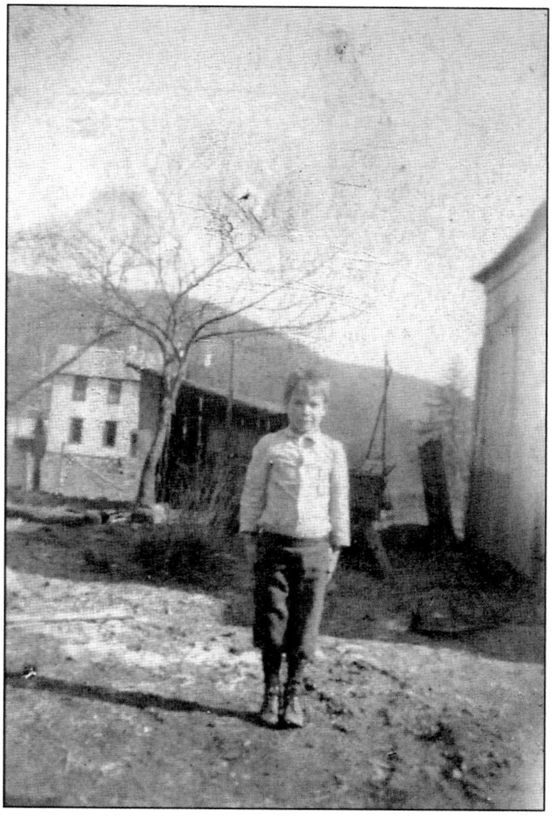

OLD MOUNT SAVAGE ROAD, 1919. Here is a rustic look at old Route 36 near Barrelville Road. The road had not been paved or bricked. Robert Martin stands on the dirt road. (Courtesy of Phyllis Reed.)

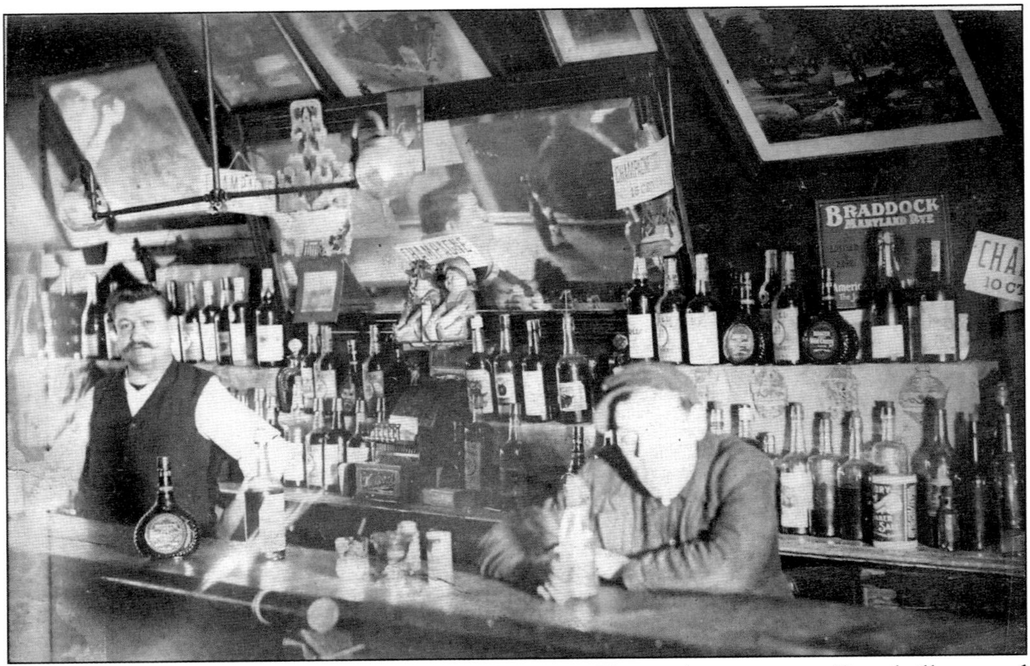

EARLY 1900S BARRELVILLE COAL COMPANY SALOON. The coal company in Barrelville owned and operated this saloon from the turn of the 20th century to the 1930s. There was also a company store and boarding house located next to the saloon. (Courtesy of Phyllis Reed.)

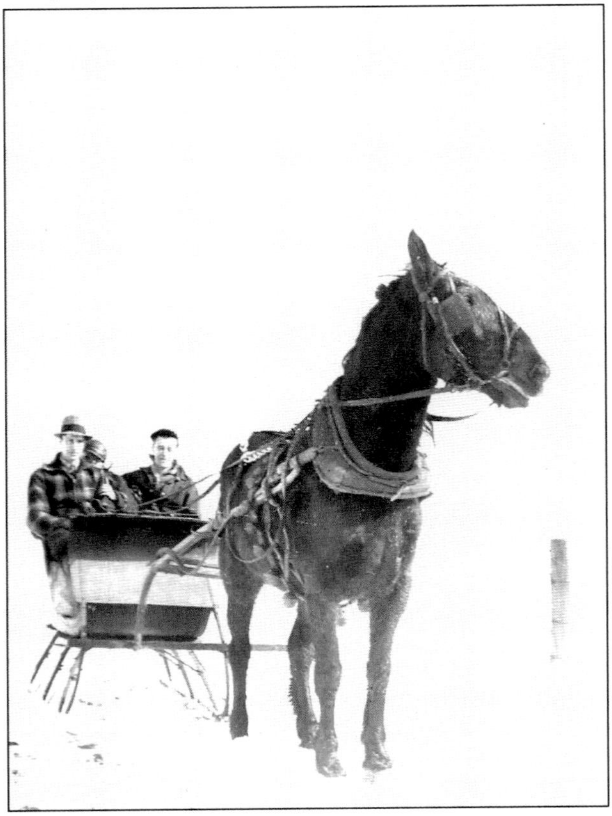

HORSE AND SLEIGH. Even after the automobile became easily available, a horse and sleigh during the winter months was still the best way to get around in the country until the mid-1950s. The country roads were not plowed and many times drifted shut.

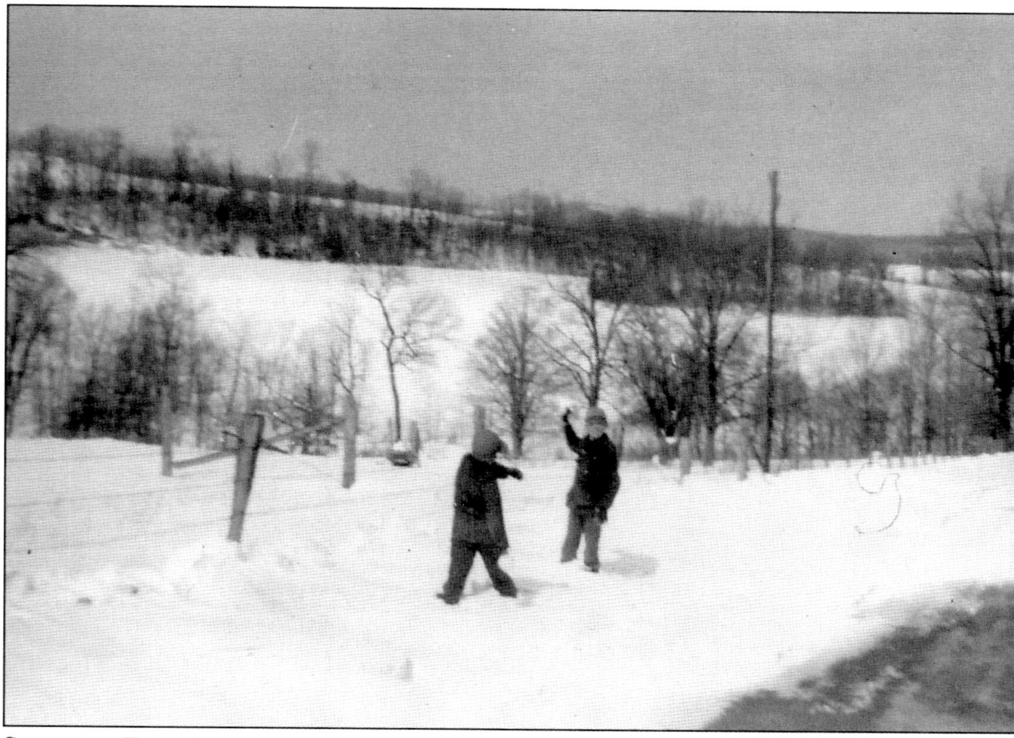

Snowball Fight! Trying to make the best of the snow, these farm boys are having a snowball fight. Sometimes this was the only form of entertainment that rural family had during the long, cold winters.

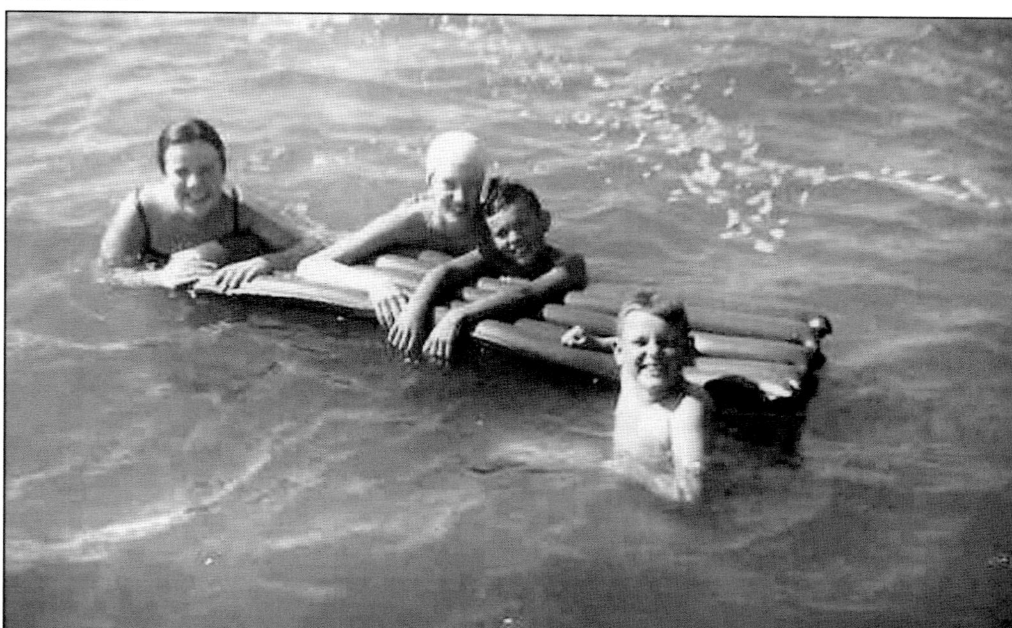

Taking a Dip. Who didn't love going to the country for a swim? These folks look like the water is refreshing. Seen here from left to right are Jeanie Jolly, Nancy Paul Hobbs, Jim Paul, and Gene Paul. (Courtesy of Theresa Swanson.)

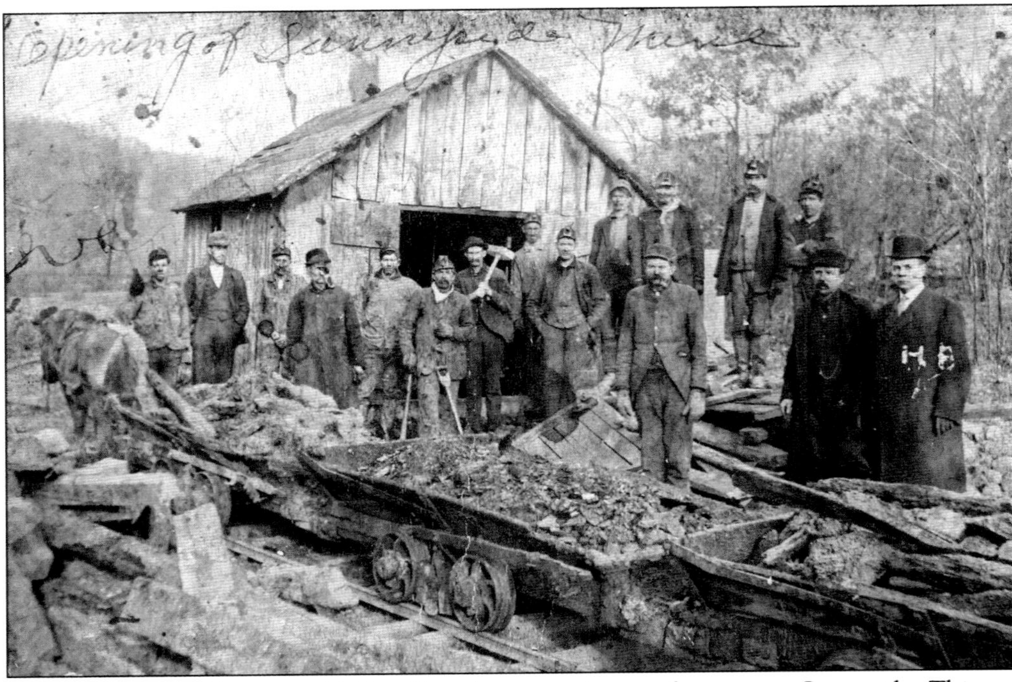

Sunnyside Mine Opening, 1880s. Here is a rare picture of miners in Sunnyside. This was taken when one of the first mines was open for coal removal in the 1880s.

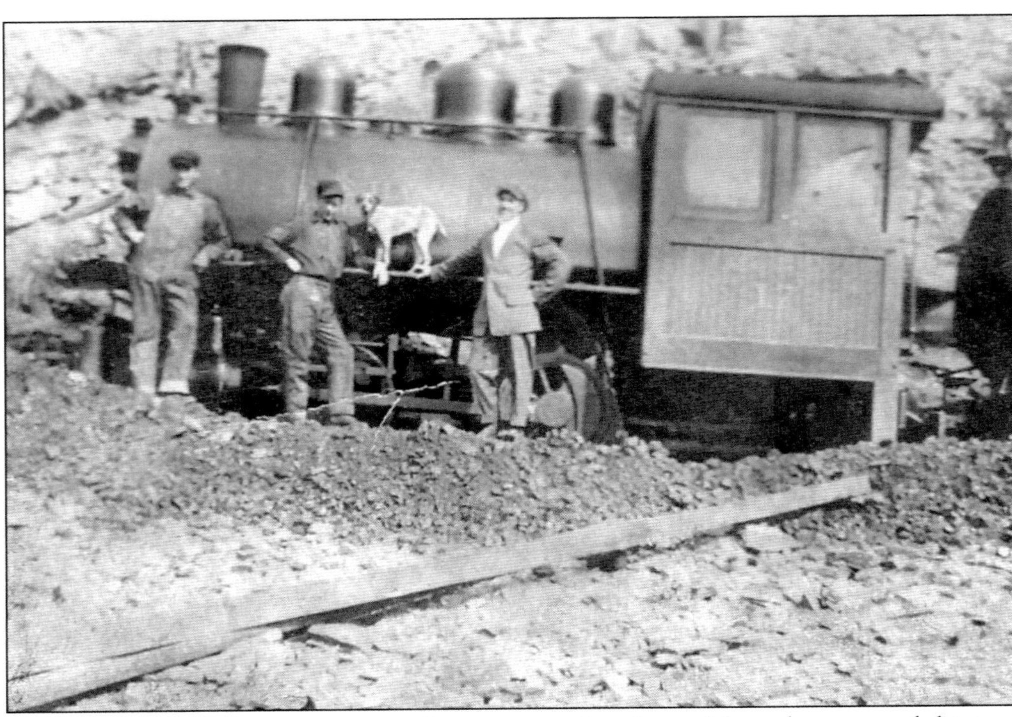

Tram Engine. The mining company that was removing the coal from the area used this tram steam engine in Barrelville. It was much like the Dinky that was used by the Union Mining Company in Mount Savage.

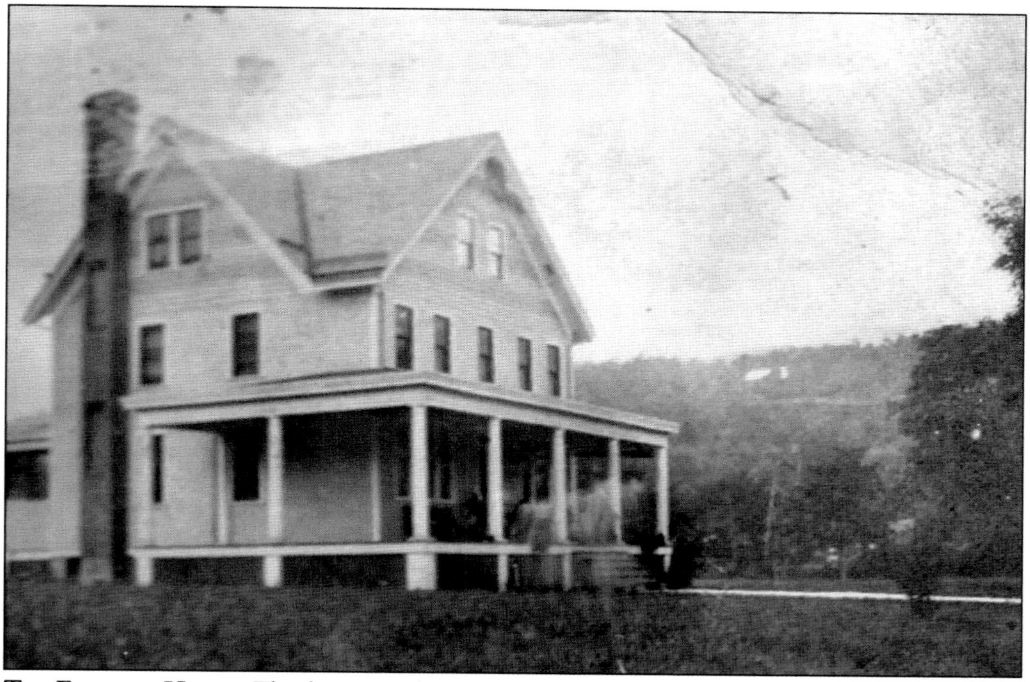

The Foreman House. The foreman of the Barrelville Mining Company and his family lived in this house that was built by the mining company in the late 1890s.

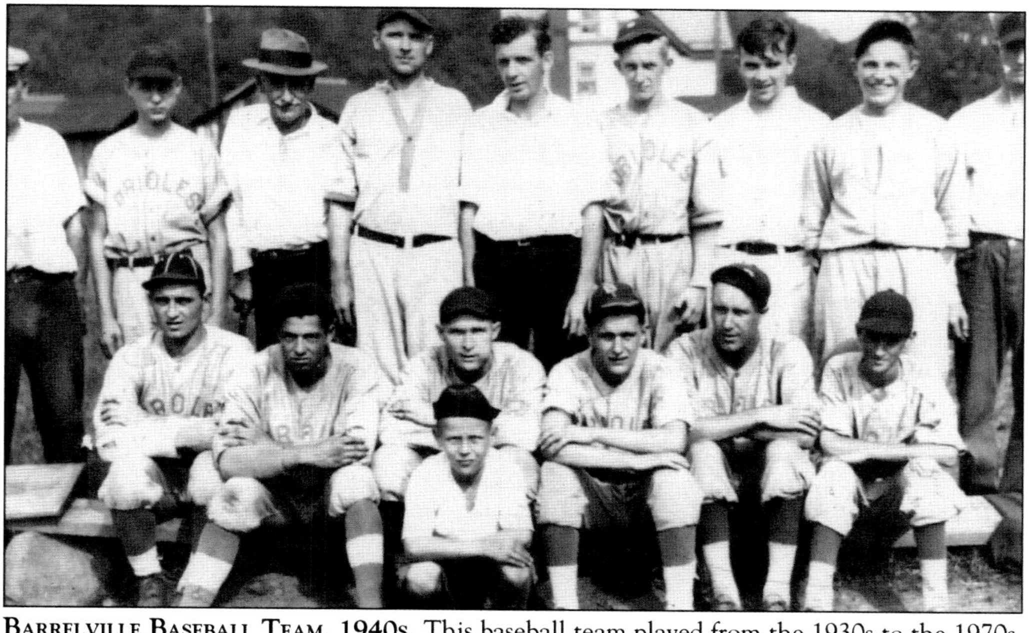

Barrelville Baseball Team, 1940s. This baseball team played from the 1930s to the 1970s. Miners who worked for the Barrelville Mining Company first started the baseball team. The field they played on was located directly behind the foreman's house.

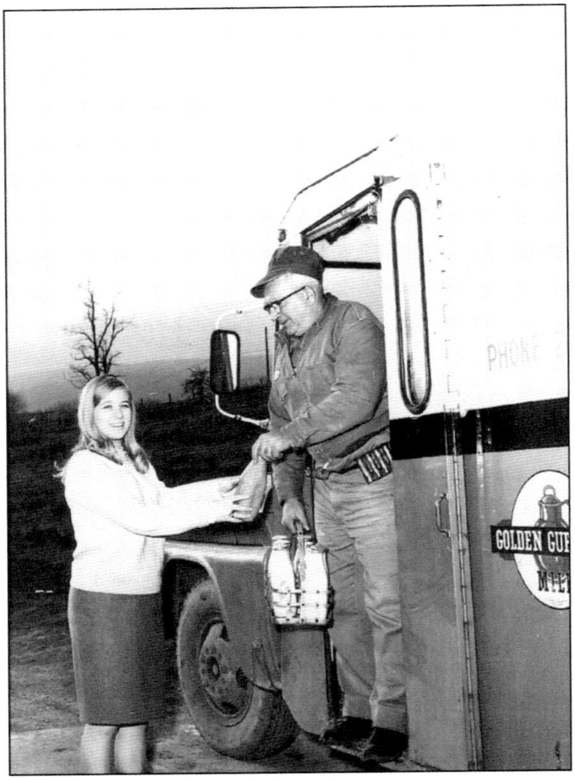

Milk Delivery. The dairy in town, Glen Savage Dairy, provided doorstep delivery. The milkman in this photo, Charlie Bittner, started working for the dairy when he was 16 years old and worked there until the dairy closed in 1968. (Courtesy of the James Robison family.)

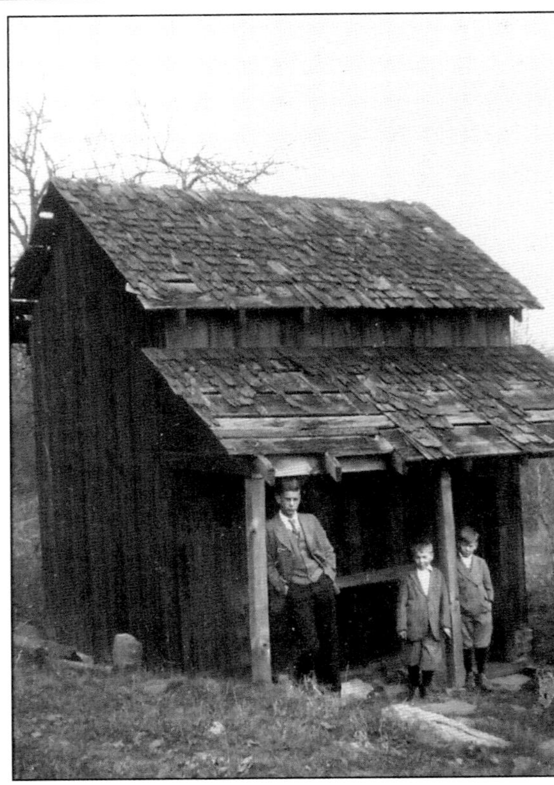

Cabin in the Woods. It was common to find cabins like this one outside of town. Many cabins were converted into moonshine operations during Prohibition. (Courtesy of the James Robison family.)

Ten

Travelling the Rows, Lanes, and Hills

The close proximity of the houses in town comes from the fact that the town was at one time a company town. But the housing situation was not the typical company town arrangement of leasing or renting the houses. Mount Savage workers were some of the best treated in the country. They could purchase the homes that were built by the company for a low cost.

These houses were not the typical, cheaply constructed company houses. They were made from log, stone, and later brick. In the usual company housing of other industrial towns, the workers had to rent poorly constructed homes. Other company town housing consisted of makeshift houses built with cheap lumber that did not have insulation. The Mount Savage Iron Works treated its laborers well. From the beginning of the population boom to the present day, the houses were owned by individuals who took pride in their homes.

The companies that established Mount Savage as an industrial town molded the town into what it is today. They donated land for churches and houses to be built. As the population grew, the town identified neighborhoods for the ethnic groups that dwelled there.

Colorful names like Calla Hill and Coke Hill were conjured up by the workers who settled there; many of the names reminded them of their homeland. The name Calla came from Calla, Ireland, and was thus named by the Irish immigrants who established homes there. Other places were simply named for the area in which they were developed, such as Old Row, the first street of row houses built in town. Coke Hill was aptly named because it was where the coke was poured into the iron furnaces fired at the foot of the hill.

Many of these names have changed since the new emergency address system came about in the 1990s. But the old timers and locals still call them by their colorful names of the past. The only street named as a street in Mount Savage is Main. The rest are just rows, hills, and lanes. The following pages will take readers on a tour of streets and residents of Mount Savage.

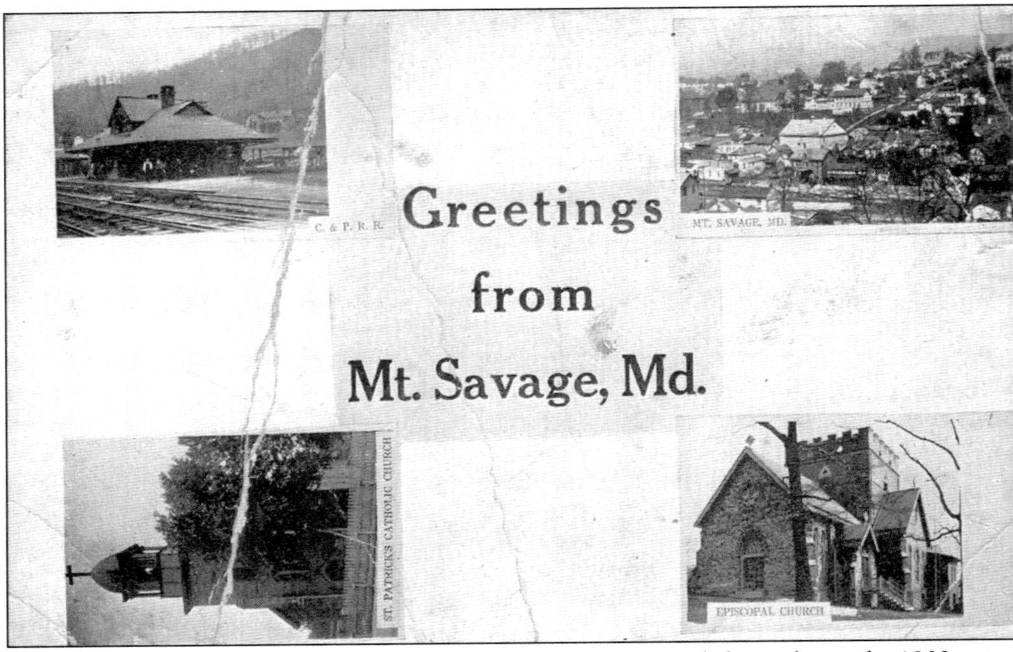

GREETINGS FROM MOUNT SAVAGE! This enthusiastic postcard from the early 1900s gives an overview of the town and was likely to spark the interest of potential visitors. (Courtesy of Gary Delaney.)

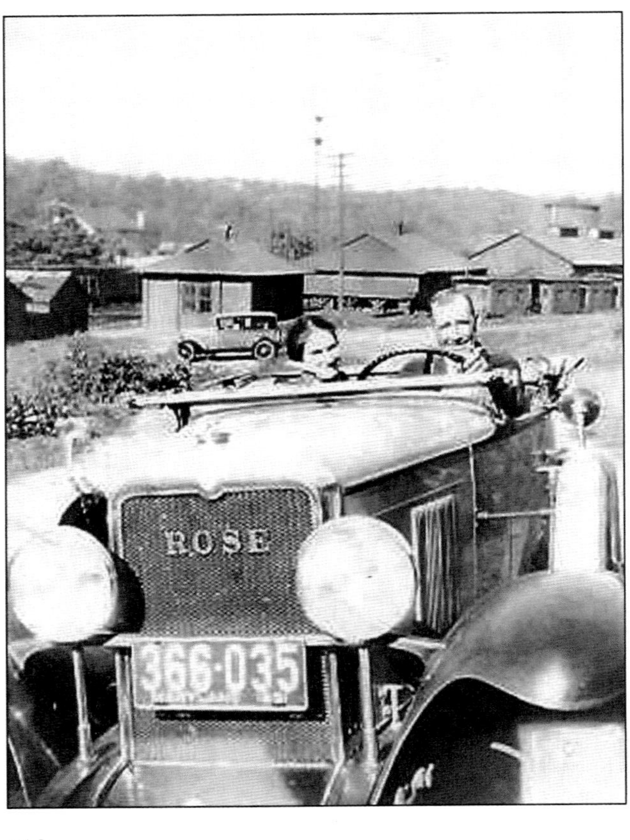

DRIVING UP RAILROAD STREET, 1935. Taking a drive in town, this couple looks happy to be out on a glorious day. In the background you can see the freight depot and other buildings from the C & P Railroad. (Courtesy of Theresa Swanson.)

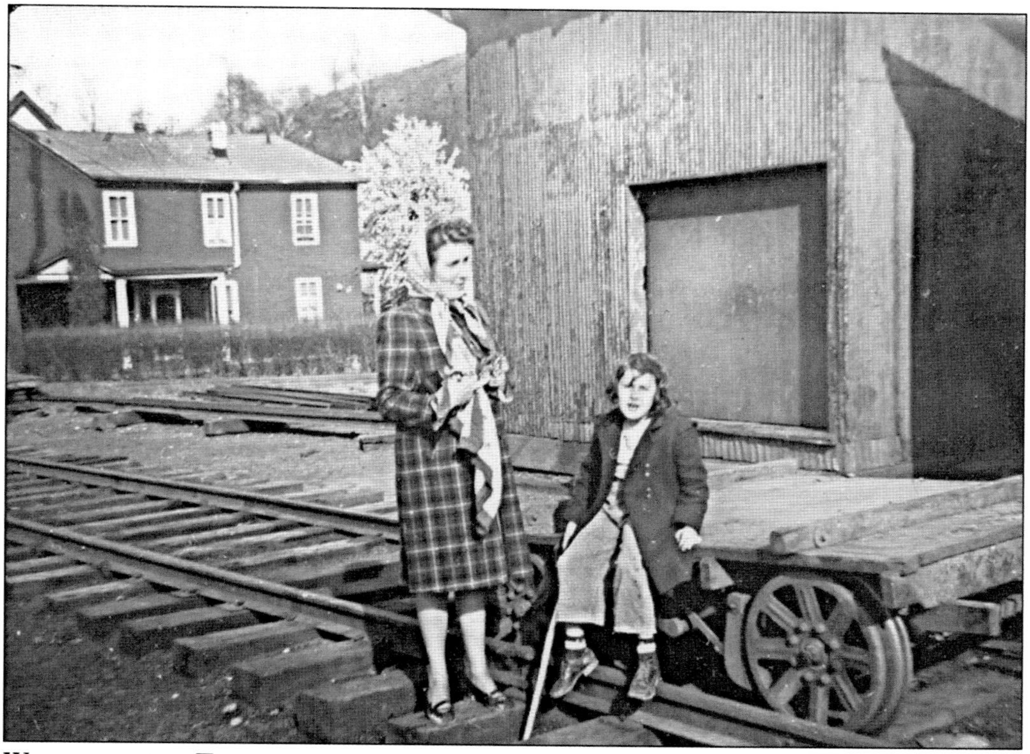

Waiting on the Train. Mother and daughter look like they are waiting on the next train. They sure do not look too thrilled about having their picture taken. (Courtesy of Gary Delaney.)

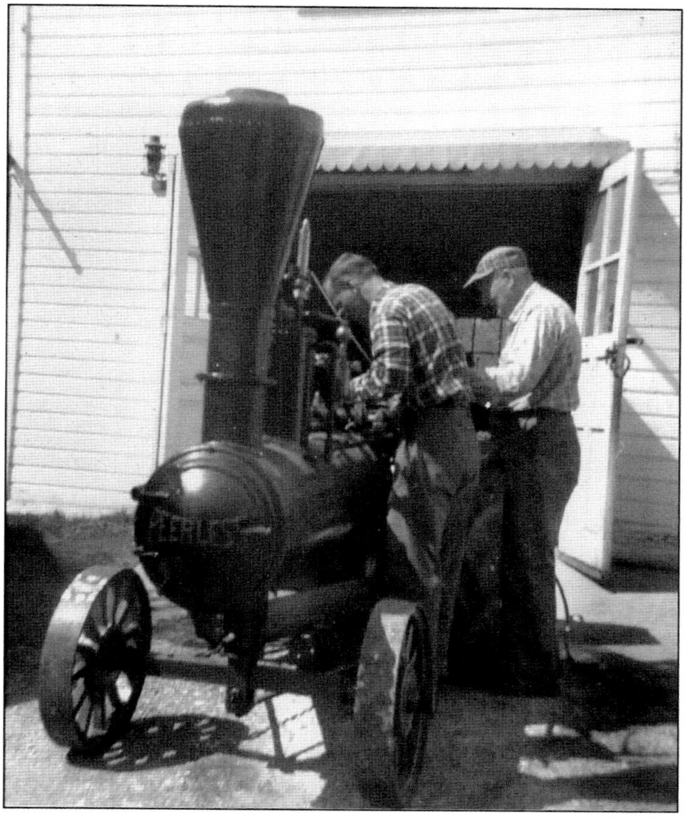

Building a Parade Train. Even after the C & P Railroad left Mount Savage, the railroading spirit flourished. Jim Lancaster and an unidentified friend construct a steam engine to use in parades. (Courtesy of Gary Delaney.)

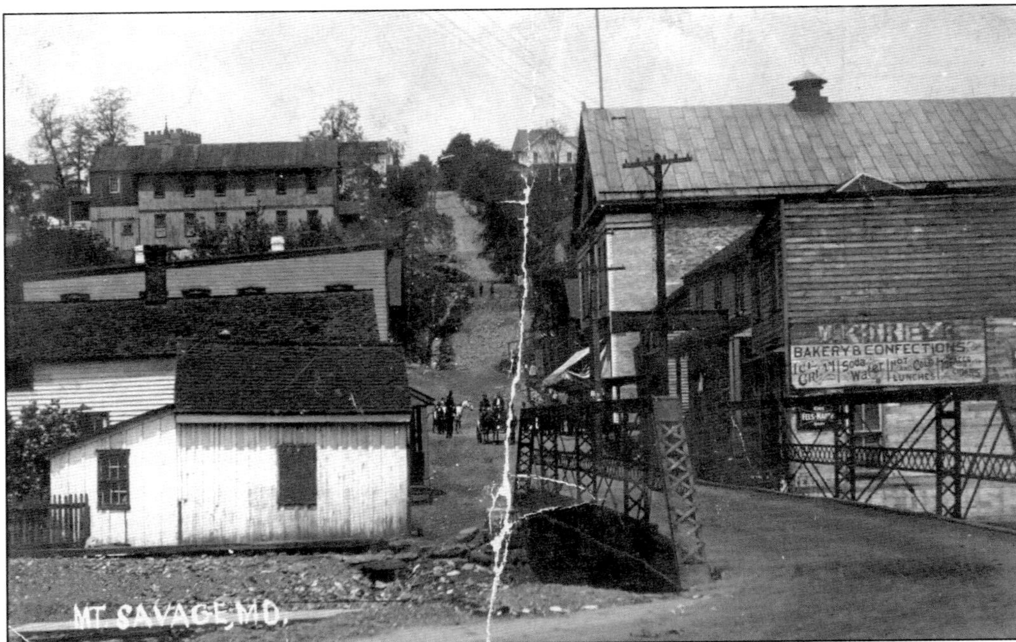

COBBLESTONE HILL, 1890s. What a great view of the steep hill of cobblestone road. The early residents of the town named the street Rocky Road because of its rough stone paving. Later, people tried to name this hill Columbia Street but the name never has stuck, even though there is a street sign with this name.

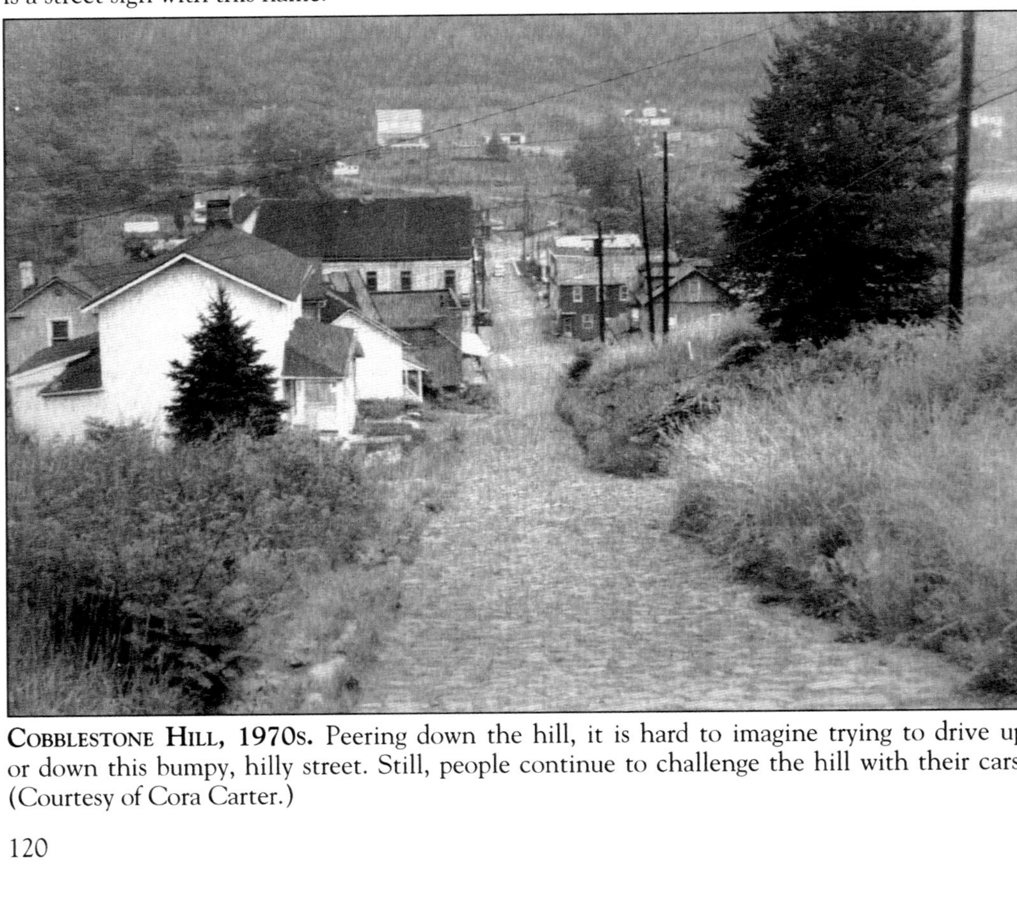

COBBLESTONE HILL, 1970s. Peering down the hill, it is hard to imagine trying to drive up or down this bumpy, hilly street. Still, people continue to challenge the hill with their cars. (Courtesy of Cora Carter.)

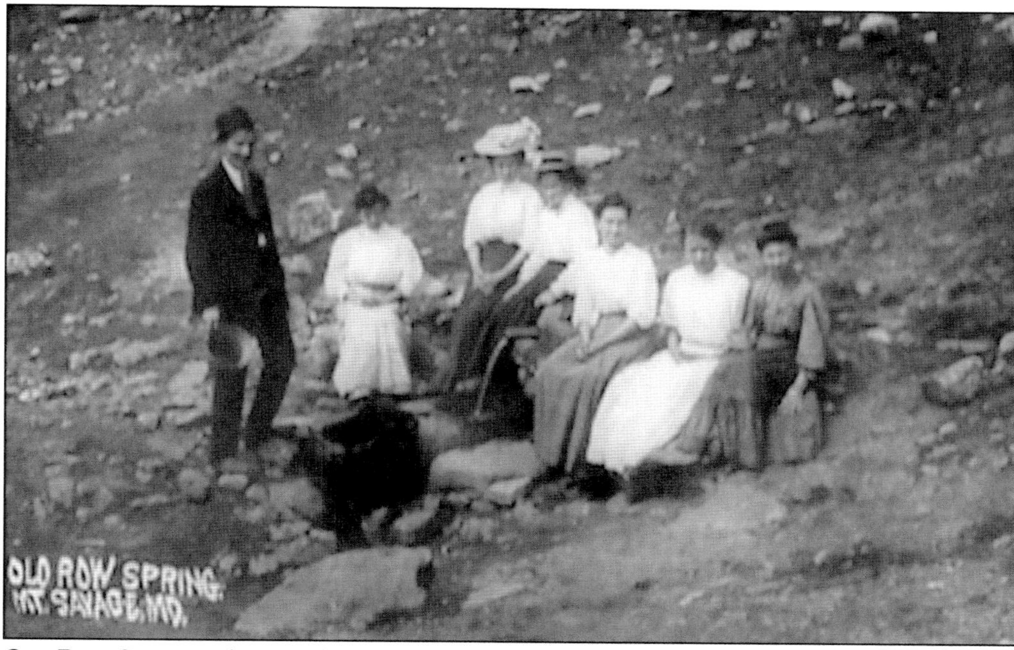

Old Row Spring. This wonderful glimpse into the past allows us to see how simple, yet hard, life was before indoor plumbing. Most of us do not know what fresh spring water tastes like or how hard it would be to carry our family's share of water back to the house. At least this group seems to be relaxing by the spring. (Courtesy of Carol Barry.)

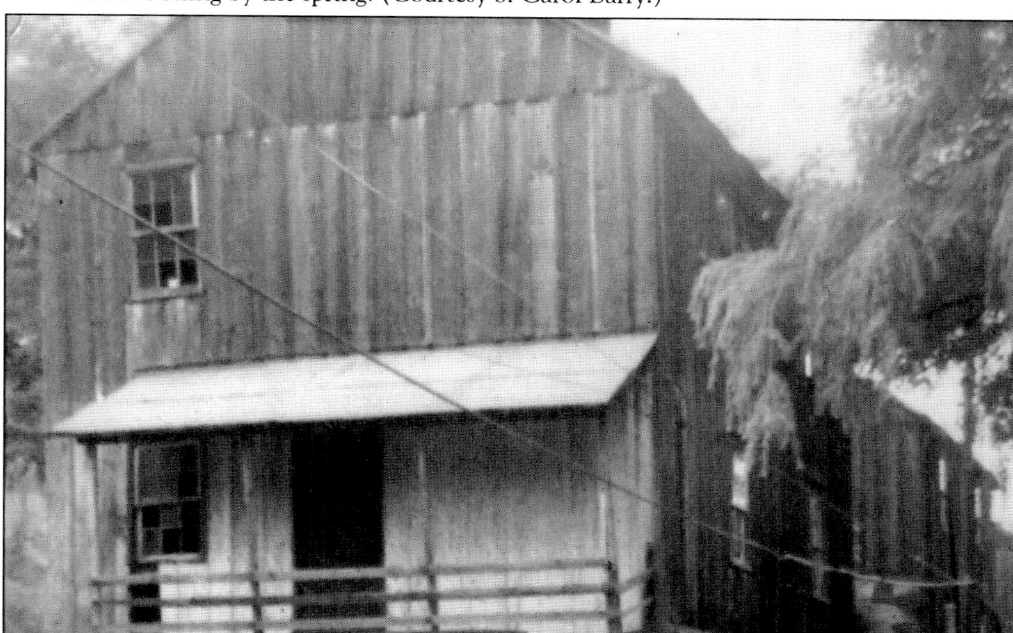

Old Row, 1960s. Cardinal Edward Mooney was born and grew up here. He went into the priesthood and flourished with his Catholic duties. He never forgot about Mount Savage; once he left, he visited when he could to see his mother. Even after his mother's death, he visited the town to pay respect to the graves of his parents and grandparents. (Courtesy of Cora Carter.)

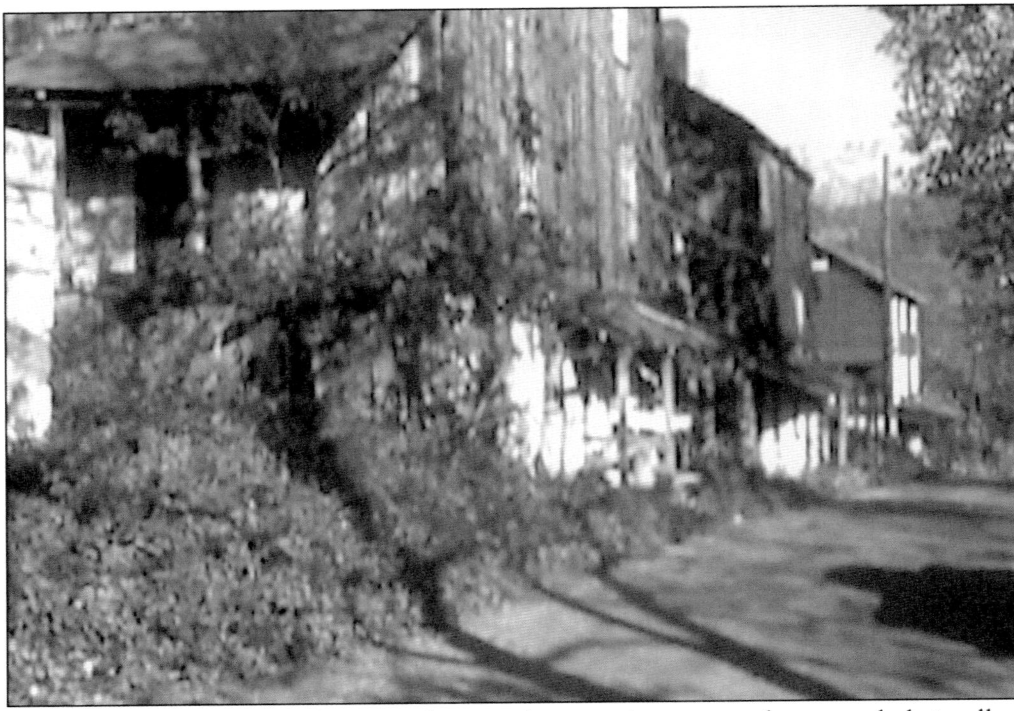

Old Row Falling Down. The years of wear and tear on the company houses took their toll on Old Row. The houses started to be abandoned or neglected in the 1950s and 1960s. (Courtesy of Carol Barry.)

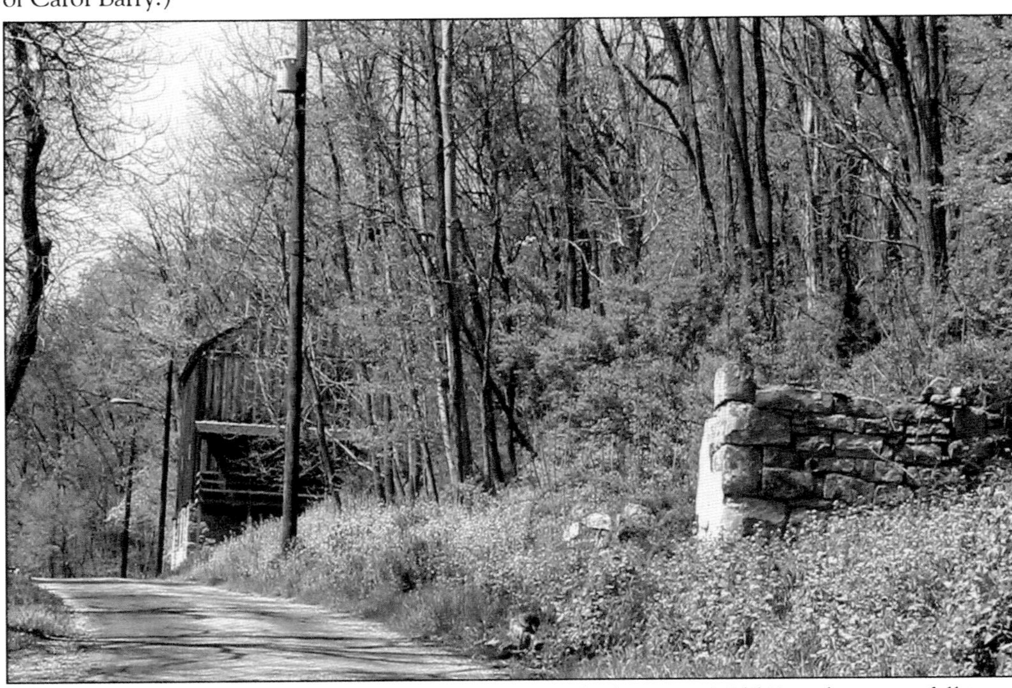

Present Day Old Row. After years of hard living, the houses of Old Row began to fall in on themselves. In the late 1960s and 1970s almost all of the houses were torn down for the safety of the community.

WORKING MEN. These two men seem to be taking a break from hauling around this Model-T tire. (Courtesy of Cora Carter.)

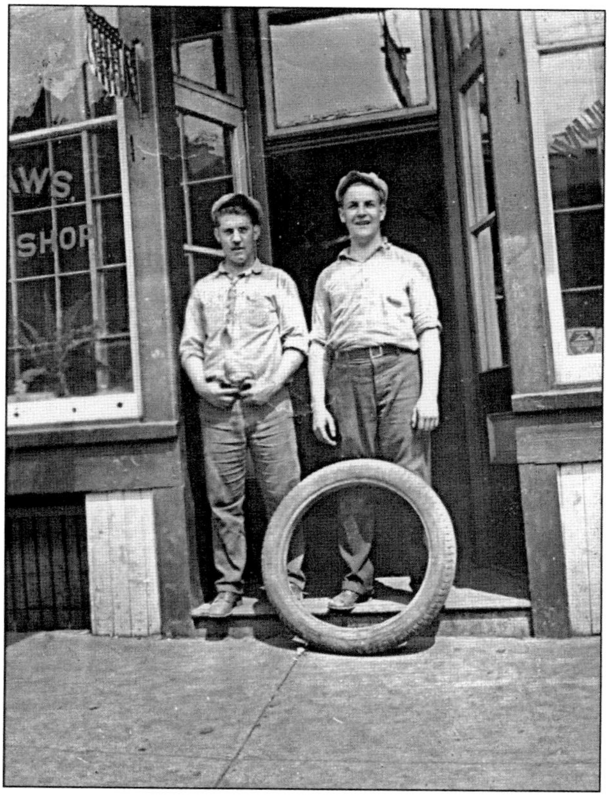

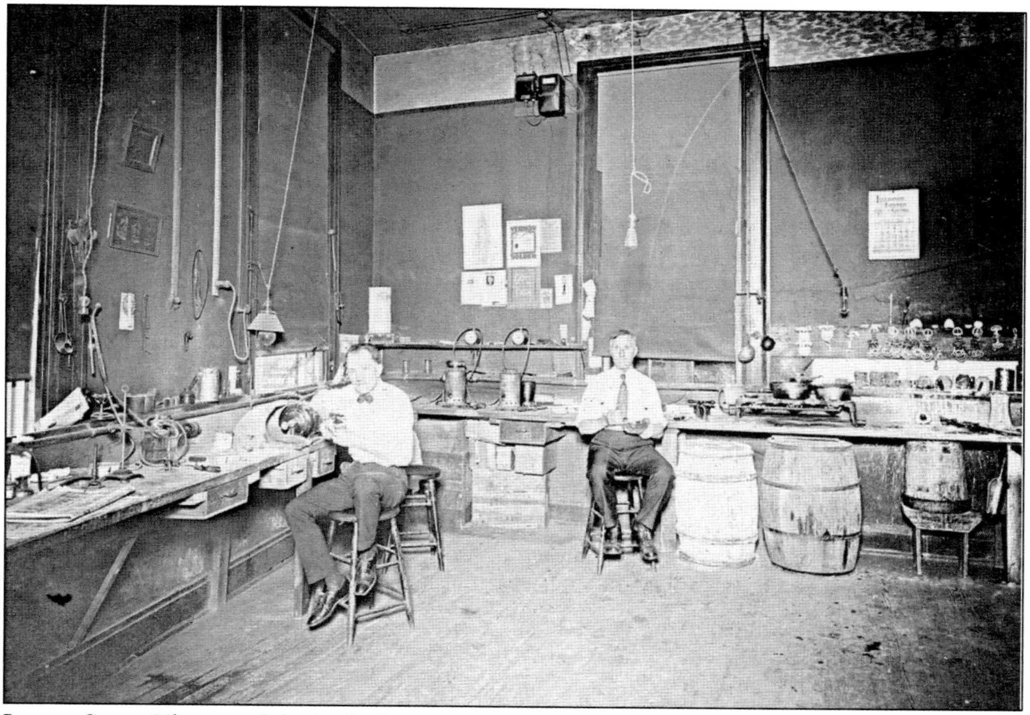

IN THE SHOP. Their work looks fairly secretive, with the blinds pulled. Whatever these men are doing, their workbenches are full of stuff. (Courtesy of Gary Delaney.)

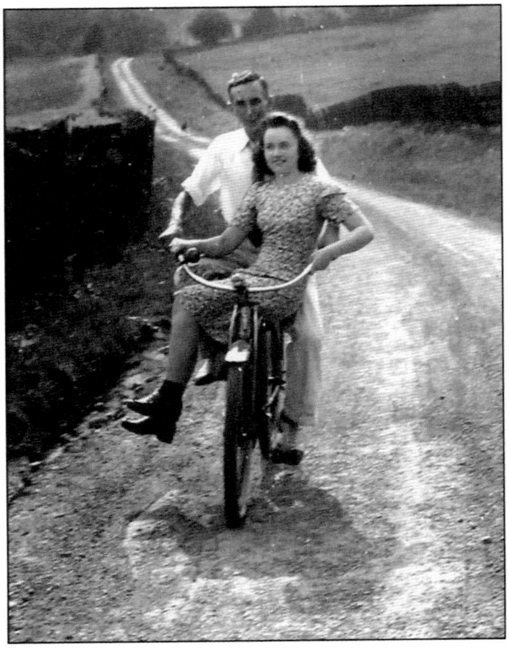

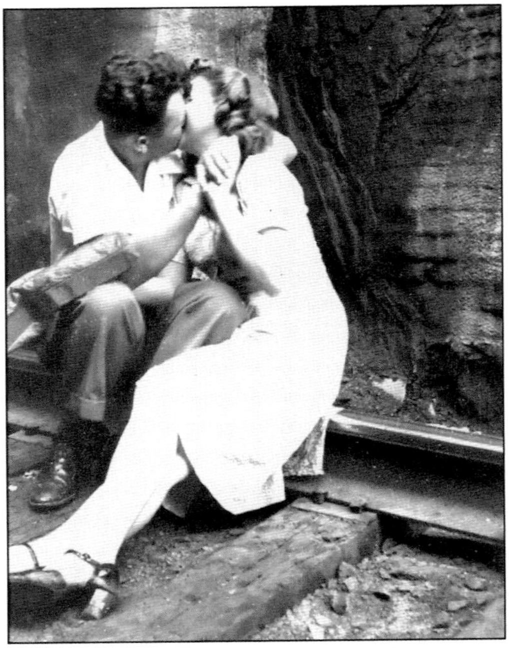

(Above left) **Hitching a Ride.** Wilma Smearman hitches a ride on her boyfriend's, Stewart Delbrook's, bicycle; the two seem to be enjoying a day on Mile Lane. (Courtesy of Wilma Delbrook, in memory of Stewart.)
(Above right) **Caught Kissing.** This couple, Raymond and Edna May Lepley, seems to have escaped to somewhere private along the railroad tracks, but they have been caught kissing. (Courtesy of Wilma Delbrook, in memory of Stewart.)

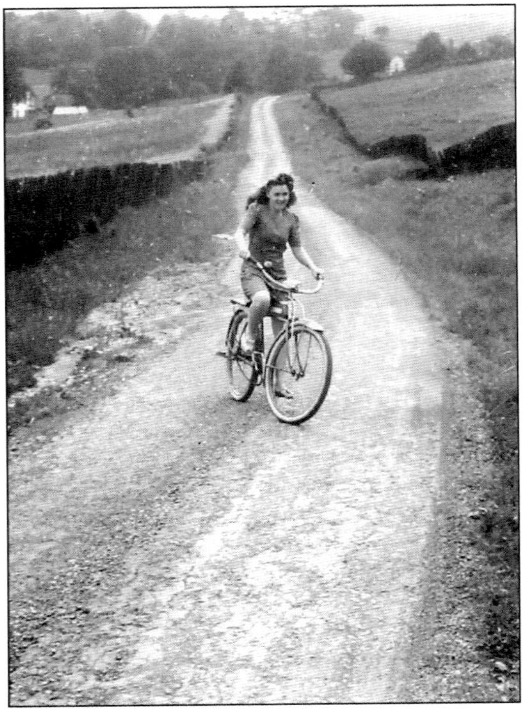

Just Riding My Bicycle. Ann Smearman looks to be enjoying the wind in her hair as she rides out Mile Lane. It is amazing to see that the entire lane was lined with picket fence. (Wilma Delbrook, in memory of Stewart.)

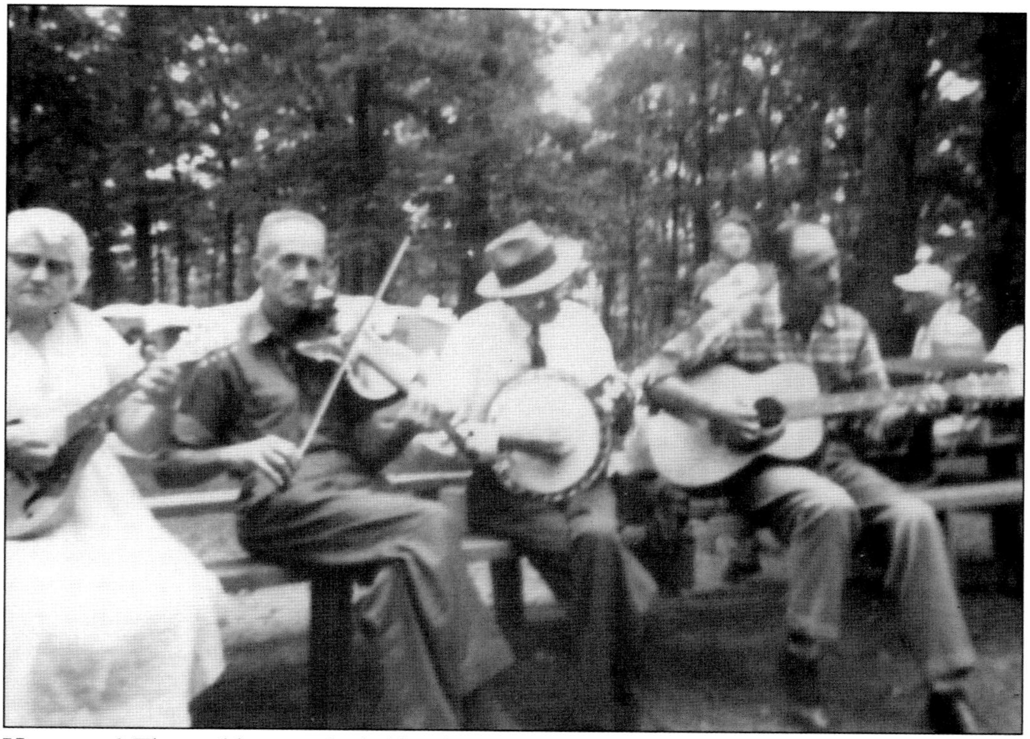

HOEDOWN! These old timers look like they are having a grand time playing some old-timey music. Playing music like this has become a lost tradition.

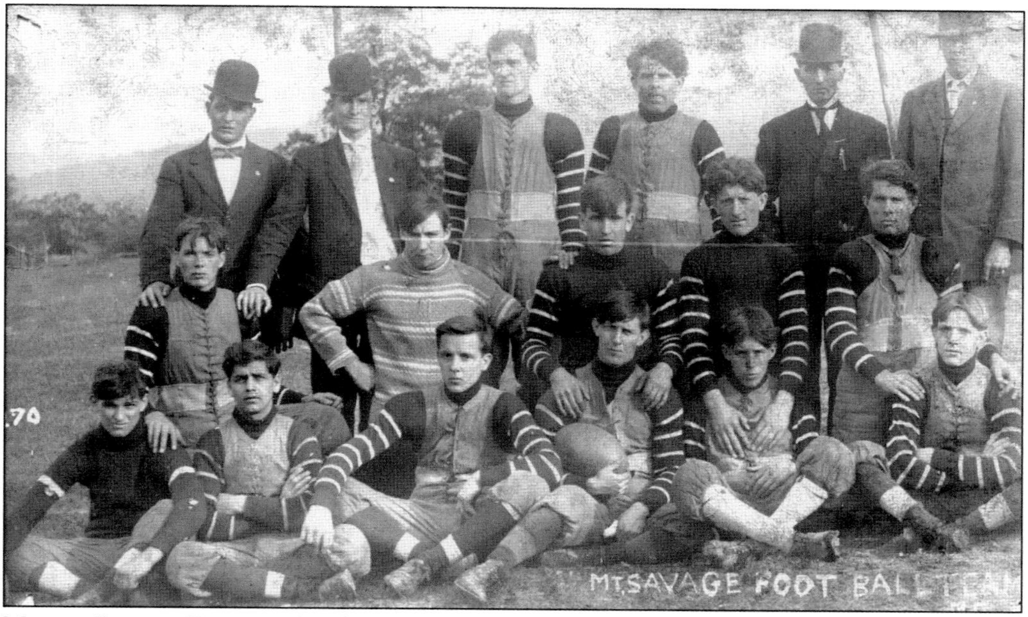

MOUNT SAVAGE FOOTBALL? Believe it or not, at one time the town did have an adult football team named the Cinder Tips. They received their name from the field they played on. The field was located at the top of Coke Hill (the first hill on New School Road) where the coke was stored to make iron ore. The field was many times covered in cinders and ash from burning the coke. (Courtesy of Gary Delaney.)

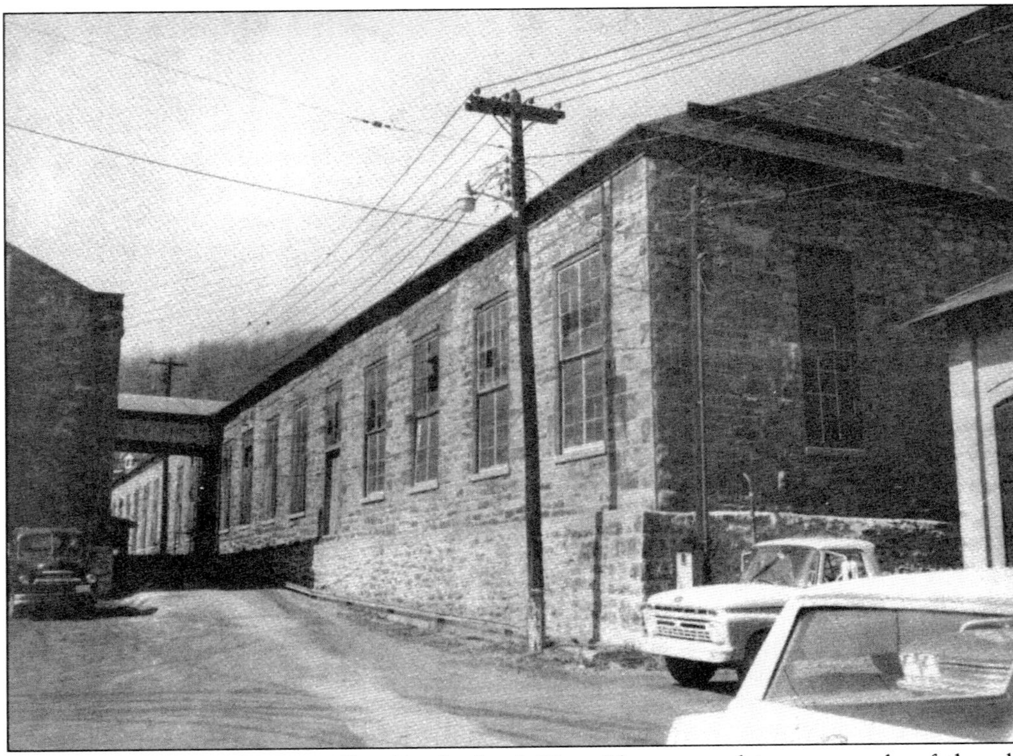

Cumberland Glass Plant. The Cumberland Glass Plant moved into a couple of the old C & P Shops in 1957. A fire in their LaVale Plant preempted the move in 1956. The glass plant ceased production in 1961. (Courtesy of Mount Savage School.)

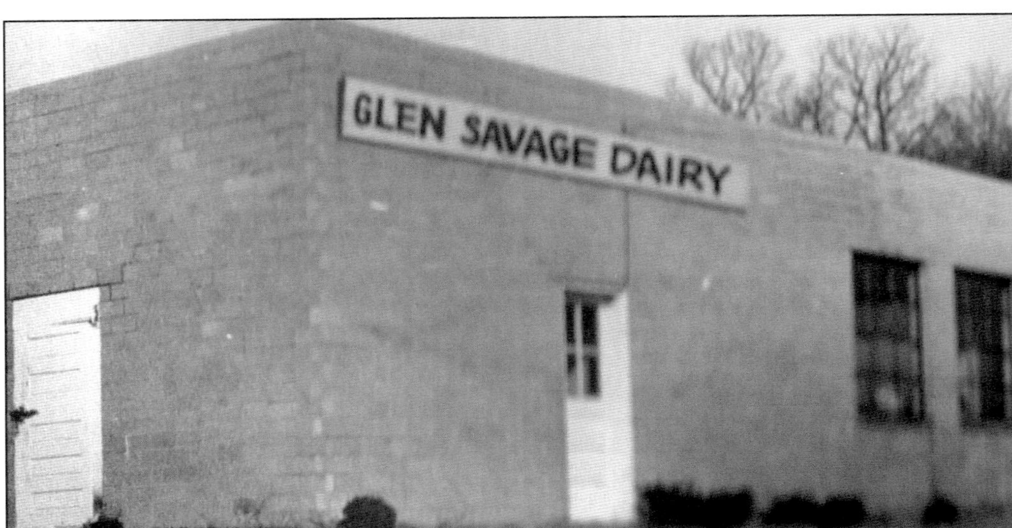

Glen Savage Dairy. The Weimer family founded the dairy in 1949. The James Robison family later operated the dairy until 1968. The dairy pasteurized and bottled Guernsey milk. The name of the dairy came from the fact that the farm where they raised cattle was located on a glen overlooking Mount Savage. (Courtesy of the James Robison family.)

DIXIE MALE SEXTET. In 1935 this singing group was formed and performed at churches and clubs throughout Allegany County. They were so liked that they won a contest at the Strand Theatre in Cumberland. As the contest winners, they sang on KDKA radio in Pittsburgh, Pennsylvania, on Valentine's Day 1936. The singers are, from left to right, (front row) Matthew McKenzie, "Peach" Blake, and Bob Wilson; (back row) Harry Crowe, Ralph Wilson, Wilbert Paul, and Robert Kirby. (Courtesy of Wilbert Paul.)

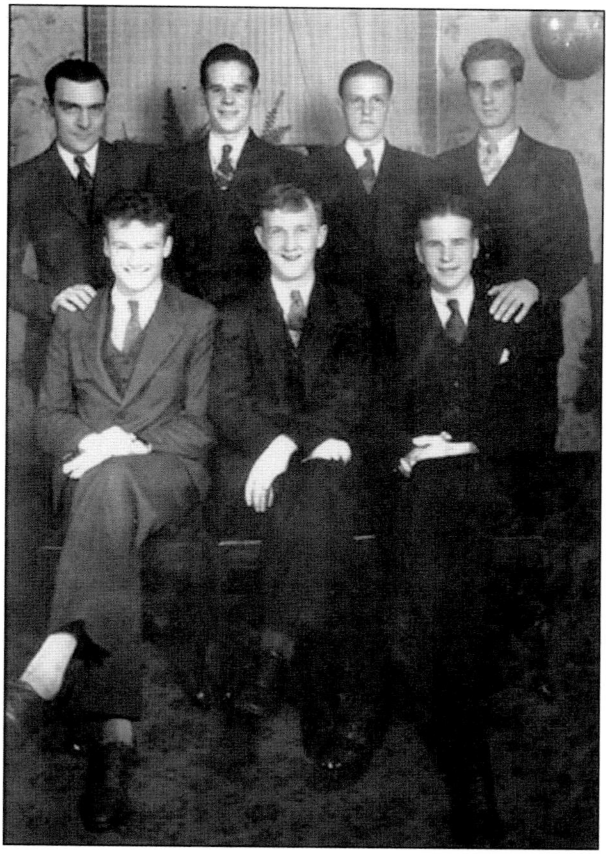

BALD KNOB PICNIC. Who could say no to a fine picnic on Bald Knob? Just thinking about the homemade preserves and iced tea that they have on their picnic blanket makes one's mouth water. (Courtesy of Wilma Delbrook, in memory of Stewart.)

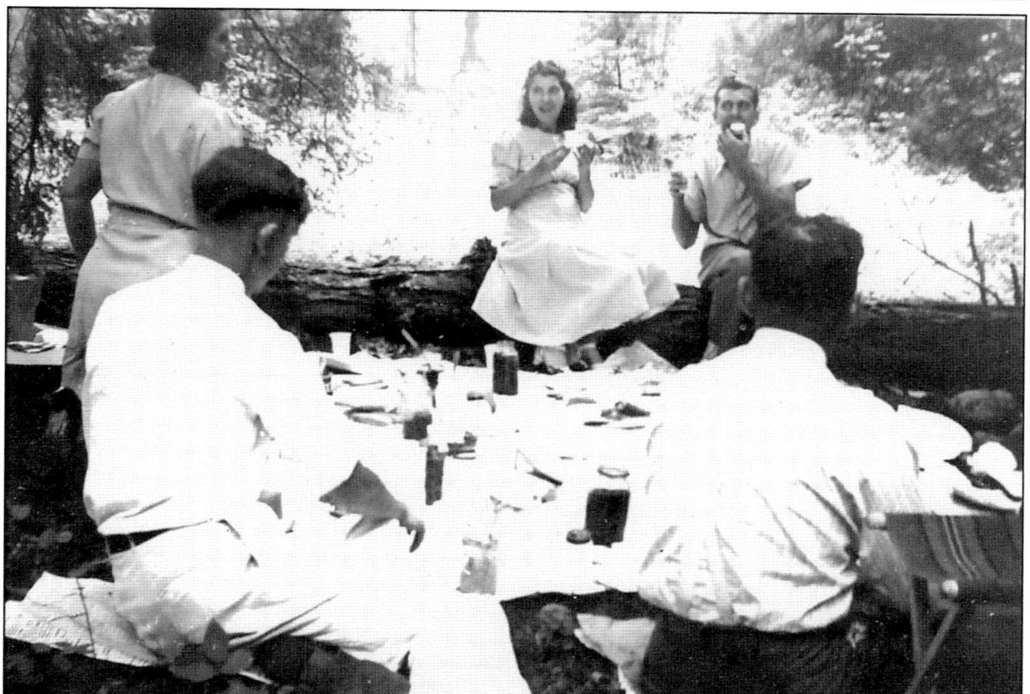

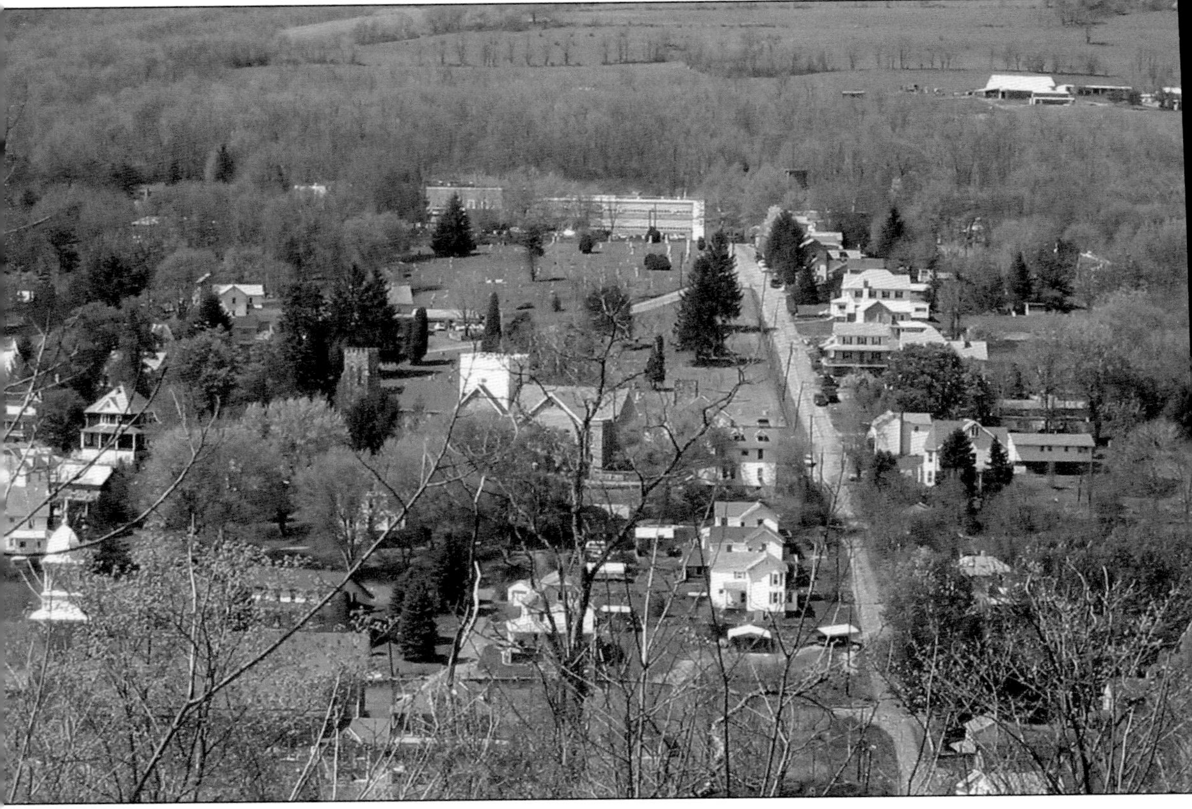

View from Mac' Hill.
There's a town in Western Maryland
Made up of Irish stock.
A few miles west of Cumberland
and east of Old Dan's Rock.
A little bit Ireland, that has acquired wide fame,
is just a quaint old-fashioned town
Mount Savage is its name.
(Courtesy of Mount Savage Historical Society.)